The Case for Sanctions Against Israel

The Case for Sanctions Against Israel

Edited by Audrea Lim

VERSO
London • New York

1 3 5 7 9 10 8 6 4 2

Verso
UK: 6 Meard Street, London W1F 0EG
US: 20 Jay Street, Suite 1010, Brooklyn, NY 11201
www.versobooks.com

Verso is the imprint of New Left Books

ISBN-13: 978-1-84467-450-3

British Library Cataloguing in Publication Data
A catalogue record for this book is available from the British Library

Library of Congress Cataloging-in-Publication Data
A catalog record for this book is available from the Library of Congress

Typeset in Minion Pro by MJ Gavan, Cornwall
Printed in the US by Maple Vail

CONTENTS

Part I ISRAEL/PALESTINE

1 FREEDOM IN OUR LIFETIME

Mustafa Barghouthi

I have lived my entire adult life under occupation, with Israelis holding ultimate control over my movement and daily life.

When young Israeli police officers force me to sit on the cold ground and soldiers beat me during a peaceful protest, I smolder. No human being should be compelled to sit on the ground while exercising rights taken for granted throughout the West.

Irrespective of what political settlement is ultimately embraced, Palestinians need a unified strategy for confronting and overcoming Israeli racism, apartheid, and oppression.

Javier Solana, just prior to completing his stint as European Union foreign policy chief, claimed Palestinian moves toward statehood "have to be done with time, with calm, in an appropriate moment." But he also added, "I don't think today is the moment to talk about that." When, precisely, is a good time for Palestinian freedom? If Israel insists on hewing to antiquated notions of determining the date of another people's freedom, then it is incumbent on Palestinians to organize ourselves and highlight the moral repugnance of such an outlook.

Palestinians have only two choices before them: either 1) continue to evade the struggle, as some have been trying to do, or 2) summon the collective national resolve to engage in it.

The latter option does not necessarily entail a call to arms. Clearly, Israel has the overwhelming advantage in this respect, in both conventional and unconventional (nuclear) weapons. Just as obviously, neighboring Arab countries have neither the will nor the ability to go the military route.

However, the inability to wage war does not automatically mean we have to surrender and eschew other means of struggle.

As powerful as it is militarily, Israel has two major weak points. First, it cannot impose political solutions by force of arms on a people determined to sustain a campaign of resistance. This has been amply demonstrated in two full-scale wars against Lebanon and in the 2009 assault against Gaza. Second, the longer the Palestinians have remained steadfast, and the greater the role the demographic factor has come to play in the conflict, the more clearly Israel has emerged as an apartheid system hostile to peace. If the ethnic cleansing of 1948 and colonialist expansionism describe the circumstances surrounding the birth of the Israeli state, the recent bills regarding the declaration of allegiance to a Jewish state and prohibiting the Palestinian commemoration of the Nakba more explicitly underscore its essentially racist character.

Ironically, just as Israel has reached the peak in its drive to fragment the Palestinian people—with geographical divides between those in Israel and those abroad, between Jerusalem and the West Bank, between the West Bank and Gaza, and between one governorate and the next in the West Bank, by means of ring roads, walls and barriers—Palestinians have become reunified in their hardship and in the challenges that confront them. Regardless of whether or not they bear Israeli citizenship, or whether they are residents of Jerusalem, the West Bank, or Gaza, they all share the plight of being victims of Israel's systematic discrimination and apartheid order.

If the only alternative to evading the struggle is to engage in it in order to resolve it, we must affirm that our national liberation movement is still alive. We must affirm, secondly, that political and diplomatic action is a fundamental part of managing the conflict, as opposed to an alternative to our struggle to resolve it. In fact, we must elevate it to our primary means for exposing the true nature of Israel, isolating it politically, and pressing for international sanctions against it.

In this context, we must caution against the plan of building state institutions under the occupation. An administration whose security services would be consuming 35 percent of the public budget—that would be constantly pressured to act as the occupation's policeman while furthering Benjamin Netanyahu's scheme for economic normalization as a substitute for a political solution—is clearly an entity geared to promoting the acclimatization to the status quo, not change.

The building of Palestinian governing institutions and promotion of genuine economic development must occur within the framework of a philosophy of "resistance development." Such a philosophy is founded on the dual principles of 1) supporting the people's power to withstand the hardships of occupation, and 2) reducing dependency on foreign funding and foreign aid. The strategic aim of the Palestinian struggle, under this philosophy, must be to make the costs of the Israeli occupation and its apartheid system so great as to be unsustainable.

If we agree on this course for conducting the struggle, then the next step is to adopt a unified national strategy founded upon the four following pillars.

1. RESISTANCE

In the face of European and American inaction, it is crucial that we continue to revive our culture of collective activism by vigorously and nonviolently resisting Israel's domination over us. These are actions that every man, woman, and child can take.

Through decades of occupation and dispossession, 90 percent of the Palestinian struggle has been nonviolent, with the vast majority of Palestinians supporting this method of struggle. Today growing numbers of Palestinians are participating in organized nonviolent resistance.

Models for this type of resistance already exist. Of particular note is the brave and persistent campaign against the separation or apartheid wall, which has spread across several towns and villages. The campaign has become increasingly adamant regardless of the high price people have to pay, including the killing of twenty Palestinian peaceful activists by the Israeli army. The resistance by the people of East Jerusalem, including in Silwan and Sheikh Jarrah, against Israeli home demolitions and the drive to Judaize the city presents another heroic model.

This strategy must retain its peaceful, grassroots character. If it does, it will revive the culture of collective activism among all sectors of the Palestinian people. This will keep the struggle from becoming the preserve or monopoly of small cliques, and will promote its growth and momentum.

President Barack Obama, perhaps unwittingly, encouraged this effort when he called for Palestinian nonviolence in his 2009 Cairo speech.

"Palestinians," he said, "must abandon violence … For centuries, black people in America suffered … the humiliation of segregation. But it was not violence that won full and equal rights. It was a peaceful and determined insistence upon the ideals at the center of America's founding."

Yet without public American complaint, the Israeli military has killed and injured many nonviolent Palestinians during Obama's term as president, most notably Bassem Abu Rahme in April 2009, killed by an Israeli high-velocity tear gas canister. American citizen Tristan Anderson was critically injured by the Israeli army the previous month by a similar projectile. Both men were protesting illegal Israeli land seizures and Israel's wall. Hundreds more are unknown to the outside world.

Another key aspect of resistance has been the movement to boycott Israeli goods and to encourage the consumption of locally produced goods. In addition to preventing the occupation power from deriving profits by marketing locally produced goods, this form of resistance can engage the broadest swath of the population—from old to young, both men and women—and revive the culture and spirit of communal collaboration. The campaigns to break the blockade against Gaza, as exemplified by the protest ships, the supply caravans, and the pressures on Israel to lift its economic stranglehold, are another major type of resistance.

A new generation of Palestinian leaders is attempting to speak to the world in the language of a nonviolent campaign of boycott, divestment, and sanctions (BDS), precisely as Martin Luther King Jr. and thousands of African Americans did in the Montgomery bus boycott in the mid-1950s. We are equally justified in using this tactic to advance our rights. The same world that rejects all use of Palestinian violence, even in clear self-defense, surely ought not to begrudge us the nonviolence employed by men such as King and Gandhi.

2. SUPPORTING NATIONAL STEADFASTNESS

The importance of this pillar of resistance is its focus on strengthening the demographic power of the Palestinian people, so as to transform their millions of individuals into an effective grassroots force. It entails meeting their essential needs to enable them to remain steadfast in their struggle, and developing Palestinian human resources as the foundation for a strong and independent Palestinian economy.

However, in order to achieve these aims, the Palestinian Authority (PA) economic plan and budget must be altered so as to put their weight behind the development of education, health, agriculture, and culture, rather than squandering a third of the budget on security. For example, the passage and immediate implementation of the bill for the national higher education fund would serve the educational needs of hundreds of thousands of young adults. In addition to elevating and developing the standards of university education, it would also help sustain the effectiveness of development aid and eventually reduce reliance on foreign support. The fund would also alleviate the school tuition burdens on more than 150,000 families, put an end to nepotism in the handling of study grants and loans, and provide equal opportunity for academic advancement to all young men and women regardless of their financial circumstances.

Equally innovative and dynamic ideas could be applied to other areas of education, and to stimulating the fields of public health, agriculture, and culture, with the overall aim of meeting Palestinian needs as autonomously as possible, and hence increasing our capacity to weather enormous pressures.

3. NATIONAL UNITY AND A UNIFIED NATIONAL LEADERSHIP

This strategic aim entails restructuring the Palestine Liberation Organization on a more demographically representative basis, and putting into effect agreements that have been previously reached in the Palestinian national dialogues held in Cairo. Over the past few years, Israel's greatest advantage and the thrust of its assault have centered around the rift within the Palestinian movement and the weakness of the disunited Palestinian leadership. In order to redress this flaw, Palestinians must adopt a new mentality and approach. Specifically, they must relinquish the practice of vying for power over a meaningless governing authority that is still under the thumb of the occupation, whether in the West Bank or in Gaza; give up the illusion that any single Palestinian party, however great it might become, is capable of leading the Palestinian struggle alone; adopt democracy and pluralistic democratic activities and processes as a mode of life, and peaceful decision-making as the only acceptable means to resolve our differences and disputes; and resist all outside pressures and attempts (particularly on the part of Israel) to intervene in our internal affairs and to tamper with the Palestinian popular will. We have no unity because the United States and

Israel have done everything they could to break down the unity government we established following democratic elections. There must be a firm and unshakable conviction of Palestinians' right to independent national self-determination.

The most difficult task that we face today is that of creating a unified leadership and strategy binding on all, from which no political or military decisions will depart, and within whose framework no single group or party has a monopoly on the decision-making process. Only with a unified leadership and strategy will we be able to fight the blockade as one, instead of evading unity for fear of the blockade. With a unified leadership and strategy we will be able to seize the initiative instead of simply reacting, and we will be able to assert our unified will instead of squandering our energies on internal power struggles in which various parties seek outside assistance to strengthen their hand against internal opponents. Only then will we be able to shift the equation that has subordinated the national liberation movement to the narrow concerns of the PA (both in the West Bank and Gaza) and turn the PA into an instrument in the service of the national liberation movement.

4. ENHANCING PRO-PALESTINIAN SOLIDARITY

That such a movement already exists and is steadily growing is heartening. However, it will take enormous efforts to organize it and coordinate its activities properly, so as to ensure that it has the greatest possible influence upon decision-makers, especially in Europe and the West. Palestinian, Arab, and Muslim communities will need to be orchestrated towards the realization of the same goals. The solidarity movement has scored significant successes with the organization of a boycott of Israeli products, including the decision by the British University and College Union to boycott Israeli academics; the amazing decision of fifty-two labor unions in Britain, with a membership of more than 7 million people, to join the BDS campaign; the decision taken by Hampshire College and some US churches to refuse to invest in the Israeli occupation; and the decision of Norway and Denmark to divest from Israeli military companies. Much work has yet to be done to expand the scope of such activities and build up the momentum of the solidarity movement.

It is with deepening concern that I recognize that the Obama administration is not yet capable of standing up to Israel and the pro-Israel lobby.

Hilary Clinton, speaking in February 2011, could only summon the term "illegitimate" to describe Israel's illegal settlements.

The Palestinian plight, which Nelson Mandela has described as the foremost challenge to the international humanitarian conscience, strongly resembles the state of South Africa at the outset of the 1980s. It took years of a concerted campaign before the South African liberation movement finally succeeded in bringing governments around to their cause. The tipping point came when major companies realized that the economic costs of dealing with the apartheid regime in Pretoria were unsustainable. In the Palestinian case, the success of an international solidarity movement is contingent upon three major factors: 1) careful organization and detailed planning, a high degree of discipline, and tight coordination; 2) a rational, civilized rhetoric that refuses to play into Israel's tactics of provocation; and 3) the recruitment of progressive movements and peoples in societies abroad, including anti-Zionist Jews and Jews opposed to Israeli policies.

None of the foregoing is new, by any means. However, these ideas have yet to be put into practice. The logical springboard for their implementation is to operate on the principle that, while the Palestinian cause is a Palestinian, Arab, and Muslim one, it is above all a humanitarian cause that cries out to all in the world who cherish humanitarian principles and values. The successes of the freedom fighters of South Africa, the anti–Vietnam War movement, and the campaigners for the independence of India stemmed primarily from their ability to forge a universal appeal. And this is precisely what we must do. Our mottos for the solidarity movement with the Palestinian people must be "the fight against the new apartheid and systematic racism" and "the fight for justice and the right to freedom." The International Court of Justice's ruling on the separation wall, and on the illegality of Jewish settlements and of altering the face of Jerusalem, is a valuable legal precedent that Palestinian governing institutions have ignored for five years. This ruling, as well as the Goldstone Report on Israel's attack on Gaza (despite Goldstone's later reversal), should now become our platform for a drive to impose sanctions against Israel, just as the UN resolution against the occupation of Namibia provided a platform for mounting a campaign against the apartheid system in South Africa.

*   *   *

The four-pronged strategy outlined above, which is espoused by the Palestinian National Initiative movement, can succeed if it is guided by a clear vision, patience, and systematic persistence. I do not expect it to win the approval of all. The interests of some, combined with their sense of frustration and despair, have deadened their desire to engage in or continue the confrontation with Israel. We also have to acknowledge that certain sectors of Palestinian society have become so dependent upon interim arrangements and foreign aid, and their attendant finances, as to put paid to the possibility of their contributing to the fight for real change. Yet the proposed comprehensive strategy does represent the interests of the vast majority of Palestinians, and holds the promise of a better future.

The Palestinian national struggle has so far passed through two major phases: the first was steered by Palestinians abroad while ignoring the role of Palestinians at home, and the second was steered by Palestinians at home while ignoring the role of Palestinians abroad. Today we find ourselves at the threshold of a third phase, which should combine the struggle at home with the campaign of Palestinians and their sympathizers abroad.

In closing, I would like to address the subject of the choice between a one-state and a two-state solution.

It is both theoretically and practically valid to raise this subject here for two reasons. First, Israel has consistently tried to undermine the prospect of Palestinian statehood by pressing for such formulas as a self-governing authority, or an interim state, or a state without real sovereignty. All of these simply mean substituting real statehood with clusters of ghettos and bantustans. Second, the changes produced on the ground by Israeli settlements and ring roads have made a viable state unrealizable. Western lethargy means the clock may run out on the two-state solution. If so, the fault will rest with the failure to halt Israeli settlement activity. Prime Minister Netanyahu's declaration that settlement construction will continue in East Jerusalem, and with the construction of West Bank housing units already under development, made a mockery of the much-ballyhooed "freeze" that expired in September 2010 after ten months.

Let us be clear: Israel has been working around the clock to destroy the option of an independent Palestinian state and, by extension, the two-state solution. But that does not leave the Palestinian people without an alternative, as some Zionist leaders undoubtedly hope. The single democratic state (not the single binational state), in which all citizens are equal in rights and duties regardless of their religious affiliations and origins, is an alternative to the attempt to force the Palestinians to accept slavery under occupation, and an apartheid order in the form of a feeble autonomous government that is dubbed a state. We Palestinians are completely accustomed to—and unwilling to accept—such false compromises.

The demise of the two-state solution will only lead to a new struggle for equal rights within one state. Israel, which tragically favors supremacy rather than integration with its Palestinian neighbors, will have brought this new struggle on itself by relentlessly pushing the settlement enterprise. No one can say it was not warned.

However, neither a truly independent sovereign state nor a single democratic state, both of which Israel dismisses with equal vehemence, can be achieved without exposing and destroying the apartheid system. This requires a strategy. Therefore, instead of allowing ourselves to become divided prematurely over whether to go for the one-state or two-state solution, let us unify behind the common aim required to achieve either: the formulation and implementation of a strategy to fight the occupation, apartheid, and racial discrimination. This will lead us to something that is absolutely necessary at this stage, which is to move from the world of slogans to the world of practical activism, in accordance with viable strategic plans that mobilize demonstrators against the wall, together with intellectuals and politicians and other sectors of society. Slogans do not end liberation struggles. Slogans without strategies and efforts to back them up remain nothing but idle wishes—or, for some, a seemingly noble way to avoid responsibility and the work that goes with it.

It is high time we realized that diplomatic endeavors and negotiations do not free us from actual struggle. We have one road that leads to a single goal: the freedom of the Palestinian people. There is nothing nobler than to follow this road to its end. This is not a project for some point in the future; it is one that cannot wait. Indeed, we should adopt the slogan of the freedom fighters of South Africa: "Freedom now, and freedom in our lifetime!"

Eventually, we will be free in our own country—either as a result of the two-state solution or in a new, integrated state. There comes a time when people cannot take injustice anymore; for Palestine, that time has come.

2 NI'LIN LIKE SOWETO

Jonathan Pollak

I was six years old in 1988, and it was the height of the first Intifada. The television screen in my parents' living room flickered with images of hundreds of people, mostly young men, demonstrating. Many were masked with keffiyehs, some were hurling rocks, some burning tires, some flying flags. Three were shot dead. The clear voice of the Israeli Channel One News anchorman announced their deaths with not even the slightest tremble. They were Palestinians and "rioters," and in the eyes of the anchorman that is all they were—nameless and dead. That same day, similar images could have been aired from Soweto, Cape Town, or Durban.

Though much time has passed, not much has essentially changed—and what has changed has changed for the worse. More than twenty years on, while South Africa, though still troubled, is free from apartheid, demonstrators are still imprisoned, terrorized, and shot on a regular basis in Palestinian villages in revolt, such as Bil'in, Nabi Saleh and Ni'lin.

The construction of Israel's wall on Ni'lin's land began in 2004, but was halted after an injunction was issued by the Israeli High Court. Despite this order and the 2004 advisory opinion by the International Court of Justice pronouncing it illegal, construction of the wall in the village resumed in May 2008, as Israeli bulldozers started clearing a path through Ni'lin's ancient olive groves. Following the bulldozers' return, residents of Ni'lin launched a rolling campaign to protest the massive land theft, using demonstrations, strikes, and direct action. In turn, the Israeli army has responded as it always does to civil resistance—by military might. Five of Ni'lin's protesters, including a ten-year-old, have been killed, hundreds seriously injured, and more than a hundred imprisoned.

Aqel Srour is the fifth and latest of Ni'lin's demonstrators to have lost their lives to Israeli bullets. Demonstrations continue, and, tragically, Srour is unlikely to be the last one killed. In fact, more unarmed protesters have since been killed in other villages. On June 5, 2009, Srour was shot dead as he ran towards another demonstrator, a fifteen-year-old, who had just been shot in the stomach. The bullet that killed Aqel, a single shot fired by a sniper, hit him in the heart. That same day, four more people were shot by snipers who lurked in the groves.

Standing a few meters away, we heard a shot fired, followed by a startling groan, and immediately started running in its direction. When I reached him, he had just collapsed. Both hands on his chest, he went down on his knees and fell backwards. His buttoned white shirt was soaked in the red of his blood. I tried ripping it open, but could not find the strength. Someone else did so a few seconds later.

Medics arrived with a bright orange stretcher. I grabbed the left side, in the middle, and we started running. The ambulance was perhaps 300 feet away. I looked in his eyes, and he looked in mine—maybe on purpose, but probably not. I could not look away from those eyes even as death took them over, their potency replaced with a void. His mouth started foaming and his skin turned yellow and stiff. We tried shouting his name and asked him to speak, to say something, anything. He was already dead.

The soldiers backtracked to their armored jeeps and drove away. We ran after them in all our rage, screaming, but they were gone. We found them only a kilometer away, in an olive grove that was left untouched near the wall. As we were shrouded by clouds of tear gas, someone's phone rang, formally announcing his death. We walked back towards the village, and half-way over, on the arid hill, I stopped alone and cried. Around me were a dozen others, crying alone too.

How many times have I cried alone this way for a friend whose life was taken? How many more times will I do the same?

At the funeral, the following day, I stood by the freshly dug grave, watching as the body was being lowered. Next to me was an old friend, a veteran of the first Intifada, perhaps one of those young men I saw on TV as a child. He muttered, as if to himself, "We have chosen this path. It was not forced upon us; we know the price we must pay."

He was right. We do know the price, and we do make our choices; but the tears that end up in our mouth still taste just as salty, and the pain does not lessen. On the contrary, it grows. And the greater it grows, the clearer the path is, and the firmer our commitment.

Clarity hits hard in the pauses between grief and rage, between anger and sadness. And there are a lot of them to spare. The support garnered by a movement of ordinary people facing military might is sometimes difficult for its protagonists to perceive in real time. The need for such support is never as clear as during funerals of those killed in the struggle.

The ability of civil uprisings to prevail depends greatly on the external support that they succeed or fail to generate, and on the ability of that support to curb the violence of repression. In the mid to late 1980s, the South African anti-apartheid movement began winning partly because the Goliath that was South Africa's army could no longer hold the line against rock-throwing Davids of the townships. Israel today, though, is more reminiscent of the South Africa of the 1960s, with an impeccable economy that has grown even at times of global economic crisis, and despite (or perhaps thanks to) its being an occupying power. When we demonstrate today, the army still comfortably holds the line against justice.

Enormous and powerful interests are vested in Israel and its occupation. A BDS movement is one way for ordinary people to take some of this power back. Boycott, divestment, and sanctions are chiefly a question of solidarity, pressure, and morale. Desmond Tutu, perhaps the person most synonymous with the South African anti-apartheid boycott movement, had said on many occasions that the BDS campaign was important in the South African case, since it was one of the most psychologically powerful instruments—its effects seemed to leave no one untouched. He also often says that it gave black people hope that the world cared, that this was a form of solidarity.

Ni'lin, just like Soweto, needs the world to stand behind it and generate significant pressure. Only this can stop the bullets and shift the tide between demonstrator and armed oppressor, between soldiers and freedom fighters. In Palestine, just as in South Africa, a strong BDS movement can make that change.

3 WHAT GOES ON WHEN NOTHING GOES ON?

Slavoj Žižek

On August 2, 2009, after cordoning off part of the Arab neighborhood of Sheikh Jarrah in East Jerusalem, Israeli police evicted two Palestinian families (more than 50 people) from their homes, allowing Jewish settlers immediately to move into the vacated houses. Although Israeli police cited a ruling by the country's Supreme Court, the evicted Arab families had been living there for more than 50 years. This event which, rather exceptionally, did attract the attention of the world media, is part of a much larger and mostly ignored ongoing process.

Two years later, not much has changed. On October 16, 2011, Israel announced plans to build 2,600 new homes in southern Jerusalem, despite condemnation from the UN, the EU, and Britain. If implemented, the plans would not only divide the Arab section of the city from the rest of the occupied West Bank, but also severely undermine the chances of a viable Palestinian state and hamper the everyday life of Palestinians. The conclusion is obvious: while paying lip-service to the two-state solution, Israel is busy creating a situation on the ground that will render a two-state solution practically impossible. The dream that underlies this politics is best rendered by the wall that separates a settler's town from the Palestinian town on a nearby hill somewhere in the West Bank. The Israeli side of the wall is painted with the image of the countryside beyond the wall—but without the Palestinian town, depicting just nature, grass, trees … Is this not ethnic cleansing at its purest, imagining the outside beyond the wall as it should be: empty, virginal, waiting to be settled?

This process is sometimes in the guise of cultural gentrification. On October 28, 2008, the Israeli Supreme Court ruled that the Simon Wiesenthal

Center could proceed to build its long-planned Center for Human Dignity—Museum of Tolerance on a contested site in the middle of Jerusalem. It is currently under construction. Frank Gehry (who else?), until he withdrew from the project in 2010, was commissioned to design the vast complex consisting of a general museum, children's museum, theater, conference center, library, gallery, lecture halls, cafeterias, and so on. The museum's declared mission will be to promote civility and respect among different segments of the Jewish community and between people of all faiths—the only obstacle (overrun by the Supreme Court's ruling) being that the museum site served as Jerusalem's main Muslim cemetery until 1948 (the Muslim community appealed to the Supreme Court that museum construction would desecrate the cemetery, which allegedly contained the bones of Muslims killed during the Crusades of the twelfth and thirteenth centuries). This dark spot wonderfully enacts the hidden truth of this multi-confessional project: it is a place celebrating tolerance, open to all ... but protected by the Israeli cupola which ignores the subterranean victims of intolerance—as if one needs a little bit of intolerance to create the space for true tolerance.

What does all this mean? To get at the true significance of news, it is sometimes enough to read two disparate news items together—meaning emerges from their very link, like a spark exploding from an electric short circuit. On September 21, 2011, Obama criticized the Palestinian bid for UN membership, stating to the world that "peace will not come through statements and resolutions at the UN." Less than one week later, on September 27, Israel announced plans to build another 1,100 new settlement units in the south of Jerusalem (outside of its pre-1967 boundaries), and the quartet—the US, EU, UN, and Russia—simply called on both sides to return to negotiations and "refrain from provocative actions," without making any mention of a settlement freeze.

So should the Palestinians stand idly while the West Bank land is taken from them day by day? When Israeli peace-loving liberals present their conflict with Palestinians in neutral "symmetrical" terms, admitting that there are extremists on both sides who reject peace, and so on, one should ask a simple question: What goes on in the Middle East when *nothing goes on there* at the direct politico-military level (i.e. when there are no tensions, attacks, negotiations)? What goes on is the incessant slow work of taking the land from the Palestinians in the West Bank: the gradual strangling of the

Palestinian economy, the parceling of their land, the building of new settlements, the pressure on Palestinian farmers to make them abandon their land (which goes from crop-burning and religious desecration up to individual killings), all this supported by a Kafkaesque network of legal regulations. Saree Makdisi, in *Palestine Inside Out: An Everyday Occupation*, described how, although the Israeli occupation of the West Bank is ultimately enforced by the armed forces, it is an "occupation by bureaucracy": its primary forms are application forms, title deeds, residency papers, and other permits. It is this micromanagement of daily life which does the job of securing the slow but steadfast Israeli expansion: one has to ask for a permit in order to leave with one's family, to farm one's own land, to dig a well, to go to work, to school, to a hospital … One by one, Palestinians born in Jerusalem are thus stripped of the right to live there, prevented from earning a living, denied housing permits, and so on. Palestinians often use the problematic cliché of the Gaza Strip as "the greatest concentration camp in the world"— however, this designation has come dangerously close to truth. This is the fundamental reality which makes all abstract "prayers for peace" obscene and hypocritical. The State of Israel is clearly engaged in a slow, invisible process, ignored by the media, a kind of underground digging of the mole, so that, one day, the world will awaken and realize that there is no more Palestinian West Bank, that the land is Palestinian-*frei*, and that we can only accept the fact. The map of the Palestinian West Bank already looks like a fragmented archipelago.

At times, the State of Israel has tried to contain Israel's excesses, as when the Supreme Court ordered the evacuation of some settlements in late 2008, when illegal West Bank settler attacks on Palestinian farmers had become a daily occurrence. But, as many observers noted then, these measures cannot but appear half-hearted, counteracting a politics which, at a deeper level, *is* the long-term politics of the State of Israel, which massively violates the international treaties signed by Israel itself. Netanyahu is proceeding full steam ahead with plans for new illegal settlements, despite widespread international condemnation. The reply of the illegal settlers to the Israeli authorities is basically: We are doing the same thing as you, just more openly, so what right do you have to condemn us? And the answer of the state is basically: Be patient, don't rush too much; we are doing what you want, just in a more moderate and acceptable way. The same story seems to continue from 1949: while Israel accepts the peace conditions proposed by the inter-national community, it calculates that the peace plan will not work. The wild settlers sometimes sound like Brünnhilde from the last act of Wagner's *Die Walküre*, reproaching Wotan that, by counteracting his explicit order and protecting Siegmund, she was only realizing Wotan's own true desire, which he was forced to renounce under external pressure. In the same way, the illegal settlers only realize the state's true desire that it was forced to renounce because of the pressure of the international community. While condemning the openly violent excesses of "illegal" settlements, the State of Israel promotes new "legal" West Bank settlements, continues to strangle the Palestinian economy, and so on. A look at the changing map of East Jerusalem, where the Palestinians are gradually being encircled and their space sliced up, says it all. The condemnation of non-state anti-Palestinian violence obfuscates the true problem of *state* violence; the condemnation of illegal settlements obfuscates the illegality of the legal ones. Therein resides the two-facedness of the much-praised non-biased "honesty" of the Israeli Supreme Court: by means of occasionally passing a judgment in favor of the dispossessed Palestinians, proclaiming their eviction illegal, it guarantees the legality of the remaining majority of cases.

And—to avoid any kind of misunderstanding—taking all this into account in no way implies any "understanding" for inexcusable terrorist acts. On the contrary, it provides the only ground from which one can condemn the terrorist attacks without hypocrisy.

Part II THE BOYCOTT MOVEMENT

4 BDS MOVEMENT CALL, JULY 9, 2005

PALESTINIAN CIVIL SOCIETY CALLS FOR BOYCOTT, DIVESTMENT AND SANCTIONS AGAINST ISRAEL UNTIL IT COMPLIES WITH INTERNATIONAL LAW AND UNIVERSAL PRINCIPLES OF HUMAN RIGHTS

One year after the historic Advisory Opinion of the International Court of Justice (ICJ) which found Israel's Wall built on occupied Palestinian territory to be illegal, Israel continues its construction of the colonial Wall with total disregard for the court's decision. Thirty-eight years into Israel's occupation of the Palestinian West Bank (including East Jerusalem), Gaza Strip, and the Syrian Golan Heights, Israel continues to expand Jewish colonies. It has unilaterally annexed occupied East Jerusalem and the Golan Heights and is now de facto annexing large parts of the West Bank by means of the Wall. Israel is also preparing—in the shadow of its planned redeployment from the Gaza Strip—to build and expand colonies in the West Bank. Fifty-seven years after the State of Israel was built mainly on land ethnically cleansed of its Palestinian owners, a majority of Palestinians are refugees, most of whom are stateless. Moreover, Israel's entrenched system of racial discrimination against its own Arab-Palestinian citizens remains intact.

In light of Israel's persistent violations of international law; and

Given that, since 1948, hundreds of UN resolutions have condemned Israel's colonial and discriminatory policies as illegal and called for immediate, adequate, and effective remedies; and

Given that all forms of international intervention and peacemaking have until now failed to convince or force Israel to comply with humanitarian law, to respect fundamental human rights, and to end its occupation and oppression of the people of Palestine; and

In view of the fact that people of conscience in the international community have historically shouldered the moral responsibility to fight injustice, as exemplified in the struggle to abolish apartheid in South Africa through diverse forms of boycott, divestment, and sanctions; and

Inspired by the struggle of South Africans against apartheid and in the spirit of international solidarity, moral consistency, and resistance to injustice and oppression;

We, representatives of Palestinian civil society, call upon international civil society organizations and people of conscience all over the world to impose broad boycotts and implement divestment initiatives against Israel similar to those applied to South Africa in the apartheid era. We appeal to you to pressure your respective states to impose embargoes and sanctions against Israel. We also invite conscientious Israelis to support this Call, for the sake of justice and genuine peace.

These nonviolent punitive measures should be maintained until Israel meets its obligation to recognize the Palestinian people's inalienable right to self-determination and fully complies with the precepts of international law by:

1. Ending its occupation and colonization of all Arab lands and dismantling the Wall;
2. Recognizing the fundamental rights of the Arab-Palestinian citizens of Israel to full equality; and
3. Respecting, protecting and promoting the rights of Palestinian refugees to return to their homes and properties as stipulated in UN resolution 194.

The Palestinian political parties, unions, associations, coalitions, and organizations representing the three integral parts of the people of Palestine: Palestinian refugees, Palestinians under occupation, and Palestinian citizens of Israel.

5 THE CULTURAL BOYCOTT: ISRAEL VS. SOUTH AFRICA

Omar Barghouti

Just as we said during apartheid that it was inappropriate for international artists to perform in South Africa in a society founded on discriminatory laws and racial exclusivity, so it would be wrong for Cape Town Opera to perform in Israel.[1]

Desmond Tutu, October 26, 2010

Since the great majority of Palestinian civil society issued its call for BDS against Israel in July 2005 to compel it to fulfill its obligations under international law, there has never been a period with as many BDS achievements as that following the Israeli massacre in Gaza in the winter of 2008–09 and the bloodbath on the Gaza-bound Freedom Flotilla in May 2010. A long-dormant sense of international public outrage at Israel's exceptional status as a state above the law, protected mainly by deep Western complicity, has been rudely awakened in reaction to these atrocities. People of conscience around the world seem to have crossed a threshold in challenging Israel's impunity through effective pressure, rather than appeasement or "constructive engagement." This has been most pronounced in the cultural field, where support for the 2004 call by the Palestinian Campaign for the Academic and Cultural Boycott of Israel (PACBI)[2] has witnessed spectacular growth.

In 2009, USACBI, a US-based campaign for the academic and cultural boycott of Israel, was formed. More than 500 academics have endorsed

---

1   "Tutu Urges Cape Town Opera to Call Off Israel Tour," *Times* (South Africa), October 26, 2010, at timeslive.co.za.
2   "Call for Academic and Cultural Boycott of Israel," at pacbi.org.

its call, not to mention the hundreds of cultural figures who have also signed on.[3]

Also in 2009, "Boycott! Supporting the Palestinian BDS Call from Within"[4] (or Boycott from Within, for short) was established, and has played an indispensable role in advocating the cultural boycott of Israel among leading arts figures and bands around the world.

In October 2010, a Norwegian petition calling for an institutional cultural and academic boycott of Israel (in line with the PACBI principles) has gathered one hundred impressive signatories—academics, writers, musicians, other cultural workers, and sports celebrities.[5] Around the same time, the European Platform for the Academic and Cultural Boycott of Israel (EPACBI) was announced, with the participation of boycott campaigns from across the continent, in full coordination with PACBI.[6]

Weeks earlier, the Indian Campaign for the Academic and Cultural Boycott of Israel had been launched, with the endorsement of some of India's most famous writers and academics.[7]

In November 2010, in a development that will be recorded as historic, artists in South Africa supporting the BDS call against Israel issued a declaration[8] titled "South African Artists against Apartheid." It followed a similar declaration in February by 500 artists in Montreal,[9] Canada, supporting BDS and, in August, an Irish pledge for cultural boycott[10]—the first national cultural boycott campaign against Israel.

---

3   US Campaign for the Academic and Cultural Boycott of Israel, "Endorse Our Call to Boycott," at usacbi.wordpress.com.
4   Boycott! Supporting the Palestinian BDS Call from Within, at boycottisrael. info.
5   "Call for an Academic and Cultural Boycott of the State of Israel," at akulbi.net.
6   PACBI, "European Platform for the Academic and Cultural Boycott of Israel (EPACBI) Brings Boycott Movement to a Higher Level in Europe," October 12, 2010, at pacbi.org.
7   "Indian Call for the Academic and Cultural Boycott of Israel," July 2010, at pacbi.org.
8   "South African Artists Against Apartheid: A Declaration," at www.south africanartistsagainstapartheid.com.
9   "500 Artists Against Israeli Apartheid," at tadamon.ca.
10   Ireland Palestine Solidarity Campaign, "IPSC 'Irish Artists' Pledge to Boycott Israel," at pacbi.org.

Academic and cultural boycott campaigns have also spread to France,[11] Italy,[12] and Spain,[13] among other countries.

In the aftermath of the flotilla attack, best-selling authors like Iain Banks, Alice Walker, and Henning Mankell explicitly advocated the boycott against Israel, as did eminent scholar Ann Laura Stoler.[14] Top artists have shunned Israel, due to its violation of international law and Palestinian rights, most often silently, without issuing public statements to that effect. News of megastar Meg Ryan's cancellation of a visit to Israel and of concert cancellations by Elvis Costello, Gil Scott-Heron, Carlos Santana, the Pixies, Faithless, Vanessa Paradis, Ladysmith Black Mambazo, Jello Biafra, Thomas Quasthoff, August Burns Red, Marc Almond, among others, has finally put to rest skepticism about the potential of the campaign. World-renowned filmmakers, from Jean-Luc Godard[15] and the Yes Men[16] to Mike Leigh,[17] have also heeded the boycott call and stayed away from Israeli festivals. John Greyson and Ken Loach have played a distinguished role in promoting the cultural boycott and popularizing its criteria and guidelines.

Support for BDS has also come from renowned authors and cultural figures of the caliber of John Berger, Roger Waters, Naomi Klein, Arundhati Roy, Judith Butler, Aharon Shabtai, Udi Aloni, Sarah Schulman, Angela Davis, Barbara Hammer, Pushpamala N., and Adrienne Rich.[18]

In September 2010, in nothing less than a watershed in the cultural boycott, more than 150 mainstream US and British theater, film, and TV

---

11   Association des Universitaires pour le Respect du Droit International en Palestine, at aurdip.fr.

12   "L'appello italiano per il boicottaggio accademico e culturale," at sites.google.com/site/icacbi.

13   Comissió Universitària Catalana per Palestina, "Col·laboració amb xarxes europees: No a l'acord EU–Israel," April 30, 2010, at cuncap.wordpress.com.

14   Ann Laura Stoler, "By Colonial Design," September 10, 2010, at pacbi.org.

15   Matthew B. Zeidman, "Jean-Luc Godard Cancels Trip to Tel Aviv Student Film Festival," *Hollywood Today*, June 3, 2008, at hollywoodtoday.net.

16   "For Once, the Yes Men Say No," letter from the Yes Men to the Jerusalem Film Festival, July 3, 2009, at pacbi.org.

17   Hannah Brown, "Mike Leigh Cancels Visit over 'Israeli Policies,'" *Jerusalem Post*, October 17, 2010, at jpost.com.

18   See various reports at www.pacbi.org.

artists issued a statement,[19] initiated by Jewish Voice for Peace, supporting the spreading cultural boycott inside Israel of its colonial settlements illegally built on occupied Palestinian territory, due to their violation of international law.[20] Frank Gehry, of Guggenheim fame, joined the supporters of this targeted boycott.[21] While falling short of endorsing a comprehensive cultural boycott of Israel, this initiative broke a long-standing taboo in the US, in particular, against calling for any pressure, let alone boycott, to be brought to bear against Israel in response to its ongoing violations of international law and war crimes. In the US context, where dissent from the bipartisan line that treats Israel as above the law of nations, often ahead of US interests,[22] may cost an artist, journalist, elected official, academic, or just about anyone else dearly, this artists' statement is beyond courageous. Condemning Israel's colonial settlements and "ugly occupation," expressing "hope for a just and lasting peace" in the region, and endorsing the logic of boycott as an effective and perfectly legitimate tool to end injustice, the statement is precedent-setting. Finally, famous US artists seem to have grasped Nelson Mandela's caution against the enticement "to read reconciliation and fairness as meaning parity between justice and injustice."[23]

This cherry-picking boycott of Israeli institutions based in colonies was

---

19   "Israeli Artists Condemn Settlements," Jewish Voice for Peace, at jvp.org.

20   Chaim Levinson and Or Kashti, "150 Academics, Artists Back Actors' Boycott of Settlement Arts Center," *Haaretz*, August 31, 2010, at haaretz.com.

21   Abe Hayeem, "Architects Against Israeli Occupation," *Guardian*, October 4, 2010, at guardian.co.uk.

22   In their book *The Israel Lobby and US Foreign Policy* (Farrar, Straus & Giroux, 2008), John Mearsheimer and Stephen Walt make a compelling and well-documented argument that Israel's influence over the decision-making apparatus is not necessarily a function of shared interests with the US but rather a result of its lobby's massive power. Without denying the almost unparalleled influence the Israeli lobby has in designing and shaping US policy in the Middle East and beyond, I wish to make a clear distinction here between the interest of the majority of the people in the US and that of the military–oil–security complex. The latter has a record of supporting war, including Israeli militarism and expansionism.

23   Desmond Tutu, "Israeli Ties: A Chance to Do the Right Thing," *Times* (South Africa), September 26, 2010, at timeslive.co.za.

initiated by some of the same figures in the Zionist "left" camp[24] who had vehemently and angrily opposed the PACBI call when it was first issued, citing the principled obligation to uphold "academic freedom" or "artistic communication channels." Suddenly, the lofty language of rejecting boycott in the cultural field in the name of protecting free speech and dialogue disappears, and the boycott becomes not only legitimate but an absolute moral duty when it fits the narrow political agenda of that Zionist "left."[25]

CHALLENGES

Despite the spectacular spread of the cultural boycott of Israel, there have been some painful exceptions where the boycott picket line has been crossed.

In a well-publicized appeal[26] to the Cape Town Opera of South Africa to cancel its "unconscionable" performance in Tel Aviv, and to respect the Palestinian-invoked cultural boycott of Israel,[27] Archbishop Emeritus Desmond Tutu wrote, "Only the thickest-skinned South Africans would be comfortable performing before an audience that excluded residents living, for example, in an occupied West Bank village 30 minutes from Tel Aviv, who would not be allowed to travel to Tel Aviv, while including his Jewish neighbours from an illegal settlement on occupied Palestinian territory." Despite this impassioned appeal, the Cape Town Opera decided to go ahead with its performance, violating the cultural boycott guidelines set by the Palestinian Campaign for the Academic and Cultural Boycott of Israel and

---

24   There is no "scientific" definition of such a camp, but for the purposes of this chapter they are defined as those who support ending a small subset of Israeli injustices against the Palestinians not out of a principled commitment to universal rights and international law, but for the sake of strengthening Israel as a Jewish supremacist, therefore racist, state.

25   For more on the inconsistencies of the Zionist "left" in dealing with the boycott of Israel, see "Boycotting Israel: Missing the Forest for the Trees," September 26, 2010, and "Boycott 'Ariel' and the Rest! All Israeli Academic Institutions are Complicit in Occupation and Apartheid," February 10, 2010, both at pacbi.org.

26   "Cape Town Opera to Go on Israel Tour Despite Tutu Plea," BBC, October 27, 2010, at bbc.co.uk.

27   See pacbi.org.

adopted by the great majority of Palestinian artists and cultural figures,[28] and by tens of leading international cultural figures.[29]

The controversy around this setback helped to expose the entrenched complicity of Israeli cultural institutions in covering up the state's multi-tiered system of colonial oppression against the Palestinian people. Crucially, it also contributed to highlighting the moral obligation of international artists to refrain, at a bare minimum, from entertaining Israeli apartheid and colluding in Israeli attempts to whitewash its crimes with a thick, deceptive cover of artistic and scientific vibrancy. The intense debate in the media about this and similar violations of the boycott has significantly raised international awareness of the crucial role the cultural boycott played in the South African anti-apartheid struggle, and its expected role in the Palestinian struggle for self-determination, freedom, justice, and equality.

There were two immediate, noteworthy outcomes of this success of the BDS movement in tarnishing the Israel "brand" in the cultural field, despite the feverish efforts by Israel and its lobby groups to re-brand the state with an expensive PR campaign. First, an impressively growing number of well-known artists have started to turn down invitations to perform in Israel, despite being offered "extreme, big numbers"[30] in fees; second, those few who finally accept such invitations are ashamed enough, due to public exposure, to attempt to provide a fig-leaf[31] for their complicity with Israel by means of a visit to the Occupied Palestinian Territories and an activity with just about any Palestinian artist or cultural institution. More often than not, however, such "fig-leafing" attempts have been futile, mainly due to increased awareness of them, and the overwhelming support for the cultural boycott of Israel among Palestinian artists and cultural institutions.

The most resilient objection to the cultural and academic boycott is in fact based on a wrong premise—that we are calling for ostracizing *individual*

---

28 "Palestinian Filmmakers, Artists and Cultural Workers Call for a Cultural Boycott of Israel," August 4, 2006, at pacbi.org.
29 "John Berger and 93 Other Authors, Film-Makers, Musicians and Performers Call for a Cultural Boycott of Israel," December 15, 2006, at pacbi.org.
30 "Boycott Targets Stars from Elvis to Elton," *Jewish Daily Forward*, May 19, 2010, at forward.com.
31 "On BDS Bashers and Their Search for Fig Leaves," June 29, 2011, at pacbi.org.

Israeli academics, writers and artists. PACBI has never done so. The 2004 PACBI Call,[32] like all subsequent PACBI documents and speeches on record, have consistently called on international artists, academics, and institutions to observe a boycott of all Israeli academic and cultural *institutions* (including formal bands and orchestras), not individuals. Unlike the South African academic and cultural boycott, which was a "blanket" boycott that targeted everyone and everything South African, the Palestinian boycott targets institutions only, due to their entrenched complicity in planning, justifying, whitewashing, or otherwise perpetuating Israel's violations of international law and Palestinian rights.

PACBI has never targeted individual artists or academics, not because they tend to be more progressive or opposed to injustice than the rest of society, as is often mistakenly assumed, but because we are opposed on principle to political testing and "blacklisting." If the UN eventually develops well-conceived and sufficiently justified lists based on widely accepted criteria of international law, as it did in the last stage of the struggle against apartheid in South Africa, then that would be a different matter; but the BDS movement, of which PACBI is a part, being a civil society movement, does not subscribe to drawing up lists to decide who is a good Israeli and who is not based on some arbitrary political criteria.[33]

ISRAEL VS. SOUTH AFRICA: APARTHEID BY ANY OTHER NAME

Those who are now hesitant to support a boycott of Israel's academic and cultural institutions while having in the past endorsed or even struggled to implement a blanket academic or cultural boycott against apartheid South Africa are hard-pressed to explain this peculiar inconsistency.

Israel operates a more sophisticated, evolved, and brutal form of apartheid[34] than its South African predecessor, according to authoritative

---

32   "Call for Academic and Cultural Boycott of Israel," July 6, 2004, at pacbi.org.
33   "PACBI Guidelines for the International Academic Boycott of Israel (Revised August 2010)," and "PACBI Guidelines for the International Cultural Boycott of Israel (Revised October 2010)," both at pacbi.org.
34   Israel's legalized, institutionalized system of racial discrimination fits the UN definition of the crime of apartheid in the 1973 International Convention of the Suppression and Punishment of the Crime of Apartheid and the 2002 Rome Statute of the International Criminal Court. See "International Convention on

statements by South African anti-apartheid leaders like Archbishop Desmond Tutu[35] and the country's past cabinet minister Ronnie Kasrils,[36] who is Jewish—among many others. From all people of conscience around the world, particularly those who opposed South African apartheid, the Palestinian cause therefore deserves the same measure of solidarity and human compassion, through an effective application of BDS against Israel until it abides by international law and respects basic human rights.

Sixty-three years after its establishment through a deliberate and systemic process of forcible displacement of a majority of the indigenous Palestinian population, Israel still practices racial discrimination against its own "non-Jewish" citizens; still maintains the longest military occupation in modern history; still denies Palestinian refugees—uprooted, dispossessed, and expelled by Zionists over the last six decades—their internationally recognized right to return to their homes and properties; and still commits war crimes and violates basic human rights and tenets of international humanitarian law with utter impunity.

Some may argue that, to them, art should transcend political division, unifying people in their common humanity. This argument ignores the political content and role of most artistic expression, particularly in situations of sustained oppression. Moreover, those parroting it seem to forget that the proverbial masters and slaves share little in common—least of all any notion of humanity. Rather than reinventing the wheel, I recall the wise words of Enuga S. Reddy, director of the United Nations Centre Against Apartheid, who in 1984 responded as follows to criticism that the cultural boycott of South Africa infringed the freedom of expression:

---

the Suppression and Punishment of the Crime of Apartheid," at icc-cpi.int, and "Treaties and International Agreements Registered or Filed and Recorded with the Secretariat of the United Nations," at treaties.un.org. Even US Department of State human rights reports have consistently accused Israel of "institutional, legal, and societal discrimination" against Palestinian citizens of the state. See, for example, "2010 Human Rights Report: Israel and the Occupied Territories," April 8, 2011, at state.gov.

35   "Tutu Condemns Israeli 'Apartheid,'" BBC, April 29, 2002, at news.bbc.co.uk.

36   Ronnie Kasrils, "Israel 2007: Worse Than Apartheid," *Mail & Guardian*, May 21, 2007, at mg.co.za.

It is rather strange, to say the least, that the South African regime which denies all freedoms … to the African majority … should become a defender of the freedom of artists and sportsmen of the world. We have a list of people who have performed in South Africa because of ignorance of the situation or the lure of money or unconcern over racism. They need to be persuaded to stop entertaining apartheid, to stop profiting from apartheid money and to stop serving the propaganda purposes of the apartheid regime.[37]

That was two decades after the Irish Anti-Apartheid Movement, in 1964, first issued a declaration, signed by twenty-eight Irish playwrights undertaking not to permit their work to be performed before segregated audiences in South Africa.[38] The next year, in 1965, the American Committee on Africa, following the lead of prominent British and Irish arts associations, sponsored a historic declaration against South African apartheid, signed by more than sixty cultural personalities. In December 1980, the United Nations General Assembly finally adopted a special resolution on the cultural boycott of South Africa, heeding consistent appeals by black organizations in South Africa that in effect censured several foreign entertainers who violated the boycott.

RE-BRANDING ISRAEL

In a recent statement, Mr. Isaac Zablocki, the director of the Israel Film Center in New York, said:

The goal of the center is to share with the public these amazing cinematic achievements coming out of a country that is normally only seen through news headlines. Through our viewing library, screenings and promotion of films, we hope to share with the public a new slice of Israeli reality … an Israel filled with innocence, humor, and ideals.[39]

---

37   "Cultural Boycott: Statement by Enuga S. Reddy, Director of U.N. Centre Against Apartheid at a Press Briefing (1984)," January 11, 1984, at pacbi.org.
38   United Nations Centre Against Apartheid, "Some Important Developments in the Movement for a Cultural Boycott Against South Africa," November 25, 1983, at anc.org.za.
39   "Announcing: New (and Enormous) Database of Israeli Films is Now Live," July 7, 2010, at cultureshuk.com.

This strikingly echoed the logic of the official Brand Israel campaign, launched by the government of Israel as early as 2005 and intensified ever since, particularly at every juncture when Israel has faced international fury upon committing war crimes, as happened in 2006 in Lebanon, in the winter of 2008–09 in Gaza, and, most recently, following the bloody attack on the humanitarian flotilla destined to Gaza. The campaign, which was developed by the directors of Israel's three most powerful ministries, focused on a new plan to improve Israel's image abroad "by downplaying religion and avoiding any discussion of the conflict with the Palestinians."[40] Non-Jewish Americans, in focus groups that were researched for the purposes of this campaign, "almost universally saw Israel only as 'militaristic' and 'religious,'" the report revealed. It went on to describe the campaign as "the latest manifestation of a growing movement—begun in America—to 're-brand' Israel, or to reinvent the country's image in the eyes of both Jews and non-Jews. The driving concept is that Israel will win supporters only if it is seen as relevant and modern rather than only as a place of fighting and religion." A former deputy director general of the Israeli foreign ministry, Nissim Ben-Sheetrit, explained upon launching the Brand Israel campaign in 2005: "We are seeing culture as a *hasbara* [propaganda] tool of the first rank, and I do not differentiate between *hasbara* and culture."[41]

After the Israeli war of aggression against the besieged Gaza Strip, Israel's image took a further steep dip, prompting the government to throw more money into the Brand Israel campaign. One of the main figures in the campaign, Arye Mekel, the deputy director general for cultural affairs in the Israeli foreign ministry, told the *New York Times*: "We will send well-known novelists and writers overseas, theater companies, exhibits. This way you show Israel's prettier face, so we are not thought of purely in the context of war."[42] And indeed, Israel has been sending ever more dance companies, orchestras, poets, and films abroad, particularly following Operation Cast Lead. The greater the number of innocent victims of Israel's incessant

---

40   Nathaniel Popper, "Israel Aims to Improve Its Public Image," *Jewish Daily Forward*, October 14, 2005, at forward.com.

41   Yuval Ben Ami, "About Face," *Haaretz*, September 20, 2005, at haaretz.com.

42   Ethan Bronner, "After Gaza, Israel Grapples with Crisis of Isolation," *New York Times*, March 18, 2009, at nytimes.com.

brutality and belligerence, the more money it needs to spend, the argument goes, to whitewash its gruesome image.

This much is now well known. What is less known or discussed in the media is a hidden aspect of the Brand Israel effort—a contract that obliges artists and writers, as "service providers" who receive state funding, to conform with, and indeed promote, state policies. Basically, the contract buys the artists' and writers' consciences, making a mockery of the "freedom of expression" mantra.

This contract was revealed in an article in *Haaretz*[43] instructively titled "Putting Out a Contract on Art," by the famous Israeli writer Yitzhak Laor. Because of the exceptional importance of this contract in understanding the organic partnership between the state and the duly complacent and complicit intelligentsia, its most relevant parts are reproduced here:

> The service provider undertakes to act faithfully, responsibly and tirelessly to provide the Ministry with the highest professional services. The service provider is aware that the purpose of ordering services from him is to promote the policy interests of the State of Israel via culture and art, including contributing to creating a positive image for Israel.
>
> The service provider will not present himself as an agent, emissary and/or representative of the Ministry.
>
> ...
>
> The Ministry is entitled to terminate this contract, or a part thereof, immediately and at the Ministry's sole discretion, if the service provider does not provide the Ministry with the services and/or does not fulfill his obligations under this contract and/or does not provide the services and/or fulfill his obligations to the Ministry's full satisfaction, and/or provides the services in an inadequate fashion and/or deviates from the timetable, and/or if the Ministry does not need the services of the service provider for any reason and/or for budgetary, organizational or security and/or policy reasons, and the service provider will make no claim, demand or suit based on the termination of the contract by the Ministry.

---

43   Yitzhak Laor, "Putting Out a Contract on Art," *Haaretz*, July 25, 2008, at haaretz.com.

HURTING THE VICTIMS OF APARTHEID?

An argument often raised to counter the case for a cultural boycott of Israel is that such a boycott, if it entails refusing to show artworks in Israel, may actually hurt the state's victims, the Palestinians, more than it would hurt Israel itself.

US filmmaker Jonathan Demme, who with Martin Scorsese cofounded Filmmakers United Against Apartheid, to protest the racist regime in South Africa in the 1980s, was asked[44] if denying American movies to all South African audiences would punish blacks as well as the white regime. He replied: "We believe the answer is no. Leaders of the [opposition] African National Congress have said they fervently want a boycott ... As far as denying the consciousness-raising among whites that American films could provide, the consensus is that it will take more than one movie or group of movies to raise the consciousness of the white rulers."

Israeli cultural as well as academic institutions will always claim that a boycott would infringe their freedom, and would punish artists and academics who are the most progressive and opposed to the "occupation" in Israeli society. In fact, this argument, aside from being quite disingenuous, is intended to deflect attention from two basic facts: first, that the Palestinian academic and cultural boycott of Israel targets institutions, not individuals; and second, that those institutions, far from being more progressive than the average in Israel, are a main pillar of the Israeli structure of colonial and apartheid oppression. Not only do the oppressed lose nothing when people of conscience boycott institutions that are persistently complicit in the system of oppression; in fact, they gain enormously from the ultimate weakening of this complicity that results from an effective and sustained boycott.

"NO REASON TO CELEBRATE"

One of the largest "branding" efforts was organized in 2008 by the Israeli government for the sixtieth anniversary of the establishment of the state. Some of the most prominent artists, politicians, academics, and others were invited to celebrate with Israel. In response, PACBI, in cooperation with the Palestinian NGO Network, took out a half-page advertisement in

44   Bob Thomas, "US Entertainment Industry Fights Racism in South Africa," Associated Press, December 20, 1987.

the *International Herald Tribune*, titled "No Reason to Celebrate Israel at 60," after having collected dozens of endorsements from prominent international cultural figures, including the late Palestinian Mahmoud Darwish (the foremost poet in the Arab World), John Berger, Ella Shohat, Ken Loach, Augusto Boal, Roger Waters, André Brink, Judith Butler, Vincenzo Consolo, and Nigel Kennedy, among many others. It read:

> The creation of the state of Israel almost 60 years ago dispossessed and uprooted hundreds of thousands of Palestinians from their homes and lands. With their peaceful lives ruined, society fragmented, possessions pillaged and hope for freedom and nationhood dashed, Palestinian refugees held on to their dream of return, and Palestinians everywhere nourished their aspiration for freedom, dignified living, and becoming whole again.
>
> There is no reason to celebrate! Israel at 60 is a state that is still denying Palestinian refugees their UN-sanctioned rights, simply because they are "non-Jews." It is still illegally occupying Palestinian and other Arab lands, in violation of numerous UN resolutions. It is still persistently and grossly breaching international law and infringing fundamental human rights with impunity afforded to it through munificent US and European economic, diplomatic and political support.
>
> It is still treating its own Palestinian citizens with institutionalized discrimination.
>
> In short, celebrating "Israel at 60" is tantamount to dancing on Palestinian graves to the haunting tune of lingering dispossession and multi-faceted injustice.
>
> There is absolutely no reason to celebrate! But there are myriad reasons to reflect, to engage, to work towards peace and justice.[45]

Well, there are plenty of reasons to celebrate. The cultural boycott of Israel, despite its young age, is already witnessing a healthy growth in the Western mainstream, and having a considerable impact on Israel's impunity and "brand." Perhaps Maxi Jazz, the front man of Faithless, a famous British band that refused to perform in Israel, captured the moment well in his explanation of his band's decision:

---

45   "60 Years of Palestinian Dispossession … No Reason to Celebrate 'Israel at 60'!" at pngo.net.

While human beings are being willfully denied not just their rights but their NEEDS for their children and grandparents and themselves, I feel deeply that I should not be sending even tacit signals that this is either "normal" or "ok." It's neither and I cannot support it. It grieves me that it has come to this and I pray every day for human beings to begin caring for each other, firm in the wisdom that we are all we have.

6 ECONOMIC ACTIVISM AGAINST THE OCCUPATION: WORKING FROM WITHIN

Dalit Baum and Merav Amir

A POLITICAL COMPROMISE

Ever since the outbreak of the al-Aqsa Intifada, the Israeli anti-occupation movement has been reinventing itself through new forms of action and solidarity work. Facing hostile denial from Israeli public opinion, large protests have been met first by a complete lack of media attention, and then by a wave of public sympathy for police and army violence against protesters. The movement, further marginalized and radicalized, has found itself reorganizing as a network of small groups, each specializing in a different form of direct action, public education, or resistance work. In this network, the feminist anti-occupation movement has found a central and leading role, both in maintaining visible opposition in the Israeli street and in creating ad hoc as well as long-term coalitions for broader efforts.

Who Profits from the Occupation? is one such specialized project of the Coalition of Women for Peace (CWP). It came into being in 2006 as a political compromise in a deep ongoing discussion inside the organization concerning our response to the July 2005 Palestinian call for BDS[1]—a call also specifically addressed to Israeli activists. CWP is an organization comprising Jewish and Palestinian women activists from within 1948 Israel, and affiliated left-feminist groups such as Women in Black, New Profile, Bat Shalom, Machsom (Checkpoint) Watch, and Tandi.[2] As a radical feminist

---

1   See Chapter 4.
2   For more information about the Coalition of Women for Peace, see coalition ofwomen.org.

organization, CWP has been haunted from its inception by dilemmas of economic justice with respect to the occupation, and by the challenges of solidarity and respective privilege within the joint movement, all of which led to the BDS discussion.

What is the role of Israelis in a movement that calls for international pressure? How can an Israeli organization continue to try to communicate and change Israeli public opinion in such a setting? What is the responsibility of Israeli Ashkenazi middle-class women who advocate economic measures that might further impoverish the poor, Mizrahi Jews, or Palestinians living in Israel? The discussion raised valid and important questions. In the tradition of consensus decision-making, it focused on existing agreements: to promote economic activism in all forms against the 1967 occupation both within Palestine/Israel and internationally. This decision included a plan for action—the initiation of a grassroots research effort, both to educate ourselves about the economy of the occupation and to serve the broader movement, using our access to this information.

Three years later, in November 2009, the general body of CWP reconvened to review the BDS discussion. Strikingly, this time support for the general call for BDS was unanimous. Throughout those three years, we had witnessed the attacks and the siege on Gaza, while the occupation in the West Bank had further entrenched itself as a form of apartheid regime—all with the support of Israeli public opinion. At the same time, the BDS movement has grown globally, and CWP has played an important part in it through its research project, entitled Who Profits from the Occupation? Through this project we have studied new facets of the economy of the occupation, and the results of our study have played an important part in showing how the use of boycott, divestment, and sanctions is justified, necessary, and potentially very effective in our work for a just peace in Israel/Palestine.

FROM COST TO PROFIT

This is not the first time that the Israeli anti-occupation movement has tried to engage with the economic aspects of the occupation. The well-worn Peace Now slogan, "Money to the [inner-city] neighborhoods and not to the settlements," was coined about thirty years ago. It has been criticized since for its simplistic formation, and presented as proof of this movement's disregard for "real" class and poverty issues. This slogan was developed into a solid argument by researchers such as Shlomo Swirski of the Adva Center, who conduct periodic studies estimating the cost of the occupation to the Israeli economy and society.[3] The argument that the occupation is very costly aims to undermine Israeli-Jewish public support for the settlements and for the ongoing occupation.[4] But the same studies show that much of the economic cost of the occupation to the Israeli public can also be viewed as income to certain parties who benefit from the colonial expansion—through the security industry and the exploitation of Palestinian resources and markets. This new perspective also calls for another line of political intervention: it is not enough to inform the Israeli public rhetorically about the costs of the occupation; it is also necessary to follow the money and expose the beneficiaries with a stake in the occupation, in order to influence their economic interests directly by applying pressure to raise the price of the occupation.

Israeli control of the West Bank and Gaza has changed over the years, but from the start and throughout, it has remained a system of economic-military control. Economic exploitation and repression have been used as tools to control the Palestinian population, and the terms of this control have been dictated by the interests of the Israeli economic elite. A potentially competitive Palestinian economy has been actively de-developed[5] and the movement of Palestinian workers and goods regulated to the benefit of the Israeli market, while Palestinian consumers have become a captive market for Israeli goods. In short, Israeli manufacturers, employers, and merchants have used economic-military control to secure profits.[6]

During the 1990s the Israeli economy underwent very rapid neoliberal reforms, which included cuts in social services and support; increased exposure to global investors, markets, and corporations; and the privatization of public services, national projects, and state assets and companies.

---

3   Shlomo Swirski, *The Price of Occupation*, Adva Center and Mapa Publishers, 2005.
4   Shlomo Swirski, *Is There an Israeli Business Peace Disincentive?* Adva Center, August 7, 2008, at adva.org.
5   Sara Roy, *Failing Peace: Gaza and the Palestinian-Israeli Conflict*, Pluto Press, 2007.
6   Lev Grinberg, "Economic Envelopment: Three Turning Points in Forty Years of Economic and Military Domination," *Theory and Criticism* 31 (Winter 2007) (Hebrew). English translation by Ami Asher, at whoprofits.org.

These dramatic changes in the Israeli economy have significantly increased the economic activity of private companies in the occupied territories, in the settlements, and at the checkpoints, providing security services, technologies, and weapons. As is the case in similar global settings, such as the American military interventions in Afghanistan and Iraq, the rise of the occupation business has seen the corporate sector develop a higher stake in maintaining the occupation.

As grassroots activists, we tackle political arguments and religious/nationalistic beliefs in the Israeli public arena, but economic interests are often more hidden and intricate, and Who Profits? was set up as an effort to expose and study these interests, in order to influence them. Corporate complicity with the occupation is a dangerous and influential force that can stifle peace initiatives or set them back. On the other hand, corporations are profit-oriented, and their involvement in these controversial endeavors can become costly for them: public campaigns may tarnish their public image, important clients or investors may choose to leave them due to ethical concerns, and complicity with human rights violations may even have legal repercussions in some countries. In a way, this increased corporate involvement in the occupation can be used to enhance civil society's reach and influence, if we can effectively demand corporate accountability.

Who Profits from the Occupation? focuses on exposing these corporate interests, in order to provide accurate, reliable, and well-documented information for such corporate accountability campaigns. As Israeli activists living inside 1948 Israel who speak Hebrew, have freedom of movement in the occupied territory, and are well acquainted with the Israeli economy and the occupation, we occupy a useful vantage point for such research. Almost all of our information comes from the companies' own publications, or from regular visits to sites in the occupied West Bank and Golan Heights. Our database of over 1,000 corporations directly complicit in the system of military-economic control has become an information hub both through an information center and through our website, whoprofits.org, supporting scores of initiatives and providing ongoing support by checking information for campaigns, both internationally and locally.

BEYOND THE BOYCOTT OF SETTLEMENT PRODUCTS

When we started our mapping of the occupation industry, the main focus of economic activism against the occupation was on settlement production. Long lists of settlement companies and products were distributed by Israeli peace organizations such as Gush Shalom, Bat Shalom, and various student organizations, as tools for consumer boycotts. These old lists were included Israeli companies based in settlements, but omitted most of the distributors of agricultural goods and products partially manufactured in the settlements, as well as companies registered elsewhere. Hence, these boycotts targeted mainly marginal products and were carried out by a small group of Israeli, mostly Jewish, activists; at best, they were implemented as discrete concerns, framed within the language of ethical shopping practices.

Besides offering an easy—perhaps much too easy—way for Israelis seemingly to distance themselves from the settlements, these initiatives did not challenge these companies with sustained campaigns, and never attempted to change corporate policies. While widespread consumer boycotts may be effective in some cases, this type of action can have no effect when the percentage of participants is almost negligible, and when these actions are not part of broader, collectively organized activism. More significantly, our research shows that settlement industries are few and their revenues are very limited, and that, for all but a handful of agricultural settlements, they do not contribute substantially to the settlements' economic sustainability.[7] In other words, even strategic corporate accountability campaigns focusing on settlement products would not go far beyond the symbolic or educational levels.

Consequently, we have decided to broaden the focus of our mapping, and include under the headline "settlement industry" the entire economic sustenance of the settlements. In addition to settlements' agricultural and industrial production, we investigate real-estate deals, the construction of settlements and infrastructure, and the provision of all vital services and utilities to the settlements. As is evident from the examples provided below, Israeli and international corporations build roads and housing units; provide

---

7   Exact figures for production in settlements are not available, since the Israeli Central Bureau of Statistics does not provide such figures, but it is estimated that the entire production in settlements is negligible. See "Israel's Unbalanced Economic Development," Avda Center, March 2011, at adva.org.

services such as public transportation, waste management, water, security, and telecommunications; offer loans; and market goods.

This wider settlement industry includes most large Israeli retailers and service providers. These companies claim to pursue a policy of "nondiscrimination," meaning that they provide equal services inside the official borders of Israel and in the occupied territory—to the Jewish-Israeli settlers. Since entrance into Israeli settlements is forbidden for West Bank Palestinians, and since these services are provided only in the Israeli settlements, their intended services map does not include the Palestinian residents of the West Bank. In other words, their policy is not only a policy of systematic discrimination; it is a facet of the ethnic segregation between Palestinians and Jews in the occupied West Bank.

DEXIA ISRAEL: FROM PUBLIC TO PRIVATE AND BACK

The increasing privatization of government services in Israel has not passed over local governance and municipalities. International corporations offer local authorities anything from waste management and public transportation services to management and financial services, and many of the public tenders for these services in Israel cover services to regional councils and municipalities of settlements in the West Bank, East Jerusalem, and the Golan Heights. This provides new opportunities for activist intervention, as exemplified by the rapid success of the campaign against Dexia Bank.[8]

In 2001, Israel privatized the Israeli Municipality Treasure Bank, a government institution providing credit and financial services to local authorities. The bank was bought by the Belgian–French financial group Dexia, and renamed Dexia Israel, while retaining most of its former functions.

In June 2007, the bank's CEO, David Kapach, was summoned to the Knesset Finance Committee by representatives of the settlement movement, after having made allegations that Dexia Israel refrained from providing loans to West Bank settlements. Kapach claimed that Dexia had no such "discrimination" policy, and he listed, for the record, at least seven Israeli settlements and three regional authorities of settlements that had received long-term loans from his bank since 2003. Little did he know that Who

---

8   For this company's page, see "Dexia Israel: (Formerly: Local Municipality Treasure Bank)," at whoprofits.org.

Profits? and the Belgian solidarity group Intal[9] had been looking for such proof of direct involvement for many months.

The loans provided by Dexia are used for the development of infrastructure, the construction of public buildings, and the provision of municipal services. Further investigation has proved that the bank provides services to other local authorities within settlements; it operates as a financial channel transferring government funds to settlements, and it provides them with loans using future public income as collateral. Moreover, the bank regularly transfers funds from the Israeli National Lottery (Mifal HaPayis) to settlements—funds used for the construction of schools and community centers, and for other projects of local development.

Intal and other Belgian groups, working with the Coalition of Women for Peace, launched a campaign called Israel Colonizes—Dexia Finances, calling on Dexia to sever all economic ties to Israeli settlement activity. This demand gained much public credence after September 2008, when Dexia bank was bailed out by the governments of Belgium, France, and Luxembourg—governments that officially oppose the construction of Israeli settlements and view them as illegal. Thus, the privatization of financial services has come almost full-circle: from Israeli government-assured support for its own controversial colonization projects, to a seemingly disinterested international publicly traded corporation, and back to substantial national ownership—this time on the part of a European public very much opposed to those same projects.

In June 2009 the management of the Dexia Group stated that financing Israeli settlements was contrary to the bank's code of ethics, and that it would stop providing new loans to West Bank settlements; furthermore, the bank announced that it had not given any new loans to settlements since June 2008. However, our research exposed records showing that the bank had continued to provide new loans to local authorities of settlements during 2009. The bank provided loans during this period totaling almost US$4 million to twelve settlements, including Kedumim, Oranit, and Immanuel, as well as to the regional council of the settlements around Hebron.

As a result of this ongoing campaign, during the annual shareholder meeting of the bank in May 2011, the president of the board of the Dexia

9   More about the organization and the campaign can be found on their website at intal.be.

Group, Jean-Luc Dehaene, announced that, since the bank could not stop funding settlements, it would completely divest from Israel and sell its shares in the Israeli bank "even at a loss."[10] Moreover, Dehaene claimed that the bank would contribute to Palestinian society in the West Bank as some form of compensation. Until that happens, however, the campaign continues.

THE BUSINESSES OF REPRESSION AND EXPLOITATION

The settlement industry does not exhaust the different ways in which corporations benefit from the 1967 occupation; our mapping identifies two other categories of corporate involvement. One consists of corporations involved in Israeli control over the Palestinian population in the occupied territories. This includes the construction and operation of the wall and the checkpoints and, in general, the supply and operation of means of surveillance and control of Palestinian movement both within the occupied territories and between them and the State of Israel. Aware of our own limited capacities, we decided not to directly investigate the military-industrial complex and the weapons industry, but they would fit well into this same category. Since 9/11 and the terror attacks in Europe, the growing market for the homeland security industry has contributed significantly to the growth of the Israeli high-tech market, where products can be "tested" on Palestinians in Israeli-controlled areas. We have seen this used as a blunt marketing strategy by sales representatives for products ranging from "anti-terrorist" surveillance systems sold for airport control to advanced weapon platforms sold to armies. One example of a seemingly benign company deeply involved in the restriction and control of Palestinian movement in the occupied territories is the South African steel and wire producer, Cape Gate, whose Israeli affiliate Yehuda Welded Mesh[11] has supplied security fencing for separation barriers in the "seam line" zone around settlements and Israeli-only roads and railroads, settlement industrial zones, and the besieged Gaza Strip. The irony is that the late founder and owner of this company, Mendel Kaplan, former president of the World Zionist Congress, wrote extensively about his opposition to apartheid in his own country, and called upon all Jews in

---

10   Eran Peer, "Dexia Israel To Be Sold "Even at a Loss," *Globes*, May 15, 2011, available online at globes.co.il.
11   For further information, see "Yehuda Welded Mesh," at whoprofits.org.

South Africa to "give leadership in the movement to abolish all discriminatory practices" as a lesson from Jewish history.[12]

The second type of corporate involvement outside the settlement industry itself consists of corporations that directly benefit from systemic advantages deriving from Israeli control of Palestinian land, people, and markets. This category includes the companies that plunder natural resources in the occupied territories, use them as a dumping ground for waste, profit from the exploitation of Palestinian labor, and benefit from access to the captive market of Palestinian consumers.

For example, many Israeli food manufacturers and distributors benefit from selling low-grade products in the West Bank, while Palestinian competitors are denied free movement through Israeli military checkpoints. Similarly, telecommunications service providers exploit Israeli control of land and airwaves in the occupied territories to penetrate the Palestinian market illegally. One aspect of that control stems from the exclusive Israeli physical control of Area C, which constitutes about 60 percent of the West Bank and stretches across all the major population centers. Israeli companies have seeded the area with hundreds of cellular antennae, while the Palestinian cellular infrastructure is limited to the main Palestinian cities. As a result, the Israeli companies have a hold over the Palestinian cellular market—especially over long-distance and international calling.[13]

Some companies fall under all three categories. The giant transnational corporation Cemex is one of the largest global suppliers of building materials, and is controlled by the Mexican tycoon Lorenzo Zambrano. Through its Israeli subsidiary, Readymix Industries,[14] the company has several plants in Israeli settlements in the occupied West Bank, in which it uses Palestinian labor. It is a partner in an aggregates quarry in the West Bank, exploiting Palestinian nonrenewable natural resources such as stone and gravel for the needs of the Israeli construction industry. Furthermore, the company has provided "concrete elements" for the construction of security walls and military checkpoints in the West Bank.

---

12   For example, Mendel Kaplan and Marian Robertson, *Jewish Roots in the South African Economy*, C. Struik, 1986: 133.

13   See "The Cellular Companies and the Occupation," August 2009, at whoprofits.org.

14   For further information, see "Readymix Industries," at whoprofits.org.

Who Profits? has prepared the corporate research for a Supreme Court petition submitted by Yesh Din in March 2009, demanding a halt to all Israeli mining activity in West Bank quarries, including the Yatir quarry co-owned by Cemex. Israeli quarries operating in the occupied territories transfer most of their output back into Israel. As stated in the petition, this type of activity violates the laws of occupation, and in some cases may be considered pillage. In May 2010, the government of Israel informed the court that it would stop all new land allocation for Israeli quarrying purposes in the West Bank, and would also cease to approve any expansion of existing quarries there. As of October 2011, the petition is still pending before the court.

ISRAEL AND THE OCCUPATION: WHERE IS THE GREEN LINE?

As we complete our mapping, one fact becomes very clear: any clear-cut distinction between the Israeli economy as a whole and the economy of the occupation can no longer be justified. The Green Line border has all but disappeared from the corporate activity map. Even if we consider only the Israeli settlements, and then again focus only on settlement construction, we discover that the major players in the Israeli economy are deeply complicit with the occupation. For instance, our findings show that all major Israeli banks have funded and supervised construction projects in the settlements. According to Israeli regulations, every construction project has to have an "accompanier" bank, which not only provides funding and loans but functions as an active partner and supervisor of the project on the ground. All major Israeli banks are thus not only aiding in the construction of settlements, but actively involved in this process. Moreover, all of the Israeli banks provide mortgage loans for homebuyers in settlements, and also provide financial services to Israeli business activities in the occupied territories and to the local authorities of settlements.[15] Most large retailers have branches in settlements; service providers provide their services; importers and exporters exploit the uneven trade agreements. The Israeli economy is highly centralized; it is often claimed that a handful of tycoons control a third of private-sector revenues, as well as most media, telecommunications, banking, and infrastructure industries.[16] Our research shows

---

15   See the executive summary of our report at whoprofits.org.
16   Assaf Hamdani, "Concentrated Ownership and Business Groups in Israel: A Legal Analysis," Policy Paper 78, Israeli Democracy Institute, November 2009.

that each of these central economic players is implicated in the occupation industry in more ways than one.

We can safely say that most of the Israeli economy is involved in the economy of the occupation: from an economic perspective, the Green Line is long gone. Choosing to call for economic activism against Israeli corporations directly complicit in the Israeli occupation, rather than calling for economic activism against all significant Israeli corporations, should be regarded as a strategic decision, since all Israeli corporations are somehow complicit, making this distinction more or less semantic.

STRATEGY FOR A BUDDING MOVEMENT

Our research project began as a tentative response to the Palestinian call for BDS: a call to put effective pressure on Israel, to practice noncooperation, and to target the ongoing support for the Israeli regime—economic, cultural, and diplomatic. Very soon, we have found ourselves in the crux of a new and exciting global movement, a movement made up of separate and very successful campaigns. We have learned that BDS is not about a prescribed set of tools or list of targets; rather, it is about moving beyond public education, protest, and symbolic actions to using our collective power and leverage to apply real, discernible pressure.

A BDS campaign should plan for success, and choose its targets accordingly. Our database is not a boycott list; in fact there is no one boycott list, and boycotting is just one tool among many. A choice of target for a campaign relies on a great deal of research, most of it local. What would be an achievable, measurable goal? What is our leverage locally? How do we build it as a movement, from one campaign to the next, toward divestment and sanctions?

Our mapping of corporate complicity in the occupation is just one tool that helps activist communities around the world to trace lines of accountability back to their own neighborhoods: to the factory in the US, the grocery store in France, or the construction site in Abu Dhabi. The occupation and colonization of Palestine is not just a solidarity issue, to be debated and studied. These lines of accountability are our way in: this is where we can influence power; this is where our power begins.

7 THE BRAIN OF THE MONSTER

Nada Elia

BDS activists who organize for the Academic and Cultural Boycott of Israel (ACBI) face a particularly pernicious, if unfounded, charge—namely, that they are censoring freedom of speech, curtailing academic freedom, and preventing scholarly and cultural exchange. In reality, the goal of ACBI is quite the opposite, since this particular aspect of the global BDS campaign aims very specifically at creating venues for academic and artistic expression, as well as cultural exchange, where they do not currently exist. Looking at historically similar examples and at which voices are being silenced, and by whom, will help to distinguish between "boycott" as a temporary strategy, and "censorship" as denial of freedom of expression.

My colleagues and I, as scholars of global, regional, gender, or ethnic studies, are often called upon to provide expert analysis about political developments around the world. This expertise is understood as the capacity to understand such developments better, to grasp and explain their complexities, and even make highly educated "guesses" about forthcoming events. And while this may be flattering, the fact is that the news anchors interviewing us, as well as the viewers and listeners, most frequently assume that such scholars do not actually contribute to making and shaping the events, but merely observe and interpret them. We need to problematize and flesh out this general perception of scholarship. I argue that academics shape the events that we observe, analyze, and comment on. That is, we are truly knowledge producers, not merely interpreters.

Interestingly, there seems to be no controversy around a direct connection between research and implementation in the "hard sciences." Instead, there is an expectation that such a connection should exist, to justify (and fund) the research. Medical scholars research cures for illnesses so that medical doctors can treat patients successfully. Aeronautic engineers draw the blueprints for spaceships. Engineers study mechanics to build bridges that support traffic. Indeed, the success of such experts is determined by the success of the products they have researched and developed. This is somewhat different in the social sciences, where there is not necessarily an expectation of a direct, pragmatic causal relationship between intellect and action, beyond the production of "academic" knowledge. Nevertheless, one of the many lessons garnered from Edward Said's *Orientalism* is that all knowledge-production is political. Narratives—literary, historical, anthropological, and so on—are informed by, and in turn inform, power dynamics and politics. And as the official production of state-sanctioned knowledge is concentrated in the academy, it becomes obvious that there is no "ivory tower," no insular forum of intellectual activity that does not translate into on-the-ground manifestations. Towards the end of *Orientalism*, Edward Said noted that, in the post–World War II era, the US academy advanced to the forefront in Orientalism, which had previously been the domain of European scholars, and that the "area specialist [now] lays claims to regional expertise, which is put at the service of government or business or both." As the US and Israeli governments rely on think tanks staffed by area specialists, graduates of the most prestigious universities, and often professors and fellows there, we must acknowledge that scholarship is not neutral, and that the academy does not exist in a bubble or an ivory tower. In fact, the more militarized a society, the more complicit its academy. And as academics, if we do not want to be part of the problem, we must be part of the solution.

The convergence of academic and sociopolitical thought was central to South African political studies professor Shireen Hassim's retrospective analysis of the role of universities in establishing and maintaining apartheid in South Africa. "In reality," Hassim writes,

> institutions of higher education do not stand outside the relations of power in society. They are implicated in defending, elaborating, and applying technologies of power and in training the elites who use that power. Although destructive uses of the natural and physical sciences—for example, the development of efficient mechanisms for killing—are acknowledged, social scientists are also implicated—for example, in developing anthropological

and philosophical arguments for the supposed racial inferiority of colonized peoples.[1]

There is no doubt that the academy in Israel is complicit in maintaining the state of apartheid in Israel, the settler-colonial country founded on the ethnic cleansing of the indigenous Palestinian people. Israel is the region's only known nuclear power, with the largest army in the Middle East and, small as the country is, the fourth-largest army in the world. Every single Jewish Israeli, male and female, is required to serve in the military, and very few get out of serving their three years, if male, or two if female. Considering the hyper-militarization of this society, it is inconceivable to think that the academy functions in a bubble. Instead, in Israel, the academy is very intimately involved in every aspect of the occupation.

There are seven main research universities in Israel, and each is directly complicit in the occupation. The Technion (Israel Institute of Technology), for example, which is most famous for applied sciences, develops research and development projects with the Israeli military—including the remote-controlled D9 bulldozer used by the Israeli military to demolish Palestinian homes.[2] The Technion has also developed the equipment to detect underground tunnels, which is used by the Israeli military to enforce its siege on Gaza; and it has partnered with Elbit Systems, Israel's largest defense electronics manufacturer and weapons research company, and the developer of the apartheid wall surveillance system.[3] Another prestigious Israeli university, the Weizmann Institute, has also partnered with Elbit Systems to create an electro-optic science program that trains students directly in the Elbit factories.[4] The engineering and architecture departments at many universities have professors and graduate students who are responsible for

---

1   Edward Said, *Orientalism*, Vintage, 1979: 184–5.
2   See, for example, "Israel to Deploy Robot Bulldozers," October 31, 2003, at bbc.co.uk, and "Israel to Use Remote Control Bulldozers," October 30, 2003, at rense.com.
3   "Elbit Systems and the Israel Institute of Technology (Technion) to Establish New Vision Systems Research Centre," at prnewswire.com.
4   As listed in the Weizmann Institute's faculty profiles, a number of senior faculty at the Weizmann Institute also hold project management and research positions at Elbit.

the design and construction of the settlements and apartheid wall. In 2008, both Hebrew University and Ben Gurion University were in competition for a grant to establish a school for military medicine, training staff to serve specifically in the Israeli army. This separation between "civilian medicine" and "military medicine" is important, as Israel's military doctors have long been suspected of involvement in the torture in Israeli jails of Palestinian prisoners—a significant number of whom are in "administrative detention," held without charge. Haifa University has a military base on its campus. Carmel College closed down an entire department because it had "too many" Israeli Arab (i.e. Palestinian) students.[5] The Herzliya Interdiciplinary Center, a very prestigious academic institute, has made support of the Israeli military an integral part of its agenda …[6]

In the humanities and social sciences, sociology books omit the Palestinian narrative; historical accounts and textbooks erase our Nakba; geography books erase the names of our towns and villages; and the archeology departments discard Palestinian artifacts, only selecting ancient Jewish finds as worthy of identification. These are all the products and teaching tools of the Israeli academy. Thus Israeli students are taught to ignore almost 2,000 years of continuous Palestinian history, society, civilization, and a deep attachment to the land. If and when our existence is recognized at all, it is generally dismissed as quasi-illegitimate, because Palestine did not exist as a nation-state, even though the very concept of "nation-state" is an eighteenth-century European idea, which should not be the determining criterion for whether a society—especially one that is not European—is grounded in its homeland or not.

Finally, most universities give upwards of 90 percent scholarships to soldiers who fought in Cast Lead, Israel's murderous war on besieged Gazan refugees in 2008–09, and 80 percent to soldiers who participated in

---

5   Faculty for Israeli-Palestinian Peace, "The Carmel Academic Center in Haifa Closes Academic Track as Too Many Palestinian Students Registered," May 27, 2009, at ffipp.org.

6   My information about the very close connections between Israeli universities and the Israeil military comes primarily from Uri Yacobi Keller's excellent and detailed report, "Academic Boycott of Israel and the Complicity of Israeli Academic Institutions in Occupation of Palestinian Territories," at usacbi.files. wordpress.com.

Defensive Shield (2002), Israel's largest military assault on West Bank cities since the 1967 war. Rewarding the soldiers thus directly disadvantages the Palestinian citizens of Israel, who generally do not serve in the army. And while Arabic is a second language in Israel, spoken by at least 20 percent of the population, no subject, except for Arabic language, is taught in Arabic at any Israeli university. Similarly, while Palestinians make up 20 percent of Israel's population and have historically been a highly educated people with illustrious scholars, today they account for less than 1 percent of the faculty at Israeli universities. Far from being a detached, neutral ivory tower, the academy, then, is the brain of the monster that generates the ideology and tools of occupation, dispossession, and violation of human rights, whereby the servants of occupation are rewarded, while its victims are alienated, discriminated against as students and scholars.

How, then, can academics outside Israel counter this? How do we make sure we are not complicit, if only by default? We do have a historical model for the boycott movement, which was used successfully in the US South, in South Africa, and in India. Writing about South Africa's struggle with apartheid, and commenting on the strategy that put an end to that brutal system of institutionalized discrimination, another South African academic, Jacklyn Cock, explains: "I think opposition to academic boycotts tends to privilege the university as an ivory tower that is divorced from its social context, and in the South African case, the notion of isolating the regime was a very significant nonviolent action."[7]

South African apartheid—like Israel with its system of violently enforced settler colonialism, displacement of the indigenous population, and institutionalized racial hierarchies—was defeated by the global boycott movement, not by "constructive engagement"—which is what then-President Ronald Reagan proposed, until the very last days of that brutal system. South African apartheid was not defeated through a boycott of South African oranges and diamonds alone, but by a comprehensive—the key word here is comprehensive—boycott that also applied to sports, culture, and the academy. Similarly, the boycott of Israel must also be comprehensive in order to be effective, meaning that it must include an academic and cultural

---

7 Personal communication with Salim Vally, quoted in Jonathan Hyslop, Salim Vally, and Shireen Hassim, "The South African Boycott Experience," at aaup.org.

boycott too. In fact, the academic and cultural boycott is the new battlefront in the Palestine-Israel conflict, as Israel seeks feverishly to fix its severely tarnished image, whitewashing its crimes with a façade of academic and cultural excellence.

Israel's academic and cultural accomplishments are Israel's glamorous, "non-military" face—a mask it uses to distract from its apartheid policy and its violations of international law and human rights. They provide the façade that Israel displays, as it seeks to refurbish its image in the wake of the massacres and other crimes it engages in, which it can no longer hide from the world, as alternative and citizen journalism become more democratic. This re-branding effort, known as the "Brand Israel" campaign, is the brainchild of a conglomerate of American marketing firms that specialize in image-making, and is funded by Israel's three most powerful ministries: the Foreign Ministry, the Prime Minister's Office, and the Finance Ministry. Though the idea began incubating around 2002, the ministries officially adopted "Brand Israel" in October 2005, aware that Israel would only win supporters if it was seen as relevant and modern, rather than merely as a place of fighting and religion. With the Zionist narrative of Israel as a "land without a people, for a people without a land" now rivaled by the image of Israel as an aggressive military power, its claims to be a democracy have come into question. Hence Israel's need to distract from that, and project academic and cultural achievements and superiority, creating a sense of affinity with other developed "First World" countries. In 2009, in the aftermath of Operation Cast Lead, Israel made a further push to improve its image by increasing its funding of the Brand Israel campaign. Speaking shortly after the Gaza massacres, Arye Mekel, the Israeli Foreign Ministry's deputy director general for cultural affairs, explained: "We will send well-known novelists and writers overseas, theater companies, exhibits. This way you show Israel's prettier face, so we are not thought of purely in the context of war."[8]

In the US, one of the earlier converts to this idea of re-branding Israel was Hillel, the international Jewish campus organization, whose executive vice president Wayne Firestone explained that the campaign would portray Israel as a place "where there are cool, hip people." The American Israel Public Affairs Committee (AIPAC), along with public relations organization

---

8   Ethan Bronner, "After Gaza, Israel Grapples with Crisis of Isolation," *New York Times*, March 18, 2009, at nytimes.com.

Israel21c, generate collaborative content for the campaign's academic and cultural events. Gay rights are also being exploited, and gay activists co-opted into this re-branding effort, which is also actively "pinkwashing" Israel's crimes. Thus even StandWithUs, an ultra-Zionist conservative group that has never before allied itself with gay rights, is now projecting Israel as the region's only gay-friendly country.[9] (Ironically, Israel prides itself on having gays openly serve in the military, with no mention of the fact that a disproportionate number of Israelis would likely declare themselves homosexual if this were grounds for not serving.) Yet this discussion among Israel advocacy groups about changing the world's perception of Israel has not been accompanied by discussion of changing those practices responsible for tarnishing Israel's image in the first place. If anything, the policies continue to become harsher: more home demolitions; expansion of settlements; recurrent indiscriminate attacks on Gaza, which remains besieged; criminalization of dissent; military responses to nonviolent demonstrations against the illegal wall in the West Bank. "Buying" into the image of Israel as a vibrant democracy and into the "brand" that Israel is projecting is to buy into the propaganda which serves to distract from the murderous reality.

Alongside its cultural and pinkwashing campaigns, Israel is also pushing to present itself as a "normal" country by offering the world's finest academic programs. Examining the academic boycott—a boycott of institutions, not individuals, as explained in the PACBI guidelines—therefore requires consideration of areas of exchange and collaborative research. Semester-abroad programs that take US students to Israel to give them a sanitized "Israel experience" are prime targets, and there are a number of campuses that are currently at various stages of planning such boycotts. Obviously, there are grounds for boycotting these semester-abroad programs as violating equal opportunity, since US citizens of Arab descent are often turned away from them.

Collaborative projects at the institutional level must also be boycotted, since these impact the Israeli academy most. Universities are not funded by student tuition, but by the research grants secured by academics. In the sciences, especially—with their need for labs, equipment, experiments,

---

9   See Jasbir Puar, "Israel's Gay Propaganda War," July 1, 2010, at guardian. co.uk, and my own "Reflections from Detroit: Standoff with StandWithUs," August 2, 2010, at inciteblog.wordpress.com.

prototypes, and so on—research can be extremely costly, and many programs seek out alliances between two universities in order to increase their
chances of getting a grant, while minimizing the cost for each university. This
is where a boycott can have the most impact, both directly and indirectly.
And this is where Israeli academic institutions are seeking "collaboration."

Some may claim that "art rises above politics, and culture builds
bridges"—but, in reality, Israel uses culture and art to cover up apartheid.
Others claim that the academic boycott "shuts down academic and intellectual exchange"—but the "freedom" one would be protecting is only the
freedom of Israeli academics, as the Palestinian right to education is very
severely jeopardized. In fact, Palestinians do not have academic freedom,
so what one would be protecting in the name of "academic freedom" is the
oppressor's privilege.[10] Indeed, before Palestinian academics called for the
academic boycott, a group of Palestinian scholars wrote a letter to all 9,000
Israeli members of the Israeli academy, our "colleagues," asking them to
endorse our call for lifting the restrictions on Palestinian scholars' freedom
of movement. Of the 9,000 Israeli professors, no more than 400 agreed to
sign the letter. The rest—about 90 percent—would not even denounce the
various closures that disrupt the Palestinian school year. Additionally, only
an insignificant minority of Israelis denounce the segregation of schools in
Israel, from day care to high school, even though it is obvious that the two
systems ("Jewish" and "Arab") are separate and unequal, with Arab schools
being chronically underfunded. A 2009 report reveals that the Israeli government invested $1,100 a year for each Jewish child's education in secular
public schools, compared to $190 for each Arab (Palestinian) child. The gap
was wider in the popular religious schools, which are also state-run, and
where Jewish students received nine times more funding than Arab students.[11] Just like the J14 (July 14) Israelis protesting in summer 2011 in Tel
Aviv and demanding affordable housing—without much thought to the fact

---

10   See also Salim Vally's excellent analysis of Israeli academics' privileges in
"The South African Boycott Experience."
11   Jonathan Cook, "Israeli School Apartheid: Arab Family Sues over 'Racist
Incitement,'" *Counterpunch*, August 10, 2009, available at jkcook.net. There is
also racism within the "Jewish schools," with Ethiopian students being sent to
underfunded, segregated schools for "foreigners," even though they are Jewish
Israeli citizens.

that Palestinians are losing their ancestral homes so that Israel can build affordable housing for middle- and working-class Israelis—the Israeli academics also ignore the harsh circumstances surrounding every aspect of academic life for Palestinians, from getting to one's school down the street, to government funding for state schools, to traveling outside the country for an education or a conference abroad. Yet this is the context in which the Palestinian call for an academic boycott of Israel is grounded: the reality that millions of Palestinians do not enjoy a right to education.

Contrary to popular belief, culture is not apolitical, music does not transcend national and linguistic boundaries, and art does not bring us together—at least not when Israel intentionally and explicitly uses art to further its political agenda, while blocking Palestinian artists and musicians from disseminating their work. In fact, the illusion that culture is apolitical plays right into Israel's strategy. Naturally, to serve their propaganda purpose, Israel's cultural ambassadors are precisely those who do show its beautiful face, rather than those who advocate apartheid and ethnic cleansing. The Idan Raichel Project sings tender songs of multicultural harmony and togetherness. The Ethiopian (Jewish) Israeli ballet troupe is a stunningly graceful illustration of how refugees can blossom into world-class artists. *Waltz with Bashir*, sponsored by the Israeli Culture Ministry, is a touching depiction of an Israeli soldier's psychological torment after the massacres of hundreds of refugees in the Sabra and Shatila camps. While boycotting specifically those Israeli cultural products that show a complex, multi-hued aspect of Israeli civilian society can be challenging, we must do so nevertheless, because of the use they are being put to. Of course, Israel would never assign an openly racist, violent settler as "cultural ambassador." Hence the boycott guidelines specify that a cultural product is subject to boycott based on sponsorship, not content. Simply put: if a performance is officially sponsored by Israel in its campaign to "fix its image," it is subject to boycott, regardless of what it presents.

Meanwhile, Palestinian artists encounter enormous, and occasionally insurmountable challenges, as they attempt to display or perform their art, including at the Museum of Children's Art in Oakland. Pro-Palestine academics face serious reprisals for presenting a Palestinian narrative or perspective in their syllabi, their lectures, their writings. In "The Trial of Israel's Campus Critics," David Theo Goldberg and Saree Makdisi reveal that no fewer than thirty-three organizations, including the very powerful AIPAC, the Zionist Organization of America, the American Jewish Congress, the Jewish National Fund, and StandWithUs, are members and affiliates of the "Israel on Campus Coalition." These organizations, Goldberg and Makdisi write, are uninterested in "the niceties of intellectual exchange and academic process. Insinuation, accusation, and defamation have become the weapons of first resort to respond to argument and criticism directed at Israeli policies."[12] The academic and cultural boycott must therefore be understood as a strategy, and embraced for what it seeks to achieve: academic and cultural freedom for all, where there currently is only privilege for some. To claim that a boycott is strictly negative is tantamount to claiming that the African Americans who boycotted the Montgomery bus system were being strictly negative, and did not want public transportation. In reality, they were boycotting public transportation in order to make it genuinely public, available to all without distinction.

ACBI, the Academic and Cultural Boycott of Israel, is a means to an end. We want culture that is not propaganda, and we want academic freedom. But culture that shows how tolerant and complex Israeli society is, without hinting at the institutionalized apartheid in Israel, remains propaganda. Until we all have academic freedom, and until the universities are not at the service of occupation and apartheid, Israeli academics' so-called academic freedom is merely the privilege of the oppressor, at the service of an oppressive state.

We social scientists, ethnic studies scholars, historians, gender studies professors, are the ones who must remind our detractors of this fact. We are the ones who must remind people that boycott is a means to an end—to freedom, dignity, human rights for all, and the implementation of international law.

---

12   David Theo Goldberg and Saree Makdisi, "The Trial of Israel's Campus Critics," *Tikkun*, September/October 2009, at tikkun.org.

8 NORTH AMERICAN COLLEGES AND UNIVERSITIES AND BDS

Joel Beinin

In October 2005 Ilan Pappe, an early supporter of the Palestinian Campaign for the Academic and Cultural Boycott of Israel (PACBI) and at that time a professor at Haifa University, accepted invitations to speak at several US universities. Students at Stanford asked him how they should respond to the call for a boycott. "You should boycott me," he replied, even though the original PACBI call for an academic and cultural boycott contained a clause apparently excluding Israelis, like Pappe, whom PACBI rightly considers allies.[1] The student organizers of Pappe's visit to Stanford were bewildered, and were left uncertain about how to interpret and implement PACBI's call.

Although the boycott is directed at Israeli institutions, perhaps boycotting some individuals—for example, anyone associated with Ariel University Center of Samaria, located in the heart of the northern West Bank—solely on the basis of their institutional affiliation would make a readily understandable political statement. At the urging of Architects and Planners for Justice in Palestine, the Spanish government banned an architectural team from Ariel University Center from taking part in Solar Decathlon 2010, a green housing competition sponsored by Spain's Ministry of Housing. The manager of the Solar Decathlon informed Ariel University Center:

> The decision was made by the Spanish government based on the fact that the university is located in occupied territory in the West Bank. The Spanish

---

1   That clause was removed in 2006 because it gave the impression that PACBI favored establishing blacklists; PACBI clarified that it does not advocate boycotting individuals. See "The PACBI Call for Academic Boycott Revised: Adjusting the Parameters of the Debate," January 28, 2006, at pacbi.org.

government is committed to uphold the international agreement under the framework of the European Union and the United Nations regarding this geographical area.[2]

Does boycotting all Israeli academic and cultural institutions make an equally clear statement? Does Ben-Gurion University, which has a number of prominent faculty members whose scholarly work is critical of Zionism and who have vocally condemned the Israeli occupation for many years, deserve to be boycotted on the same basis as Bar-Ilan University, which was the incubator for Ariel University Center and maintains its own branch in the West Bank—and whose orthodox religious intellectual environment tolerated, and some would say encouraged, the extreme right-wing politics of people like Yigal Amir, the assassin of former Israeli Prime Minister Yitzhak Rabin? Even if all Israeli academic and cultural institutions deserve, in principle, to be boycotted, is it a better strategy to apply a comprehensive approach or to focus on the most egregious cases, like Ariel University Center and Bar-Ilan University, which are institutionally integral to the occupation project?

Such concerns led the Booker Prize–winning art critic, novelist, and painter John Berger to explain his position in a letter he appended to the December 2006 statement of ninety-four authors, filmmakers and others endorsing the call for a cultural boycott of Israel issued by the British Committee for the Universities of Palestine.[3] Berger explained,

> Boycott is not a principle. When it becomes one, it itself risks becoming exclusive and racist. No boycott ... should be directed against an individual, a people, or a nation as such. A boycott is directed against a policy and the institutions which support that policy either actively or tacitly ...
>
> How to apply a cultural boycott? ... For academics it's perhaps a little clearer—a question of declining invitations from state institutions and

---

2   Yaheli Moran Zelikovich, "Spain Boycotts Ariel College for Being on 'Occupied Territory,'" *Ynet*, September 22, 2009, at ynetnews.com.

3   "John Berger and 93 Other Authors, Film-Makers, Musicians and Performers Call for a Cultural Boycott of Israel," December 15, 2006, at electronicintifada. net. See also his article launching the boycott in Britain, "We Must Speak Out," *Guardian*, December 15, 2006, at guardian.co.uk.

explaining why. For invited actors, musicians, jugglers or poets it can be more complicated. I'm convinced … that its application should not be systematised; it has to come from a personal choice based on a personal assessment.

For instance: an important mainstream Israeli publisher today is asking to publish three of my books. I intend to apply the boycott with an explanation. There exist, however, a few small, marginal Israeli publishers who expressly work to encourage exchanges and bridges between Arabs and Israelis, and if one of them should ask to publish something of mine, I would unhesitatingly agree and furthermore waive aside any question of author's royalties. I don't ask other writers supporting the boycott to come necessarily to exactly the same conclusion. I simply offer an example.

Canadian journalist Naomi Klein applied Berger's example in arranging her visit to Israel/Palestine on the occasion of the publication of the Hebrew translation of her bestseller, *The Shock Doctrine*.[4] Instead of working with her former commercial publisher, Bavel, Klein allowed a small, anti-occupation press, Andalus, to publish the book, and she donated her royalties to Andalus. That was apparently acceptable to the international network, BDSMovement.net, since it posted on its website Klein's interview with Jewish Voice for Peace deputy director, Cecilie Surasky, in which Klein explained her actions.[5]

The July 9, 2005, call for "Boycott, Divestment and Sanctions Against Israel Until It Complies with International Law and Universal Principles of Human Rights" is somewhat narrower in scope than PACBI's call.[6] But it leaves open the question: Is BDS directed against the occupation, the existence of the state of Israel, or Israel's current undemocratic character, which institutionalizes discrimination against the 20 percent of its citizens who are not Jews? In fact, Israel's occupation extends far beyond the West Bank and the Gaza Strip; the entire state is built on occupied and colonized lands. Is ending the "greater occupation" an objective of the boycott?

The case of Intel's manufacturing facility at Kiryat Gat illustrates both the

---

4   Naomi Klein, "Boycott, Divest, Sanction," *Nation*, January 8, 2009, at naomiklein.org.

5   Cecilie Surasky, "Analysis: Naomi Klein Boycotts Life as Normal in Israel," September 2, 2009, at bdsmovement.net.

6   "Palestinian Society Call for BDS," July 9, 2005, at bdsmovement.net.

righteousness and the complexities of dealing with the "greater occupation." The Intel factory is located on land designated for a Palestinian state according to the 1947 UN Partition Plan. During the 1948–49 war, the Israeli army surrounded the area (the Faluja pocket) and the defending Egyptian forces but did not occupy it. Before the Egyptians withdrew at the end of the war, they secured a written Israeli guarantee of the personal security and property of the 3,100 Palestinian residents and refugees in the villages of Faluja and 'Iraq al-Manshiyya. The Israeli army disregarded its explicit commitment, frightened the Palestinians into fleeing, confiscated their lands, and destroyed the villages. In 1955, Kiryat Gat was constructed on the lands of 'Iraq al-Manshiyya. Intel's Fab 18 plant was established there in 1999, and represented the largest foreign direct investment in Israel at the time.

This story was broken in the United States in 2002 by *San Francisco Chronicle* technology reporter and Jewish Voice for Peace member Henry Norr, after a contentious exchange with his editors about whether or not it was "technology news."[7] (The *Chronicle* fired Norr for breaching his professional obligation to maintain "objectivity" in 2003, after he was arrested in a demonstration on the day the US invaded Iraq—an event he was not covering for the paper.)

In July 2008 Intel inaugurated a new fabrication facility at Kiryat Gat, known as Fab 28. Fab 28 embodies the largest private-sector investment (sweetened with a substantial government subsidy) ever made in Israel. It was projected to contribute about 2 percent to Israel's GDP—a little more than the total of annual US aid (about $3 billion).[8] Intel's collaborators in this project include several major Japanese firms: Tokyo Electron, Hitachi High Tech Instruments, Hitachi Kokusai Electric, Nikon, DNP, Daifuku, and Shinko.[9] The original Fab 18 plant was turned over to Numonyx Israel,

---

7   Henry Norr, "Intel Chip Plant Located on Disputed Israeli Land," *San Francisco Chronicle*, July 8, 2002, at sfgate.com. See also Benny Morris, *The Birth of the Palestinian Refugee Problem Revisited*, Cambridge University Press, 2004: 521–5. According to the testimony of a survivor originally reported by Sharif Kana'na and Rashad al-Madani in Kafr Faluja and quoted by Morris, the Israeli army "created a situation of terror, entered the houses and beat the people with rifle butts."

8   *Globes*, July 1, 2008, at globes.co.il.

9   "Intel Recruits Japanese Equipment Companies for Fab 28," *EE Times Asia*, November 10, 2006, at eetasia.com.

the local subsidiary of an Intel joint venture with STMicroelectronics, which produces flash memory.

This historical background provides a principled reason to boycott the products of the Intel and Numonyx fabrication plants in Kiryat Gat. But taking on Intel would be a monumental task. A very large number of computers contain the advanced chips Intel manufactures at Kiryat Gat, and there are legions of users of the flash memory that Numonyx fabricates there. Moreover, sixty years after the expulsion of the residents of Faluja and 'Iraq al-Manshiyya, perhaps a campaign with more immediate resonance would win wider publicity.

Caterpillar supplies Israel with D9 bulldozers, which the Israeli army weaponizes and has used to build the separation barrier, or apartheid wall, since 2002. A D9 killed Evergreen State College student and International Solidarity Movement member Rachel Corrie in Rafah in March 2003. Since then, the Sisters of Loretto, the Sisters of Mercy, and Jewish Voice for Peace, with support from the US Campaign to End the Israeli Occupation and others, have conducted a shareholders' campaign aimed at ending sales of Caterpillar bulldozers to Israel.[10] In related actions, in February 2006 the Church of England voted to divest itself of £2.5 million in Caterpillar stock. The United Church of Christ, Presbyterian, and United Methodist churches of the US have seriously discussed divestment from Caterpillar. After seven years of trying to engage Caterpillar over its violations of Palestinian rights, the Presbyterian Church's Mission Responsibility Through Investment committee announced in September 2011 that it would recommend that the 2012 church General Assembly make a decision to divest from Caterpillar.[11] It will also recommend divestment from Motorola Solutions and Hewlett-Packard. US churches have not taken such steps previously largely due to pressure by Jewish organizations across the spectrum, from Americans for Peace Now to the pro-Likud Zionist Organization of America, which have threatened to smear them as "anti-Semitic."[12]

---

10   See "Our Report from the Caterpillar Shareholder's Meeting," at jewish voiceforpeace.org.

11   Bethany Furkin, "MRTI Recommends PC (USA) Divestment of Three Companies," September 12, 2011, at pcusa.org.

12   "United Methodist Church and Selective Divestment," at jewishvoicefor peace.org. For an example of the institutional Jewish response, see Josh Gerstein,

Caterpillar's sales to the Israeli army were a key element in the successful campaign of Hampshire College Students for Justice in Palestine (SJP). This highly regarded small, private college in western Massachusetts became the first US institution of higher learning to divest from companies that profit from Israel's occupation. Like most institutions, Hampshire's endowment fund is ultimately controlled by the board of trustees, and is invested in stocks, bonds, and other financial instruments. SJP argued that certain companies operating in the West Bank were engaged in manufacturing war materiel or in human rights violations, and that investing in those firms violated Hampshire College's longstanding policies on socially responsible investment. On February 7, 2009, the board of trustees voted to sell its shares in Caterpillar, Terex, Motorola, ITT, General Electric, and United Technologies. Hampshire's president acknowledged that "it was the good work of SJP that brought this issue to the attention of the committee," while members of the board of trustees denied this.[13] Building on its success, Hampshire SJP and allied groups hosted a national campus BDS conference in November 2009.

The strategy applied at Hampshire might work at other institutions with strong guidelines for socially responsible investment, thus avoiding the argument that Israel is being singled out as a special case. (Israel *is* a special case; no other country so massively violating human rights receives nearly $3 billion a year in aid from the US government. Egypt was a close second, at least until the popular uprising that began on January 25, 2011—though there were credible reports of torture and detention without charges after ex-President Mubarak's ouster on February 11.) But when students cannot readily know where their institution's endowment is invested, and institutions have a less than robust standard for socially responsible investment, other approaches must be explored. A divestment campaign launched in 2007 by Stanford Confronting Apartheid by Israel (SCAI) stalled on these points,[14] as did several campus efforts that preceded the Hampshire campaign.

"Presbyterian Church Proposals Could Reopen Wounds with Jews," *New York Sun*, June 23, 2008, at nysun.com.

13   Hampshire Students for Justice in Palestine, "Hampshire College Becomes First US University to Divest from Israeli Occupation," *Indypendent*, February 12, 2009, at indypendent.org.

14   Belatedly responding to a student campaign for divestment from

SCAI renewed its divestment campaign in 2011, after fruitless "dialogue" aimed at persuading Jewish students not to smear them as "anti-Semites." Soon after resuming the divestment campaign, SCAI changed its name to Students for Palestinian Equal Rights, in an effort to focus discussion on divestment rather than on whether or not Israel can properly be called an apartheid state. If one believes that Israel is an apartheid state, and a very good case can be made for that view, there is arguably a cost to such tactical flexibility; but Stanford students obviously thought they were outweighed by the benefits. In any case, by the beginning of the 2011–12 academic year, Stanford students advocating divestment had not been able to determine whether Stanford invested in firms complicit with the Israeli occupation. It almost certainly does. As a private institution, however, Stanford is not required to make its investments public. Perhaps this is a project for Wikileaks.

Following Israel's reoccupation of the West Bank in 2002, and in response to a call by Archbishop Desmond Tutu,[15] divestment campaigns were launched at Princeton, Harvard, MIT, Yale, Tufts, Columbia, the University of Pennsylvania, and the public universities of California, Illinois, and North Carolina. Following the South African model, most of them called for general divestment from all companies doing business in Israel. But the campaign at Penn sought divestment from "companies whose business promotes the Israeli occupation, especially firms that sell arms to Israel and firms based in illegal settlements in the West Bank and Gaza." But the organizers did not specify which of those companies were in Penn's investment portfolio. At Columbia, which probably had the best-organized effort, students and faculty demanded that the university divest from "companies that manufacture and sell arms to Israel." After researching the stock holdings in the endowment fund, the Columbia campaign targeted Boeing, Caterpillar, General Electric, and Lockheed Martin.

---

apartheid South Africa, in 2002 the Stanford board of trustees amended its weak "Statement on Investment Responsibility," originally adopted in 1971. The statement stipulates that divestment is a serious consideration for the trustees when they "conclude that a company's activities or policies cause substantial social injury." That is to say, under no circumstances is Stanford required to divest.
15   Desmond Tutu, "Build Moral Pressure to End the Israeli Occupation of the Palestinian Lands," *International Herald Tribune*, July 14, 2002.

These early campaigns were met with exceptional hostility, regardless of how their objective was formulated. Columbia President Lee Bollinger called the comparison of Israel with apartheid South Africa "grotesque and offensive."[16] In an address to students and faculty on September 17, 2002, Harvard President Lawrence Summers, alluding to the divestment call, argued that "serious and thoughtful people are advocating and taking actions that are anti-Semitic in their effect if not their intent."[17] (Summers, who resigned in 2006 after a no-confidence vote by the faculty in the wake of comments he made questioning women's aptitude for science and engineering, went on to direct President Obama's National Economic Council until the end of 2010, when he returned to Harvard.) Several years and two wars later, while rabid denunciations of BDS are still common, a wider audience is prepared to consider the tactic.

If research reveals where an institution's endowment is invested, particularly nefarious types of company may be easier targets for divestment campaigns than the range of all firms that do business in Israel, or firms whose activity in the occupied territories is incidental to their operations. Some 100 Israeli firms are listed on the NASDAQ. Among them are Elbit Systems, Gilat Satellite Networks, and Magal Security Systems—all major suppliers of equipment for the separation barrier, or apartheid wall. Elbit also supplies unmanned aerial vehicles to the Israeli army, which have been used in combat in the West Bank and Gaza Strip. US-based holding companies own major shares of Israeli firms involved in the occupation. Shamrock Holdings of California owns 38 percent of the Orad Group, which is involved in building the barrier/wall and checkpoints, and 18 percent of Ahava Dead Sea Laboratories, which manufactures and markets beauty products at Mitzpe Shalem, a West Bank settlement near the Dead Sea.

Most people do not buy Caterpillar bulldozers or military equipment or own stock in these firms, making boycott or divestment campaigns focused on such firms difficult beyond the context of institutional investors. So, although makeup has not killed anyone in Israel/Palestine, individual students and faculty may find it more accessible to participate

---

16   "President Lee Bollinger's Statement on the Divestment Campaign," November 7, 2002, at columbiadivest.org.
17   On this incident see Judith Butler, "No, It's Not Anti-Semitic," *London Review of Books*, August 21, 2003, at lrb.co.uk.

in the "Stolen Beauty" campaign to boycott Ahava products launched by Code Pink.[18]

In addition to Caterpillar, prominent US firms supplying military equipment to Israel include Boeing (Apache helicopters), Northrop Grumman (weapons, cluster bombs), General Dynamics (weapons, cluster bombs, phosphorus bombs), General Electric (engines for Apache helicopters), L-3 Communications (weapon and communication systems), Motorola Solutions (wireless communications), United Technologies (missile systems, helicopters), Raytheon (weapon systems), and Lockheed Martin (F-15 and F-16 fighter jets). Many university endowments hold shares in these firms, because they are quite profitable. Why would they not be, with annual US government military-related expenditures in the range of $1 trillion, including Foreign Military Sales financing of more than $4.5 billion, of which $1.8 billion goes to Israel?

Another easy target is Africa Israel Investments Ltd., whose majority shareholder is the Russian-Israeli diamond dealer and settlement supporter Lev Leviev. Africa Israel subsidiary Danya Cebus has undertaken construction projects in the settlements of Ariel, Modi'in Ilit, Maale Adumim, Har Homa, Tzufin, and Adam. Its Anglo-Saxon Real Estate subsidiary maintains an office in Ma'ale Adumim and sells housing in the West Bank.[19]

Adalah–NY, the "New York Campaign for the Boycott of Israel," has targeted Leviev. Following its interventions, at least four Hollywood stars complained about their pictures being displayed wearing Leviev's diamond jewelry on the celebrity photo page at www.leviev.com. Consequently, the entire page was removed from the website.[20]

In September 2009, Adalah–NY called on the largest higher-education pension fund in North America, Teachers Insurance and Annuity Association, College Retirement Equities Fund (TIAA-CREF), to divest its $257,000 of holdings in Africa Israel. In addition to TIAA-CREF, pension funds of university personnel are also invested in Fidelity and Vanguard. The holdings of these funds are detailed in their quarterly reports, readily

---

18   See Code Pink's "Stolen Beauty" campaign at stolenbeauty.org.
19   For full details, see Adri Nieuwhof, "Africa-Israel Under Scrutiny for Settlement Construction," June 22, 2009, at electronicintifada.net.
20   See Adalah–NY: The New York Campaign for the Boycott of Israel, at adalahny.org.

available online. This campaign could have been an effective way to engage college and university faculty and administrators in the BDS movement. But Adalah and its supporters were embarrassed to learn that TIAA-CREF had actually sold its shares of Africa Israel several months previously, for financial reasons.[21] Despite this setback, a divestment campaign directed at TIAA-CREF may still be a viable project, because it holds shares in many other companies that profit from the occupation.

In 2010 Jewish Voice for Peace (JVP) launched a campaign urging that TIAA-CREF "stop investing in companies that profit from the Israeli occupation of the Gaza Strip and the West Bank, including East Jerusalem."[22] JVP's general statement on BDS clarifies that it "supports divestment from and boycotts of companies operating in or from occupied Palestinian territory, exploiting Palestinian labor and scarce environmental resources, providing materials or labor for settlements, or producing military or other equipment or materials used to violate human rights or to profit from the Occupation." Caterpillar and Elbit have been prominently mentioned as candidates for divestment. Although JVP's demand is much more limited than the 2005 Palestinian BDS call, the Boycott National Committee has endorsed JVP's TIAA-CREF campaign.

The corporate and institutional sales division of Israel Bonds markets Israeli bonds to university endowment funds. With an interest rate under 3 percent, Israeli bonds have not historically been considered investment-quality instruments (at current market interest rates, this may no longer be the case); they have functioned primarily as an emotional statement of "support for Israel." Among the educational institutions holding these bonds are the University of Florida, the University System of Maryland, and Marquette University.[23]

Buying Israeli bonds has been a popular way for US trade unions, which have historically had close ties to Israel's Histadrut labor federation, to

---

21 "TIAA-CREF Clients Ask Fund to Divest from Leviev's Africa-Israel Due to Israeli Settlements," at adalahny.org.
22 Jewish Voice for Peace website, at jewishvoiceforpeace.org.
23 Erin Cohen, "Wild to Be Honored by Israel Bonds," *Wisconsin Jewish Chronicle*, May 20, 2005, at jewishchronicle.org; "University of Florida Hillel Students Donate $17,000 in Israel Bonds to University Foundation," April 18, 2005, at hillel.org.

support Israel. The AFL-CIO and its affiliates are the largest non-Jewish holders of Israeli bonds in the world, with total holdings reported in the range of $5 billion. At many universities the faculty, graduate research and teaching assistants, or clerical and maintenance workers, are unionized. The United Auto Workers union has organized on campuses to compensate for its declining membership in the auto industry. It represents over 11,000 teaching assistants, readers, and tutors at University of California campuses, and over 6,000 in the California State University system, as well as faculty, graduate assistants, or workers at Columbia, Cornell, the New School, the University of Massachusetts, the University of Washington, Boston University, and others. The UAW may hold as much as $785,000 in Israeli bonds.[24] The American Federation of Teachers, which represents faculty at some institutions, holds $600,000 in Israeli bonds.[25]

After the 1967 war, the Detroit-area Arab Auto Workers Caucus unsuccessfully demanded that the UAW sell its Israeli bonds. Since that effort, there had not been any divestment campaigns targeting trade unions until very recently. Before the September 2009 Connecticut AFL-CIO convention, over sixty union members and others called on the Connecticut AFL-CIO leadership to sell its $25,000 in Israeli bonds. Teacher and union member Stanley Heller addressed the convention and extracted from President John Olsen a promise that the federation's executive board would consult with Washington officials and vote on the issue later in the year; but nothing has come of this effort. In December 2009, Labor for Palestine, which is affiliated with the al-Awda Right to Return Coalition, sent an open letter to AFL-CIO President Richard Trumka urging divestment from State of Israel bonds, as well as wider boycott and sanctions measures. But there has been no visible public campaign around this issue.

Colleges and universities are common venues for cultural events featuring Israeli writers and artists of all sorts. In February 2009 the Minnesota Break the Bonds Campaign called for a boycott of the Batsheva Dance Company's performance at the University of Minnesota in Minneapolis. A very small

---

24 Doug Henwood, "UAW Finances (cont.)," *Left Business Observer*, January 3, 1998, at mail-archive.com.
25 Marcy Newman, "How Many Israel Bonds Does Your Union Own?" US Campaign for the Academic and Cultural Boycott of Israel, April 17, 2010, at usacbi.wordpress.com.

but spirited demonstration was held outside the performance venue, but the show went on. The connection between dance and denial of the rights of the Palestinian people may not be readily apparent, but the link is real. After the 2006 Lebanon War, the Anholt National Brands Index included Israel for the first time in its annual survey of national brands. Anholt discovered that "Israel's brand is, by a considerable margin, the most negative we have ever measured in the NBI, and comes in at the bottom of the ranking on almost every question."[26] In response, Israeli officials launched a "Brand Israel" campaign, whose objective is to divert attention from the Palestinian-Israeli conflict and the negative image it creates for Israel by promoting positive images of Israel. The Israeli consul general in Toronto, Amir Gissin, announced his intention to make Toronto a "test market for the Israel Brand," including "a major Israeli presence at [the 2009] Toronto International Film Festival"[27]

In September 2009 a small group of filmmakers and others drafted a declaration announcing their objection to the Toronto International Film Festival, featuring a "Spotlight on Tel Aviv" as part of their "City to City" program. This very focused protest argued that, knowingly or not, TIFF was collaborating with the "Brand Israel" campaign. The Toronto Declaration was worded carefully:

> We do not protest the individual Israeli filmmakers included in City to City, nor do we in any way suggest that Israeli films should be unwelcome at TIFF. However, especially in the wake of this year's brutal assault on Gaza, we object to the use of such an important international festival in staging a propaganda campaign on behalf of what South African Archbishop Desmond Tutu, former US President Jimmy Carter, and UN General Assembly President Miguel d'Escoto Brockmann have all characterized as an apartheid regime.[28]

---

26   "A Country with a Bad Reputation," *Ynet*, November 22, 2006, at ynet news.com.

27   Andy Levy-Ajzenkopf, "Brand Israel Set to Launch in GTA," *Canadian Jewish News*, August 20, 2008, at cjnews.com

28   "Toronto Declaration: No Celebration of Occupation," open letter to the Toronto International Film Festival, September 9, 2009, at torontodeclaration. blogspot.com.

The Toronto Declaration was endorsed by over 1,500 signatories, including Harry Belafonte, Jane Fonda, Julie Christie, Danny Glover, Naomi Klein, Eve Ensler, and sixty-three Palestinians and Israelis, including Elia Suleiman and Udi Aloni. Its publication prompted frenzied denunciations accusing the signers of anti-Semitism, censorship, blacklisting, and even advocating "the complete destruction of the Jewish State." These hysterical claims were based on a willful misreading of the text of the Toronto Declaration. Jane Fonda was put under extraordinary pressure and issued a statement of clarification, but kept her signature on the declaration.[29] In response to the fabrications and pressures, Jewish Voice for Peace gathered 7,500 additional signatures in twenty-four hours, and assembled a fact sheet refuting the "Blizzard of Lies" circulated by the entire Jewish establishment, including Jeremy Ben-Ami, executive director of the recently established "pro-Israel, pro-peace" lobby, J Street.[30]

Boycotting the Batsheva dance troupe's appearance in Minneapolis is in principle no different from protesting the "Spotlight on Tel Aviv" at the Toronto International Film Festival. Both events were part of the same "Brand Israel" campaign. However, the Toronto Declaration received immeasurably more attention in Canada, the United States, and even Israel. Apparently, tactical moderation and focus on a clear, limited target (along with the media power of Hollywood stars) was more effective. The Toronto Declaration did not call for a boycott, which some of its signatories who drew the most media attention (like Jane Fonda) would not have supported. But it achieved a similar effect, which is why it was so viciously attacked. So, in this case, less was more.

The experience of the University of California–Berkeley Students for Justice in Palestine campaign for divestment suggests a similar conclusion. The first effort, in 2001, demanded that the university divest all its holdings from firms that do business in Israel. The university did not do so. Pro-divestment students occupied several buildings in response, and a very vociferous and bitter debate ensued. But the campaign petered out. In a tactical shift at least partly inspired by the 2009 victory at Hampshire College, the renewed 2009–10 SJP campaign targeted two arms manufacturers which

---

29　Jane Fonda, "An Intense Ten Days," September 16, 2009, at jane fonda.com.

30　"Fighting the Lies—Toronto International Film Festival," at jvp.org.

profit from the most egregious aspects of the Israeli occupation of the West Bank and the Gaza Strip—General Electric and United Technologies. The details of this effort are taken up elsewhere in this volume. Here it is sufficient to note that, although the campaign failed to achieve divestment, it was a huge success in two arenas—extensive regional and even national media attention was focused on the issue for weeks; and a strong, highly visible, and inspiring alliance was built among Arab, Israeli, Muslim, and Jewish students and faculty who supported divestment. JVP put an enormous effort into supporting SJP and the divestment bill. The close relations forged as a result are an enduring asset of the BDS movement. Not only are they a concrete demonstration that BDS is not anti-Semitc; even more importantly, they embody the kind of human relationships it is possible to create if people share a common commitment to justice, equal rights, and self-determination for Palestinians.

This survey of BDS efforts in which colleges and universities have engaged, and which they might consider in the future, illustrates a wide range of approaches and targets. Unlike Scandinavia, Spain, and Britain, the North American environment, while more open to debate than ever before, is still largely unreceptive to the notion that Israel is or should be made a pariah state. It is impossible and undemocratic to suppress any of the voices in the BDS movement. Mass movements usually contain many currents of opinion, and this is entirely legitimate. But if BDS is to be seen as a reasonable and effective tactic in a relatively hostile milieu, its targets should be selected to send the most accessible message possible.

One of the two main tendencies in the BDS movement sees it as a campaign against Israel, or at least against the Zionist character of the state. The second main tendency envisions the more limited objective of ending Israel's occupation of the West Bank and imprisonment of the Gaza Strip. These differences may, but do not necessarily, involve selecting different targets and, just as importantly, different framing messages.

Focusing our concerns on the fate of peoples rather than the future of states may make it unnecessary to resolve these differences. Rolling back the Israeli occupation of the territories seized in 1967 is a requisite first step toward relieving the agony of the Palestinian people living under that occupation, shifting the local and global balance of forces, and mobilizing the political consciousness necessary to begin a discussion about what would be required for a regional resolution of the conflict guaranteeing democracy, equality, human rights, security, and national rights for the Palestinian and Israeli peoples, no matter how many states may be left on the map.

9 SIX YEARS OF BDS: SUCCESS!

Hind Awwad

As the world watched the Arab Spring, many Palestinians saw traces of Palestine's revolution, particularly of the first Intifada—the popular uprising of 1987—and in the beautiful spirit of the young revolutionaries. The fall of the regimes in Tunisia and Egypt was celebrated in Palestinian households not only because it promised a return of Arab resistance, a constant dimension of the Palestinian cause but hijacked by the dictatorships for so many years, but also because it was a reminder that Palestine continues to bring people together: those struggling in many places around the world against injustice of all kinds.

As we continue to watch the revolutions unfold—from Wall Street to Madrid, from London to Seattle—we can see Palestine in every Tahrir Square. The Egyptian spring is partly a result of the previous regime's heavy complicity in maintaining Israeli occupation and colonization; the Egyptian student mobilizations in solidarity with Palestine during the second Intifada, in 2000, were important precursors to January 2011. The injustice resulting from Israel's occupation, colonization, and enforcement of apartheid is heavily linked with corporate greed, environmental degradation, education cuts, and privatization of healthcare that are today being protested in North America and Europe. The channeling each year of billions in US tax dollars away from education, healthcare reform, and social services at home, to support Israel's military machine, has linked the struggle for Palestinian rights with the causes of equality and social justice in the US and elsewhere. The BDS movement has provided a way for us to break our collective chains.

In 2005, one year after the International Court of Justice had ruled that Israel's wall, built on occupied Palestinian territory, was illegal—and inspired by the South African anti-apartheid struggle—a majority of Palestinian civil society called upon people of conscience all over the world to impose broad BDS initiatives against Israel.

The comprehensive rights-based approach of the call for BDS is perhaps its most important attribute. This is exemplified by the three demands that it makes: for an end to the occupation and return to the pre-1967 boundaries; for recognition of the fundamental human rights of Palestinian citizens; and for the right of Palestinian refugees to return. These demands address the injustice done to all Palestinian people, and do not reduce Israel's oppression to occupation. Twenty years of the sham "peace process" have given the false impression—often dominant even today—that the Palestinian people are only those in the Occupied Palestinian Territories (OPT), and that Israel's occupation is its only form of oppression of Palestinians. This has marginalized the majority of the Palestinian people—those inside Israel and in the diaspora—and their rights; and it has allowed Israel to get away, unquestioned, with its more severe and legally problematic forms of oppression. The BDS movement has worked on changing the discourse addressing Palestinian rights to include the rights of *all* Palestinians. The movement has called for an end to Israel's multi-tiered system of oppression, comprising occupation, colonization, and apartheid—the latter including systematic legal discrimination against Palestinians in Israel, and a sixty-three-year-old denial of Palestinian refugees' right of return.

Setting the record straight on Palestinian rights—and reinserting both Palestinian citizens of Israel and, crucially, Palestinian refugees, at the center of the debate—could not have been achieved without a strong Palestinian leadership. The Palestinian BDS National Committee (BNC), established in April 2008, has emerged as the principal anchor of and reference for the global BDS movement. The BNC, the broadest Palestinian civil society coalition, is made up of the largest coalitions, networks, and unions of Palestinian citizens of Israel and refugees, as well as of those living in the West Bank and Gaza. The BNC has consistently provided a strong and unified Palestinian voice, and continues to lead and guide the global BDS movement, while fully respecting the principle of context sensitivity—the idea that the call for BDS should be implemented in each community in a way that suits the particular circumstances in the local environment, as decided by local activists.

Over the past six years, BDS has provided the most effective vehicle of solidarity with the Palestinian people and a successful way of challenging Israeli impunity. The victories the BDS campaign has achieved have exceeded all expectations for such a young movement, even when compared with South Africa's BDS campaign. In particular, the campaign has grown rapidly in the wake of the 2008–09 Israeli massacre in Gaza and the attack on the Freedom Flotilla. The movement has now expanded far beyond the confines of a traditional solidarity movement to include active and dedicated participation from trade unions, faith groups, mainstream NGOs, and political parties. A quick review of some of the largest and most successful campaigns reveals this growth.

One of the most successful BDS campaigns is that against Veolia, a French multinational involved in developing the Jerusalem Light Rail (JLR), an illegal tramway linking Jerusalem with illegal Israeli settlements, and cementing Israel's hold on occupied territory, in addition to Israel's involvement in a variety of waste and transport infrastructure services for illegal settlements. The French multinational has been successfully targeted all over the world, but especially in Europe. In Stockholm, a civil society campaign led to Veolia losing out on a €3.5 billion contract for the operation of the city's metro system. The determined and internationally coordinated campaign against Veolia has led to its loss of contracts totaling more than €5 billion in France, England, Wales, Ireland, and Australia combined. In late 2010, Veolia and Alstom, another French multinational involved in the JLR, announced that they would sell their shares in the operating consortium. The fact that both Veolia and Alstom are being replaced by Israeli companies with little experience, rather than by well-known international companies that would be more qualified to take their place, can only be seen as a success for the campaign: no international companies are willing to become targets of our highly effective and visible movement. The BDS movement is showing corporate supporters of Israeli apartheid that there is a price to pay for their active complicity. The campaigns against Veolia and Alstom will continue until they cease to be complicit, and provide appropriate reparations.

Churches in the UK, Sweden, the US, and beyond are investigating and implementing their own BDS campaigns, largely in response to the Kairos document—a document prepared by prominent Palestinian leaders calling on churches around the world "to say a word of truth and to take a position of truth with regard to Israel's occupation of Palestinian land." Kairos Palestine unambiguously endorses BDS as one of the key nonviolent forms of solidarity that international faith-based organizations are urged to adopt: "We see boycott and disinvestment as tools of justice, peace and security."[1]

Trade unions have historically been at the forefront of struggles against injustice, particularly that against South African apartheid. Trade unions in South Africa, France, Belgium, Ireland, Sweden, Italy, Australia, Canada, Brazil, India, Norway, and elsewhere have recently adopted aspects of the BDS campaign. In the UK, the Trades Union Congress, representing seven million workers, is about to embark on activities to educate its entire membership about the necessity of boycotting Israeli apartheid. The trade union congresses of South Africa, Ireland, Scotland, and Brazil, and many individual unions around the world are in the process of severing links with the racist Histadrut labor federation. Just days after Israel's attack on the Freedom Flotilla in May 2010, the Swedish Dockworkers Union, heeding the Palestinian trade union movement's call to block Israeli ships, blocked five hundred tons of cargo coming from Israel. They were joined by the heroic action on the part of ILWU Local 10's dockworkers in Oakland, California, who blocked an Israeli ship from docking for twenty-four hours, and by dockworkers in South Africa, India, Turkey, and beyond. The CUT— the largest and most important trade union in Brazil, representing over 20 million workers, has recently endorsed BDS as the basis for its solidarity activism, and is working on a program to spread BDS among its membership. Labor-led sanctions within the BDS framework have become the leading form of solidarity with the Palestinian people within the international trade union network.

The academic boycott—arguably the most challenging of all forms of boycott—has widely spread the debate on the entrenched complicity of Israeli academic institutions in planning, justifying, and perpetuating the state's colonial and apartheid policies, including its war crimes in Gaza, Jerusalem, and beyond. The May 2010 Congress of the British University and College Union (UCU) made history by voting to boycott the Ariel University Center of Samaria (AUCS), an Israeli colony-college in occupied Palestinian territory, and to sever all relations with Histadrut, the

---

1   See Chapter 15.

racist Israeli labor body that is a key pillar of the Israeli state's apartheid policies. University workers in the Canadian Union of Public Employees passed a motion calling for an academic boycott of Israel in February 2009. Academics also vowed to pressure their institutions to sever financial relationships with Israel. Recently, the University of Johannesburg made history by severing links with the University of Ben-Gurion, becoming the first university in the world to sever links with an Israeli academic institution. Students in the US, the UK, and elsewhere have organized campaigns for the boycott of Israeli products, and for divestment from companies profiting from Israel's occupation. In the wake of Israel's attack on Gaza in January 2009, students in thirty-three college campuses in the UK "occupied" parts of their campus demanding, among other things, divestment from Israeli companies and companies profiting from the occupation. In February 2009, Hampshire College in the US became the first to divest from companies complicit in Israel's occupation, just as it had been the first in the US to divest from apartheid South Africa. In 2010, students at UC Berkeley worked on a well-organized and publicized divestment campaign, winning support from Archbishop Desmond Tutu, Naomi Klein, Judith Butler, Hedy Epstein, and other notable figures. Jewish Voice for Peace has organized a campaign calling on pension giant TIAA-CREF to divest from five companies supporting the occupation. Their campaign has been endorsed by a number of organizations and student groups across the US.

Creative consumer boycott campaigns have provided an excellent way to engage wider sectors of the general public in the BDS movement. Code Pink's "Stolen Beauty" campaign targeting Ahava, an Israeli cosmetics company manufacturing its products in a settlement, has been successful in convincing a number of retailers to drop Ahava in the US, Canada, and the UK. The campaign has spread to Canada, Australia, and parts of Europe as a result of its creative protests and use of social media. In France, a large coalition of more than a hundred NGOs and five political parties has organized a campaign for the boycott of Agrexco, Israel's largest exporter of agricultural produce. Agrexco has been targeted with popular boycotts, blockades, demonstrations, and direct action throughout Europe. In Italy and the UK, campaigners took direct action pressuring supermarkets to drop the Agrexco brand. In September 2011, Agrexco was ordered into liquidation.

As with South Africa, sanctions by governments and official bodies have been implemented only after boycott and divestment have become widespread at the grassroots level. In the six short years of the Palestinian BDS campaign, we have witnessed a number of government actions in the form of sanctions. To name a few, an Israeli academic team from Ariel College was excluded from a prestigious competition on sustainable architecture organized by the Spanish Government in 2009, because the college is located in a settlement in the West Bank. The Norwegian government's pension fund, the third-largest in the world, divested from Elbit Systems in 2009 at the recommendation of the ethical council, due to the company's involvement in supplying Israel's illegal wall with security appliances, and the Israeli army with drones. A year later, the Norwegian government's pension fund divested from two other Israeli companies as a result of their activities in the settlements. Deutsche Bahn, a government-owned German railway operator, has ceased its involvement with the Israeli A1 rail project, which cuts through the occupied West Bank.

Perhaps the most visible form of BDS action is in the realm of cultural boycotts. Far from being "above politics," Israeli cultural institutions play a key role in the "Brand Israel" campaign of the Israeli foreign ministry, boosting the state's image and whitewashing its colonial policies and war crimes. A growing number of cultural superstars have joined the cultural boycott of Israel and are refusing to provide cultural cover for Israeli apartheid. Artists that have canceled concerts and events in Israel include, among others, Gil Scott-Heron, Elvis Costello, the Pixies, Mike Leigh, Klaxons, and Gorillaz Sound System. Most significantly, Hollywood superstars Meg Ryan and Dustin Hoffman canceled their attendance at the 2010 Jerusalem Film Festival following the attack on the Freedom Flotilla. In addition, cultural figures such as John Berger, Roger Waters, Ken Loach, Judith Butler, Naomi Klein, the Yes Men, Sarah Schulman, Aharon Shabtai, Udi Aloni, John Greyson, Adrienne Rich, and John Williams have explicitly supported the Palestinian cultural boycott of Israel. A number of cultural figures have also refused to participate in Israel's official cultural events for political reasons, including Augusto Boal, Roger Waters, André Brink, Vincenzo Consolo, and Nigel Kennedy; and cultural figures such as Bono, Björk, Jean-Luc Godard, Snoop Dogg, and others have declined offers to take part in events in Israel—or have agreed but then canceled without giving explicit political reasons.

Another measure of success for the global BDS movement can be gauged from Israeli reactions to the BDS campaign. In July 2011, the Israeli Knesset passed a law that essentially criminalizes boycotts of Israel, as well as individuals and organizations calling for them. The Reut Institute, a prominent Israeli think tank, has categorized the BDS campaign as a "strategic threat" that could turn into an existential threat. Furthermore, key Israeli politicians have issued alarmist statements about the growth of the BDS movement and the isolation of Israel. After Prime Minister Netanyahu's speech to the US Congress in May 2011, he spoke with Knesset member Binyamin "Fuad" Ben-Eliezer. "Listen, Bibi," growled Ben-Eliezer, "I congratulate you on your hug from Congress, but it will not take us off the path to confrontation. Our situation in Europe is very bad. President Obama said everything we wanted him to say … As a former industry and trade minister, I tell you: The markets are closing. We will suffer a devastating economic blow."

President Shimon Peres has also voiced fear that Israel might be subjected to economic boycotts and sanctions. "There's no need for boycotts," he said. "It would suffice for ports in Europe or Canada to stop unloading Israeli merchandise. It's already beginning."

Deputy Prime Minister Ehud Barak has also chimed in on the subject. "There are elements in the world, quite powerful, in various countries, including friendly ones, in trade unions, [among] academics, consumers, green political parties," he warned, "and this impetus has culminated in a broad movement called BDS … which is what was done with South Africa."

Since its initiation, the BDS movement has expanded and achieved effectiveness far beyond what was originally imagined to be possible in just over six years. The call of the movement is increasingly being answered by mainstream and powerful actors. Cultural superstars, global financial institutions, major trade unions, faith groups, political parties, governments, and individuals of conscience of every kind—all are beginning to take action. Our global movement has in fact begun to isolate Israel.

10 BDS IN THE USA, 2001–2010

Noura Erakat

On April 26, 2010, the student senate at the University of California–Berkeley upheld, by one vote, an executive veto on SB 118—the student body resolution endorsing divestment of university funds from General Electric and United Technologies, two companies that profit from the Israeli occupation of East Jerusalem, the West Bank, and the Gaza Strip. Proponents of the resolution needed fourteen votes to override the veto and, as sixteen senators had spoken in favor of doing so, it appeared a simple task.

But the vote at Berkeley had shifted the gaze of national pro-Israel organizations from Capitol Hill westward, begetting an unlikely alliance between the hawkish American Israel Public Affairs Committee (AIPAC) and its self-proclaimed liberal rival, J Street. The two groups collaborated in lobbying efforts on campus to sustain the veto. Ultimately, two senators changed their votes and a third abstained, bringing the final count to thirteen in favor of overriding the veto and five opposed. While adherence to student body procedure has blocked the divestment measure, the numbers indicate the strong support for divestment on Berkeley's campus, and can be regarded as a milestone in the BDS movement.

The strident response to Berkeley's resolution from off-campus groups reflected the fact that the BDS movement was being taken more seriously by its opponents than ever before. Berkeley students had been at the forefront of BDS efforts since February 6, 2001, the day Ariel Sharon became Israeli prime minister. They erected a mock checkpoint on campus and unfurled banners exclaiming, "Divest from Israeli Apartheid." Within the span of three years, this first university-based divestment campaign spread to dozens of other American campuses, as well as into churches and community organizations. Yet the movement did not gain international legitimacy and elicit serious treatment until a call for BDS came from Palestinian civil society in 2005.

Since then, and especially since the resounding failure of the international community to hold Israel to account for war crimes committed during Operation Cast Lead, the assault on Gaza in the winter of 2008–09, the notion of extra-governmental tactics targeting Israeli human rights violations has permeated mainstream institutions. No longer the passion of idealistic students alone, BDS demands have reverberated within American retail stores, corporations, and international multilateral organizations.

The movement's deepening acceptance among mainstream stakeholders correlates with the steady decline of faith in efforts to achieve a negotiated two-state solution to the Israeli-Palestinian conflict. While heads of state fail to extract the most modest commitments from Israel, such as a settlement freeze, BDS activists have increased compliance (albeit incrementally) with international law among corporations and institutions that have distanced themselves from, or divested their holdings in, settlement-related enterprises.

BDS victories to date, at least in the United States, have targeted Israeli policies in the occupied territories, the notion being that what should be boycotted and sanctioned is the occupation, rather than Israel itself. But the movement draws inspiration from similar efforts aimed at apartheid South Africa in the 1980s, coupled with the 2005 call emanating from Palestine that includes a demand for equality for Israel's Palestinian citizens and the right of return for Palestinian refugees. This genealogy makes BDS abhorrent to many loyalists of the two-state solution. J Street, for example, sees the movement as an attack on Israel's character as a Jewish state. In his blog entry opposing the Berkeley resolution, Isaac Luria of J Street complains that the movement

> fails to draw a clear distinction between opposition to the post-1967 occupation and opposition to the existence of the state of Israel itself as the democratic home of the Jewish people. Even if it was not the intent of the students who drafted this bill, its passage is now being seized on by the global BDS movement as a victory in its broader campaign.

BDS activists insist that they emphasize rights, as opposed to political solutions, precisely to escape the debate over whether Israel and Palestine should be one or two states. They recognize, however, that the fruition of the 2005 demands may lead to an Israel that is a state of all its citizens irrespective of religion. Hence it is inevitable that BDS will be anathema not only to AIPAC, but also to J Street and Arab-American partisans of the two-state solution like Hussein Ibish of the American Task Force on Palestine.

In arousing the ire of both the right and the left ends of the spectrum of permissible opinion on Israel–Palestine in Washington, the BDS platform and movement cuts to the heart of the conflict over the Israeli-Palestinian conflict—and could become central to the conflict itself.

VISIONS OF JUSTICE

At the World Conference Against Racism in Durban, South Africa, in 2001, NGOs and activists equated Israel's racially discriminatory policies throughout Israel proper and the occupied territories with apartheid, and advocated BDS as the strategy of choice for fighting back. Ever since, the activists have drawn upon the general definition of apartheid laid out in the 1973 International Convention on the Suppression and Punishment of the Crime of Apartheid: policies "designed to divide the population ... by the creation of separate reserves and ghettoes for the members of racial groups [or] the expropriation of landed property [or] the persecution of organizations or persons ... because they oppose apartheid." Then, in 2004, a group of Palestinian intellectuals and academics issued a call for the academic and cultural boycott of Israel.

On July 9, 2005, a year after the International Court of Justice's historic advisory opinion declared the route of Israel's wall illegal, 170 Palestinian civil society organizations issued a call for BDS. The tripartite strategy is rooted in economic logic: Israel must comply with international law because non-compliance is too politically and economically costly to maintain, and must do so by "ending its occupation and colonization of all Arab lands and dismantling the wall; recognizing the fundamental rights of the Arab-Palestinian citizens of Israel to full equality; and respecting, protecting and promoting the rights of Palestinian refugees to return to their homes and properties as stipulated in UN Resolution 194."

This call marked a significant shift in the movement for Palestinian self-determination. Most importantly, it emphasized the rights of Palestinians everywhere, irrespective of which state they live in today or where they envision living tomorrow. Omar Barghouti, a founder and steering committee member of PACBI and a drafter of the 2005 document, explains that "the fundamental pillar of the BDS call was its rights-based approach that does not endorse any particular political solution to the Arab-Israeli colonial conflict, but insists that for any solution to be just and sustainable it must address all three basic rights stated in the call."

Not everyone considers the affirmation of all three rights to be a neutral act. The likes of J Street view it as threatening to Israel's self-proclaimed identity as a Jewish state, because the return of refugees in appreciable numbers would render Jews a small minority. Those committed to the two-state solution on the "pro-Palestinian" side, like Ibish, have interpreted the call as a repudiation of the state-building project in place since 1993 and a return to the liberation model. But it was important to the BDS drafters to represent the interests of all Palestinians, and not just those living within the elastic boundaries of a future Palestinian state. Hence the call's second clause demands the full equality of Israel's non-Jewish Palestinian citizens.

It is logical that this clause would be inserted, given the participation in the drafting of Ittijah, the umbrella network of Palestinian NGOs in Israel, which demands equal treatment before the law irrespective of race, ethnicity, national origin, and religion. From the perspective of the BDS organizers, therefore, objecting to this clause amounts to rejecting Palestinians' self-definition as a unified national body. Still, for supporters of Palestinian human rights who prefer to indict the occupation only, the second clause is an affront to their solidarity. For these supporters, ending Jewish privilege within Israel may be desirable, but it exceeds the mandate of a movement for Palestinian self-determination. Despite its best efforts to transcend political solutions, therefore, the BDS call has been read as an implicit endorsement of the one-state solution.

Perhaps surprisingly, several Palestinian NGO representatives within the occupied territories initially opposed the BDS call as well. They viewed the comprehensive approach to Palestinian rights as a veiled endorsement of the one-state solution, and hence a blow to the Palestinian Authority and a subversion of the strategic direction of the Palestinian national movement since the late 1980s and enshrined by the "peace process" of the 1990s. Drafters of the call, including PACBI, Ittijah, Badil, and Stop the Wall, invested a tremendous amount of time and energy in explaining that the fundamental emphasis on rights was necessary to redress the concerns of a cohesive Palestinian national body, as opposed to endorsing a particular political solution. Ultimately, the Council of National and Islamic Forces in Palestine, the coordinating body for the major political parties in the occupied territories, along with the largest PLO mass movements, facilitated the acceptance of the BDS call by major sectors of Palestinian civil society within the occupied territories and beyond. Constricted by the parameters of the "peace process," the Palestinian Authority has neither endorsed nor repudiated the BDS call, though it has launched a narrower boycott of settlement-produced goods. In January 2010, Prime Minister Salam Fayyad staged the burning of $1 million in settlement products, and created a National Dignity Fund to support the production and distribution of Palestinian-made goods. Unlike the 2005 call, the PA initiative perpetuates a state-centric approach to resolving the conflict, and therefore does not attempt to represent the rights of a unified Palestinian national body.

Barghouti explains that the call for equality within Israel remains the least popular element of the call among solidarity activists—even more controversial than the right of return, because it goes beyond calling on Israel to rein in its occupation policies in the Palestinian territories and demands that Israel rectify its domestic policies to afford non-Jewish Arab citizens full equality. But, as Barghouti asks, "If a political system is built on a foundation of inequality and would collapse if equality set in, is it a system worth keeping?"

MAINSTREAMING BDS

Barghouti's rhetorical question is precisely what makes BDS so controversial. Though BDS is in fact a reform movement, one that seeks to alter corporate and state behavior, it has been viewed as radical. Mark Lance, a Georgetown philosophy professor and cofounder of Stop US Taxpayer Aid to Israel Now (SUSTAIN), explains that, when his group first approached cohorts with the idea of divestment in 2001, they were hostilely dismissed as naïve. The established solidarity organizations feared such a tactic would alienate average Americans, who were ready to support a Palestinian state but not to criticize Israel or call its internal policies into question. SUSTAIN redirected its energy at young global justice groups, Lance continues, and waited for the time for BDS to ripen. Within two years, the US Campaign to End the Israeli Occupation, the "connective tissue" of American Palestine solidarity groups, had incorporated numerous BDS activists.

Established in 2001 with a $20,000 grant and a few dozen member organizations, today the Campaign has grown to more than 300 members and boasts a budget of $250,000. In 2005, the Campaign endorsed the BDS call and mounted a campaign against Caterpillar, manufacturer of the heavy bulldozers used by the Israeli army to raze Palestinian homes. Phyllis Bennis, a Campaign cofounder and steering committee member, explains that Caterpillar emerged as a target for its role in the destruction of Palestinian olive trees and the murder of Rachel Corrie, the Evergreen State College student run over by a bulldozer in 2003 while trying to prevent a home demolition. Soon, Bennis says, "the discussion moved from the tactical targeting of Caterpillar to the strategic effort to build a campaign against corporations profiting from occupation."

The Campaign's focus, which reflects its member groups' prerogatives, has continued to shift. In 2006 the coalition adopted an anti-apartheid framework, which expounds on the discriminatory treatment of Israel's non-Jewish citizens, and in 2009 it endorsed the academic and cultural boycott of Israel, another controversial strand of the BDS movement. The Campaign's progression from divesting from occupation to boycotting Israel may be a bellwether of change in mainstream organizations that have joined the BDS movement but have limited their activism to targeting war-profiteering corporations involved in the occupation.

Code Pink, the women's peace group famed for head-to-toe pink attire and unabashed disruption of business as usual on Capitol Hill, coalesced in opposition to war in Afghanistan and Iraq. According to member Nancy Kricorian, Code Pink expanded its mandate to include the occupation of Palestine when it joined the Campaign in 2006—but the gesture was largely symbolic, as the group's work remained focused on Afghanistan and Iraq. This quiet engagement became much louder in the aftermath of Operation Cast Lead, when Code Pink brought Palestine to the front and center of its agenda, to the dismay of several members and funders. Undeterred, the women's group has since taken two solidarity delegations to Gaza, co-led the Gaza Freedom March in January 2010, and launched Stolen Beauty—a boycott of Ahava, the settlement-manufactured cosmetics line. Since its inception in June 2009, Stolen Beauty has pressured Oxfam into suspending its goodwill ambassador, *Sex and the City* star Kristin Davis, for the duration of her contract as an Ahava spokeswoman, and pushed Costco, a national wholesaler, to take Ahava products off its shelves.

Despite these achievements, which have been covered in the *New York Post* and elsewhere, Kricorian notes that her group still uses the "A-word" gingerly. While BDS can be presented within the framework of corporate accountability and war profiteering, the term "apartheid" is controversial. "This word still triggers people's emotions in a way that shuts off dialogue. It is a trigger because of its history in South Africa, but in the case of South Africa, most people would not have dreamed of saying that apartheid was necessary for security's sake, or that it was a good idea to keep blacks in bantustans."

Fayyad Sbaihat, a former University of Wisconsin student and a leading member of al-Awda Wisconsin, which garnered faculty senate and union endorsement of divestment across the twenty-five University of Wisconsin campuses in 2005, explains that the first and strongest opposition to BDS came from long-time allies who feared that the movement would drive away liberals or induce a backlash in Israel. "It was a hindrance in the short term," says Sbaihat.

Not only was BDS too much to ask of the "fair-weather friends" of Palestine, but also it was too much for them to accept or live with the apartheid analogy. However, part of the appeal of BDS as we recognized it was getting the uninterested to begin asking questions and then questioning Israel's character, and using the apartheid analogy was a way to provoke questions from the casual observer.

Glenn Dickson hopes to present precisely this challenge to the Presbyterian Church USA. At its 2004 General Assembly, the 2.3 million–strong church endorsed divestment from companies profiting from Israeli occupation by an overwhelming vote of 460 to 41. Despite receiving threats to burn down houses of worship and pressure from Congress to rescind the resolution, the church has reaffirmed its commitment to corporate engagement at subsequent general assemblies, where support for divestment has only increased. In 2006, seventeen of the 170 overtures submitted to the assembly opposed the divestment resolution, while in 2008 only two overtures protested the church's stance. Today, the Presbyterians' Mission Responsibility Through Investment Committee has denounced Caterpillar for profiting from the non-peaceful use of its products, and continues to explore divestment from Motorola, ITT, Citibank, and United Technologies for their role in sustaining the occupation.

Dickson is the retired Presbyterian pastor who introduced the 2004 divestment resolution. He did not consider including boycott at the time because he felt that, unlike divestment, which lends itself to corporate engagement, boycott precludes dialogue. He rightly predicted divestment's potential to excite controversy despite the church's legacy of principled divestment from South Africa, Indonesia, and Sudan, among other human rights violators. Today Dickson and his colleagues are thinking of introducing the concept of apartheid at the 2010 General Assembly because "it will help people to realize that Israel is as bad as South Africa in its poor treatment of people of color ... Because most people in the US see Israel as a benevolent democracy and see Palestinians as terrorists, reframing who Israel is will help us."

BLESSING OR BURDEN?

Notwithstanding its popular association with South Africa's experience, the term "apartheid" is not a requisite element of the BDS strategy, though it may be a useful instrument of branding in itself. Like the US Campaign, Code Pink, and the Presbyterians, activist groups have launched BDS campaigns without adopting the loaded term, only to adopt it later as their advocacy efforts developed. Even Students Confronting Apartheid by Israel, a group at Stanford University for whom the term was obviously central, has used it tactically at most.

According to Omar Shakir, a founding member of the group who is now at Georgetown, the Stanford students wanted to make apartheid central to demonstrate the power disparity inherent in the Israeli-Palestinian conflict and move beyond the language of "two sides," which can imply that Israel and the Palestinians have equal resources to draw upon. When campus opposition focused on the asymmetry between the South African and Palestinian cases, however, Shakir and his colleagues dropped the framework and focused instead on divestment criteria, including the disparate treatment of Israel's non-Jewish Arab citizens. The method here was to describe the violation rather than call it by name. "In the beginning," Shakir comments, "the opposition focused on apartheid more than our goal of divestment … We liked the way we did it because we could pick and choose; we weren't wedded to apartheid."

The apartheid framework is both a blessing and a burden. On the one hand, because the South African experience is so well known and so roundly condemned, mere mention of apartheid forces pro-Israel advocates to defend an entrenched system of racial discrimination and oppression rather than rally support for Israel's security. On the other hand, the two cases are far from identical. No South African blacks were allowed to vote or participate in government, as are Palestinian citizens in Israel. Neither were blacks subjected to military offensives or debilitating humanitarian blockades, as are Palestinians in the Gaza Strip; and nor were tens of thousands exiled as refugees to raise subsequent generations in the diaspora. Despite these differences, in the BDS movement there is general consensus that the apartheid framework is effective, especially in the symbolic realm. As Lisa Taraki, a Birzeit University professor and PACBI steering committee member, comments, "All historic analogies are fraught with problems, but in this case … I think this line of argument has been very successful on the whole, and has put Israel's supporters in a very uncomfortable position, to put it mildly."

That activists deploy the "A-word" tactically does not diminish their sincere belief that the framework is apt. To the contrary, Shakir and Taraki's attitudes are responses to detractors whose focus on the analogy's fine print is an attempt to dismiss it for lack of perfect symmetry. Such attempts are misguided because, although the South African experience makes the apartheid paradigm more compelling, it is by no means the yardstick against which to measure all occurrences of apartheid, whether in Israel–Palestine or elsewhere. Perhaps only a legal forum like the International Court of Justice can settle this tension. In the meantime, public discussions of Israeli apartheid continue to constitute a battle for domination at the symbolic level.

STRATEGIC CONSIDERATIONS

Activists have waged this battle offensively for six years in their organizing of Israeli Apartheid Week. Originally limited to educational activities in

Toronto and New York, today it spans forty cities worldwide, including, for the first time in 2010, Beirut.

Adalah–New York's BDS campaign is an organic outgrowth of Israeli Apartheid Week organizing. Unlike other groups, Adalah-NY began with the apartheid framework first and moved toward the divestment tactic later. The success of its campaign against Lev Leviev, an Israeli diamond mogul whose companies support the expansion of settlements in East Jerusalem and the West Bank, has made it a premier example of BDS organizing in the US. Lubna Ka'abneh of Adalah–NY explains that the apartheid analogy constituted a cornerstone of the group's outreach work "so that our [US] audience could make the connection to their own experiences." Ka'abneh and her cohorts have discovered that American audiences relate much more easily to narratives of institutionalized racial discrimination than those of occupation. Hence they work to draw parallels between the Civil Rights movement and the Palestinian movement to achieve freedom and equality.

Since launching its campaign in 2008, Adalah–NY has effectively pressed the Danish pension fund PKA and Danske Bank to exclude Leviev's enterprise, Africa Israel, from its investment portfolio; encouraged the second largest Dutch pension fund to divest from Africa Israel; and convinced UNICEF, Oxfam, the British government, and several Hollywood stars to distance themselves from the entrepreneur. Adalah–NY's success in simultaneously highlighting Israel's discriminatory character while choosing the occupation as its BDS target both captures the movement's strategic possibilities and reflects its political maturity.

The history of efforts at Berkeley is telling as well. While originally written to combat Israeli apartheid, and therefore target all companies with subsidiaries worth $5,000 or more within Israel, the student body resolution SB 118 eventually limited itself to two American corporations profiting from Israel's military occupation. "Divestment is ultimately about students engaging the administration," comments Abdel-Rahman Zahzah, a founding member of the Berkeley campaign and now a leader of similar efforts in Beirut. Zahzah notes that Berkeley students did not start out with a political strategy in 2001. Instead they issued abrupt threats to the administration: "Divest all your holdings from apartheid Israel or we'll take over academic buildings." While activists did occupy Wheeler Hall twice, they did not come close to achieving divestment until nine years later, when students introduced SB 118 in the student senate.

The tactical shift is derived in part from Hampshire College's monumental success in becoming, in 2009, the first American institution of higher education to divest from Israel. Ilana Rossoff, a leading student organizer at Hampshire, explains that their campaign was a direct response to the Palestinian BDS call. Her fellows were motivated by the opportunity "to stand behind and re-empower Palestinians in their own national struggle." Still, to avoid debilitating opposition, the students developed a strategy that targeted Israel's occupation "but did not try to make moral arguments about Israel as a nation-state."

The students won over the college's board of trustees when, in February 2009, the trustees voted to divest Hampshire's holdings from Caterpillar, United Technologies, General Electric, ITT, and Terex—companies that supply the Israeli military with equipment and services for use in the occupied territories. Under pressure from Alan Dershowitz, one of several self-appointed policemen of American discourse about Israel–Palestine, Hampshire's administration denied that its decision was linked to Israeli human rights abuses and trumpeted its other investments in Israeli firms. The minutes of the board of trustees' meeting nevertheless reveal an explicit link: the college president "acknowledged that it was the good work of Students for Justice in Palestine that brought this issue to the attention of the committee." And, of course, the students took care to claim that Hampshire was divesting from the Israeli occupation, not from Israel.

THE LOGIC OF BDS

While the Hampshire and Adalah–NY successes have made indelible marks, most campaigns cannot demonstrate their work's impact in measurable units. Instead, the virtue of BDS has been its ability to challenge Israel's moral authority—arguably the most coveted weapon in its arsenal. Israel was not a major recipient of US aid dollars until the aftermath of the Six-Day War, which greatly enhanced Israel's image as a David facing down an Arab Goliath. In June 1968, the Johnson administration, with strong support from Congress, approved the sale of supersonic aircraft to Israel and established the precedent of US support for "Israel's qualitative military edge over its neighbors" (actually, any possible combination of its neighbors). Since then, no American politician seeking high office has spoken of Middle East peace without first stressing US commitment to the security of Israel.

BDS campaigns puncture holes in this security narrative by assuming an offensive posture. By asserting that Israel is worthy of BDS treatment, activists compel Israel's defenders to explain the logic of its policies, such as the imprisonment, at one time or another since 1967, of 20 percent of the entire Palestinian population. When the conversation is taken to its logical end, as it is increasingly often, pro-Israel spokespersons are forced to declare that Palestinians' mere existence is a security threat.

In a recent address in Herzliya, site of an important annual security conference in Israel, Harvard fellow Martin Kramer leapt straight to the bottom of this slippery slope. He argued that when the proportion of adult men in the Arab and Muslim world reaches 40 percent of the population, their propensity to violence increases because they have become "superfluous" in society. Kramer not only dismissed political explanations for radicalization in favor of simple demography—dubious social science, to say the least—he concluded by encouraging the deliberate stunting of population growth among Palestinians as a matter of national security policy. The address, as Kramer said himself, was "memorable."

Its legitimacy continually eroded by such pronouncements, Israeli structural discrimination will still find allies among Christian Zionists, who beseech God and Israel to hasten Armageddon; within the defense industry, which wishes to protect its net earnings; and among those American Jews who, for one reason or another, remain blind to Palestinian suffering. These allies are formidable, but they are not the broad spectrum of Americans whose backing Israel needs to safeguard its moral authority. For this reason, AIPAC's executive director, Howard Kohr, dedicated his address at the group's 2009 annual conference to warnings of the dangers of BDS, which he lamented was "part of a broader campaign not simply to denigrate or defame Israel but to delegitimize her in the eyes of her allies."

The Reut Institute, an Israeli think tank, concurs. In its 2009 study, "Building a Political Firewall Against Israel's Delegitimization," Reut concludes that a network of activists working from the bottom up and from the periphery to the center has succeeded in casting Israel as a pariah state, and warns that, within a few years, the campaign may develop into "a comprehensive existential threat." In its presentation to the Knesset, the institute recommended that the government mitigate this threat with a multi-pronged strategy, including ending its control of the Palestinian population in the occupied territories.

Taraki says that such statements show that BDS is having an effect. Unlike efforts at dialogue, which reinforced power discrepancies by creating "a false sense of symmetry [that] does not acknowledge the colonizer–colonized relationship," BDS tackles the Israeli state head-on. The proper response to ending Israel's impunity is the application of pressure, and "the logic of BDS is the logic of pressure."

On the horizon is the burgeoning movement for academic and cultural boycotts. Although launched a year before the 2005 BDS call, the campaign for academic and cultural boycott does not enjoy the support of economic BDS campaigns. Some argue that culture should be immune from politics, and that boycotting intellectuals infringes academic freedom. Others contend that Israeli intellectuals are the best allies within Israel of the global movement for peace with justice. A close examination of the PACBI call makes it clear that boycott is restricted to Israeli institutions and entities that are complicit in justifying, promoting, supporting, or otherwise perpetuating Israel's occupation, colonization, and apartheid. Today, this call could not be more relevant, as Israel rolls out its "Brand Israel" campaign, intended to rehabilitate its hobbled image through the media of popular culture. Irrespective of form, Barghouti says, BDS is "the most effective form of solidarity with the Palestinian people today." Its nonviolent and universal nature makes it "Israel's worst nightmare."

Part III INTERSECTIONS

11 SOUR ORANGES AND THE SWEET TASTE OF FREEDOM

Ronnie Kasrils

The international boycott and isolation of apartheid South Africa lasting from the sixties to the nineties was most readily symbolized by the refusal to buy Outspan oranges and Cape grapes, by the targeting of the iconic Barclays Bank, and by vigorous protests at rugby and cricket tours.

Touring European cities as members of an agitprop theatre group, a quartet of us ANC members, all dressed in black, would produce onstage a golden Outspan orange and begin nonchalantly tossing it to one another. "Come to beautiful South Africa," the first of us would declare, "land of blue skies, boundless sunshine and … apartheid." The orange would sail from one to the other, each in turn providing statistics such as: "South Africa, where 87 percent of the land is exclusively in the hands of the white population, and 13 percent assigned to the blacks … the average age of whites is seventy-two years, and blacks forty years," and "the infant mortality rate for whites is twenty-seven per 100,000 and for black children 150 per 100,000." We would toss the orange around until the final announcement: "Every time a South African product is purchased internationally represents another brick in the wall of our existence—so says Prime Minister B. J. Vorster." Vorster, who was prime minister of South Africa from 1966 to 1978, was a staunch supporter of apartheid. Following that, the shameful orange would be tossed into the audience with the words: "So swallow that!" Audiences would applaud in acclaim. On one memorable occasion in a packed London hall, the orange sailed straight for the Tanzanian ambassador, who caught it as though it was a hot coal and threw it aside with alacrity. It was a marvelous indication of how well the boycott call had become a material force.

Those were the days when our national fruit tasted very sour indeed. Rugby, a strange sport invented at a school in England, has been regarded by white South Africans as a virtual religion for over a century. I recently viewed archival film material of South Africa's then all-white Springbok rugby team touring New Zealand in 1966. At every town, large or small, the populace received the legendary visitors with absolute adulation. The 1982 tour was vastly different. By then the international anti-apartheid campaign, reflecting the heightened resistance within South Africa, was in full swing. On that occasion tens of thousands of New Zealanders turned out in disgust over apartheid, and pelted the visitors with rotten fruit and insults. Matches were disrupted by angry crowds who fought pitched battles with the strong police presence. In the end the tour had to be called off. The different reception from previous tours could not have been more dramatic, and illustrated the fact that the international boycott of apartheid South Africa was gaining strength by leaps and bounds.

It is important to point out that the catalyst for the international boycott campaign emerged from the experience and success of South Africa's early internal, domestic boycotts. These were undertaken as part of the mass resistance to apartheid laws, associated with the 1950s defiance campaigns, by embattled black South Africans themselves. The initial boycott actions involved the humble potato, grown extensively by commercial white farmers. The boycott was directed at those farmers, who used black pass offenders[1] as virtual slave laborers provided by the police, and notoriously subjected them to daily humiliation, beatings, and even death in the potato fields.

In fury at the appalling slave-like conditions on those farms, the call for a boycott on all potato products, including potato crisps, mobilized enormous pressure against the agri-business interests concerned. Much as the refusal to buy potatoes was a symbol of internal struggle against apartheid, so subsequently was the international community's refusal to buy South African oranges a symbol of solidarity with that cause.

---

1 Black South Africans were compelled by apartheid law to carry passbooks—identification documents permitting them to be in designated "white areas" for the purposes of employment only. Failure to produce the necessary documentation resulted in their immediate arrest.

Commenting on the significance of international solidarity in crushing the pernicious system of apartheid, and on the similarities between the South African and Palestinian struggles, the distinguished Nobel Peace Prize recipient, Archbishop Desmond Tutu, wrote:

> The end of apartheid stands as one of the crowning accomplishments of the past century, but we would not have succeeded without the help of international pressure … a similar movement has taken shape, this time aiming at the end to Israeli occupation … These tactics are not the only parallels to the struggle against apartheid. Yesterday's South African township dwellers can tell you about today's life in the occupied territories … If apartheid ended, so can the occupation, but the moral force and international pressure will have to be just as determined. [2]

The impact of such statements should never be underestimated, as they prove the old adage that "the truth hurts." They in fact resulted in Archbishop Tutu becoming a victim of the Zionist propaganda machine's long list of targets. An invitation for him to address a university in the United States was summarily withdrawn after complaints were received absurdly branding this patron of the South African Holocaust Centre an anti-Semite, simply because he dared to speak the truth. But apartheid could not silence him, and neither could they. Their lies were quickly exposed precisely because of the worldwide public outcry that ensued, resulting in the university's apology for their baseless actions.

"Determined international pressure" does not occur in a vacuum. This became apparent not only in the case of South African apartheid, but also in calling for the withdrawal of American troops from Vietnam. The Vietnamese campaign stands out as one of the most successful invocations of international support, as an important element of a broader, multi-dimensional struggle for freedom and independence. Indeed, this approach greatly influenced the South African liberation movement, as the South African movement is now influencing the Palestine liberation movement. In all cases, international solidarity is an element of the movement's strategy,

---

2   Ian Urbina and Desmond Tutu, "Against Israeli Apartheid," *Nation*, June 27, 2002, at nation.com.

alongside unifying the oppressed inside their country in active struggle against a common foe.

Throughout history, all manner of tyrants have employed the strategy of "divide and rule" to keep oppressed peoples weak and to crush their resistance—a tactic the Palestinians know all too well. Unity has always therefore been a fundamental part of struggle, and in South Africa we sought to go beyond the vanguard—the oppressed—and "isolate the center of reaction," which involved neutralizing and winning over the oppressor's social base, both nationally and internationally. The conscientious objector movements that developed in the US and South Africa—much like those in Israel today—serve as a powerful illustration, where conscripts publicly stated their refusal to participate in an unjust war. In South Africa, the few whites who initially stood shoulder-to-shoulder with fellow blacks in the liberation struggle were met with particular venom by the state, having undermined the mythology of white supremacy and a white unity based on a deliberately fostered psychosis of racial hatred and fear. Over time, ever more whites came to oppose apartheid actively, while many more lost confidence in the system. The comparison with Israeli Jews courageously opposing their government is especially pertinent to their white counterparts in apartheid South Africa, or to America's anti-war movement of the 1960s and '70s.

In this way no one element of the overall strategy was exclusive, where the people's struggles inspired international support, just as international support in turn inspired the people's struggles, each coalescing and reinforcing one another.

In both Vietnam and South Africa, success lay in the two-pronged strategy that paired a strong international solidarity movement with a local struggle of the oppressed already buttressed by a moral superiority over their opponents and the justness of their cause. In the prophetic statement of the Vietnamese revolutionary icon, Ho Chi Minh, echoed by ANC leaders: "Our resistance war will be victorious because it is a just cause approved and supported by the people of the world."[3]

In the end, those struggles found universal support, despite the Cold War divisions fracturing the world. Freedom-loving peoples were able to

---

3   Former Prime Minister of the Democratic Republic of Vietnam, Pham Van Dong, "Ho Chi Minh Thought Will Light Our Path Forever," Gioi Publishers, 2002.

rise above the threat of "red, black, yellow, or terrorist peril" peddled by the oppressor, enabling them to join together, collectively expressing their demands for justice.

I have chosen to deal with the aforementioned concepts of the justness of the cause, moral high ground, and unity in action to illustrate the point that, if any element of an overall strategy is to be successful, then it must flow from those central tenets. This I believe is distinctly relevant to the mobilization of international support for the BDS campaign against Israel. I believe the campaign is gaining much ground, and will succeed in its objectives.

Nonetheless, there are still lessons to be drawn from the evolution of our international efforts to isolate apartheid South Africa.

First, as I have mentioned, the international boycott emerged from the successes of our early domestic, internal boycotts, which were in fact undertaken throughout the course of the struggle. I raise this because these boycotts not only served as a valuable means for securing internal mobilization, but also demonstrated to the outside world that the call for international isolation stemmed from the very people themselves. This is a message that was constantly emphasized, illustrating that those engaged in the international campaign were not working on behalf of black South Africans, but in conjunction with them.

The explanation of the late ANC president, Chief Albert Luthuli, in his 1959 appeal to the British people is instructive here:

> It has been argued that non-white people will be the first to be hit by external boycotts. This may be so, but every organisation which commands … non-white support in South Africa is in favour of them. The alternative to the use of these weapons is the continuation of the status quo and the bleak prospect of unending discrimination. Economic boycott is one way in which the world at large can bring home to the South African authorities that they must either mend their ways or suffer for them.[4]

This speaks directly to those concerned about the suffering of Palestinians but who continue to oppose the boycott, claiming that it will harm those

---

4   "Statement (Jointly with Chief A.J. Luthuli and Peter Brown) Appealing to the British People to Boycott South Africa," December 1959, at v1.sahistory. org.za.

whose cause it seeks to advance. In fact, many companies singled out by the BDS campaign are directly complicit in the occupation—such as the Mexican company Cemex, which illegally mines occupied land and provides construction materials for security walls and checkpoints in the West Bank.

Second, we should not forget the modest origins of the vast anti-apartheid movement that came to encompass non-governmental and international organizations, the great majority of the world's governments, and the dedicated individuals we associate with the movement today.

It was initially established as a boycott movement in Britain, South Africa's former colonizer and main trading partner, in June 1959, focusing specifically on South African products. As the late president of Tanzania, Julius Nyerere, who spoke at its launch, argued, "We are not asking you, the British people, for anything special. We are just asking you to withdraw your support from apartheid by not buying South African products."[5] It only developed into the worldwide movement that we know following the Sharpeville massacre of 1960, expanding its activities beyond the boycott of South African products to encompass the academic, cultural, and sports boycotts, as well as campaigning for divestment and sanctions.

The point here is that it took some time for the movement to build itself up into the formidable force that it ultimately became over a period of exactly thirty years. This is not to say that there were no early accomplishments—there were many; but we were able to advance them by specifically targeting those areas that could effectively communicate our message, yet were relatively simple to achieve.

The sports boycott serves as an example. It cut straight to the hearts of white South Africans, who ultimately lent their support to the negotiations process of 1990–94, as they were thoroughly sick and tired by then of being treated like lepers on the sporting front! What began with an Olympic ban imposed in the 1960s was soon to be followed by the massive protests undertaken on many a cricket pitch and rugby field—in countries like Britain, Ireland, New Zealand, and Australia—which captured the world's attention. These actions eventually resulted in apartheid South Africa being excluded from each and every major sporting fixture internationally.

---

5 "The Anti-Apartheid Movement: A 40-Year Perspective," June 25–26, 1999, South Africa House, London, at anc.org.za.

I am by no means advocating that we ignore sanctions and divestment. Indeed, it has been argued that it was divestment that eventually broke the back of apartheid, when, following the declaration of the state of emergency in 1985, sections of the international banking community refused to renew South Africa's loans. The process began in 1985, when America's Chase Manhattan Bank ended business with South Africa—swiftly followed by several other US banking concerns. A veritable body-blow was the decision by Britain's Barclays Bank to withdraw from South Africa. Barclays was the oldest and most important foreign bank operating in South Africa, and was regarded as a pillar of SA–UK cooperation. The Anti-Apartheid Movement (AAM) in Britain had succeeded in motivating a critical mass of British university students to close their accounts—Barclays had long targeted them as the future business and professional elite. AAM members took out nominal shares in Barclays, and at the bank's annual general meetings protested at its association with apartheid South Africa. I have spoken to former ministers of the apartheid government who confessed to me that when Barclays withdrew from South Africa they were shaken to the core—knowing that things simply had to change if South Africa was to survive. No longer able to raise funds abroad, the apartheid regime's aggression and militarism plunged the country into a spiraling financial and economic crisis, from which it was unable to recover.[6] This clearly signifies the importance of all dimensions of struggle.

But sanctions and divestment, largely reliant on action by countries and institutions, are slower to build momentum for the movement, unlike the boycott, which is primarily dependent on the actions of individuals and consumers.

If one looks at Israel, the boycott of goods produced in the illegal settlements is a clear, appropriate, and ready objective to mobilize around. This by no means exempts all Israeli products from being boycotted. Similarly, campaigns for Israel's exclusion from the Union of European Football Associations (UEFA) and the World Cup, the Olympics, and the Eurovision Song Contest, and boycotting its academic institutions could also be considered immediate and high-profile options. We need to bear in mind that, as sports was to white South Africans, so is international academic acceptability a particular Achilles heel of the Israeli elite. Israel's diamond-processing

---

6   Ibid.

industry, its arms trade, its security and information technology, its finance and banking sector—all are big targets around which strategies of boycott and sanctions need to be strategized.

Third, the anti-apartheid movement's real strength lay in its mass-based, grassroots support, especially in Britain, Western Europe, North America, and Australasia, where government backing for the campaign was less than forthcoming until much later. These were the traditional trading partners of apartheid South Africa, whose governments needed to be pressured.

The AAM was able to galvanize this depth and breadth of support because, much like the liberation movement that it flowed from, it was a broad front, providing a home to those of all colors, creeds, and persuasions. All that was required was a commitment to working for apartheid's demise. It tapped into issues that those on the ground could easily identify with. For example, in Ireland it drew on the experience of the ravages of British colonialism, while in America it evoked the devastation of slavery and racism. It was also readily able to adapt its campaign methods, ensuring that they were relevant to specific conditions, recognizing that strategies appropriate in one local or national context were not necessarily effective in others.

It is this very approach that underpins the BDS campaign, and which must remain at the forefront of our efforts. We cannot allow any unnecessary divisions to derail us from our ultimate goal, ensuring that we always focus on that which unites us.

Fourth, much of the anti-apartheid movement's work was concerned with disseminating information and public education. This was geared to exposing the nature of apartheid, unmasking the myths and scare tactics propagated by the regime, which closely resembled those of its Zionist counterpart. At the same time there was no relenting on the cultural and academic boycott of South Africa. While there were notable exceptions regarding the country's academics, educators, writers, dramatists, artists, and so on, they were a minority in comparison to those who worked in one way or another to shore up the apartheid system. There could therefore be no relenting on an all-embracing campaign of total boycott and isolation in all fields, for making exceptions in one particular area meant undermining the campaign in its entirety. At the same time, this did not negate supporting and encouraging those genuinely disposed to take a stand against injustice, and we were pleased and ready to meet with such academics and artists as individuals abroad, and later in seminars and conferences that were especially convened when the timing later became appropriate. As with the claim that the boycott of products would negatively affect black labor, so too there were arguments that the anti-apartheid elements within South Africa would be deprived of the "free flow of information" by cultural and academic isolation. The example of Chief Albert Luthuli's response to such arguments, that continued discrimination and the status quo were far worse, was clearly understood in its entirety. Regarding the "free flow of information," it can be cogently argued that it is precisely a cultural and academic boycott that forces people to focus their minds on the abnormality and injustice of the society they live in, and in most cases condone. In other words, it forces people—yes, even intellectuals—to wake up from their complacency.

As the BDS campaign unfolds, we must ensure that we are thoroughly prepared to engage in a similar endeavor to the anti-apartheid campaign. Incidentally, in the sixth year since its inception it is progressing at a greater speed than the South African example! We need to reject the claim that there should be even-handedness in dealing with the Israeli culprit and the Palestinian victim, and that Israel's brutality is motivated simply by security concerns. In so doing, we must bring to light Israel's entrenched system of colonialism, racism, apartheid-style separation, and denial of Palestinian human rights, which is akin to that of apartheid South Africa. This is, after all, the fundamental source of the conflict.

It is this truth that resonates with Archbishop Tutu's testimony, in which he states, "Some people are enraged by comparisons between the Israeli/Palestinian conflict and what happened in South Africa ... For those of us who lived through the dehumanizing horrors of the apartheid era, the comparison seems not only apt, it is also necessary ... if we are to persevere in our hope that things can change."[7] And without a doubt, we South Africans who fought apartheid have been unanimous in finding Israel's methods of repression and collective punishment far, far worse than anything we saw during our long and difficult liberation struggle. Israel's indiscriminate, widespread bombing and shelling of populated areas, with scant regard for the civilian victims, was absent in South Africa because the apartheid system relied on cheap black labor. Israel rejects outright

---

7   Archbishop Desmond Tutu, "Realizing God's Dream for the Holy Land," *Boston Globe*, October 26, 2007, at boston.com.

an entire people, and seeks to eliminate the Palestinian presence entirely, whether by voluntary or enforced "transfer." It is clearly this that accounts for Israel's greater degree of sustained brutality in comparison to apartheid South Africa.

This provides all the more reason why it is so necessary for world opinion and action to assist the beleaguered Palestinian people. It is through the BDS campaign, in conjunction with the internal struggles of the Palestinian people, that we can ensure that those who have thus far refused to acknowledge this truth are eventually pressured into accepting that they have no option but to do so. And, as South Africans, we pledge our unqualified support for this campaign, not only because we are obligated as former beneficiaries of generous international support, but also, as our former president, Nelson Mandela, has stated: "We know too well that our freedom is incomplete without the freedom of the Palestinians."[8]

One thing is for sure: our oranges now taste extremely sweet, and our national rugby team, together with all other sporting pursuits, receives the praises of a free people once more. This is indeed the sweet taste of freedom worth struggling and sacrificing for. But every time I eat a South African orange I think of how necessary and possible a worldwide boycott of Zionist Israel is, and that we must never relent in our support for freedom and justice for the Palestinians. Such an outcome will benefit all the people of the region, be they Muslim, Christian, or Jew—just as the end of apartheid liberated the white people along with the blacks. The encouraging events of peaceful change by mass uprisings in Tunisia and Egypt; the unfolding of the so-called Arab Spring; the mass protests in Israel itself of Palestinian youth against the lack of equal rights, and of the Jewish population against economic hardship resulting from the occupation and subsidization of the illegal settlements—all of these show that change is everywhere on the agenda. The international BDS campaign can only inspire those thirsting for a just, peaceful solution inside Israel and in the occupied Palestinian territories to greater and bolder efforts.

---

8   Nelson Mandela, address at the International Day of Solidarity with the Palestinian People, Pretoria, December 4, 1997, at anc.org.za.

12 IN THE LONG SHADOW OF THE SETTLER: ON ISRAELI AND US COLONIALISMS

David Lloyd and Laura Pulido

During Operation Cast Lead, Israel's brutal assault on Gaza in January 2009 that killed more than 1,400 Palestinians, defenders of the offensive invoked a tendentious analogy. What, they asked, would the US do if terrorist groups in Tijuana fired rockets at San Diego? The implication was that the US military would launch an assault of comparable viciousness to punish both the terrorists and the civilian population that passively or actively sheltered them. This rationalization is premised on the understanding that an overwhelming military response is legitimate conduct for a "civilized" nation, a term that is usually reserved for colonial powers. This language draws upon deeply embedded Orientalist ideologies in which Israel is the civilized force in the desert, while, in relation to Mexico, the US is not only seen as the civilized force, but also as the competent, legitimate, and powerful leader of the region. Thus, not only would the US be well within its rights to protect itself, but such an exercise would be necessary to maintain established power relations. The inequality that characterizes US–Mexican relations is fueled by a racism that dates back to the Spanish conquest, was solidified during the Mexican-American War, and has continually been rearticulated against both Mexico and the ethnic Mexican population in the US over the course of the twentieth and twenty-first centuries. Its latest manifestation began in the 1990s, with growing anti-immigrant sentiment and the militarization of the US/Mexican border, both of which reached a crescendo in the wake of 9/11.

In this context, the analogy between Gaza and Baja California found ample resonance. But Israel's defenders inadvertently set in motion comparisons that work in a sense counter to their intentions. The statement aimed at putting the Palestinian population of Gaza beyond the pale of civilization, at dehumanizing them as terrorists while normalizing Israel's violent occupation and expropriation of their lands. But it actually activated the histories it sought to occlude, and unwittingly suggested the historical and contemporary connections that might be forged between peoples whose common struggles are too often seen as entirely remote and disconnected. It resonated with the very things that have cemented the bonds between Israel and the US—not with the shared defense of civilization and democracy, but with the shared histories of settler colonialism, occupation, and expropriation. If the analogy resonated in the US, it resonated less with the immediate plight of the victims of terrorism than with the psychic residues of such histories, with the residues of the settler colonials' siege mentality, and with the disproportionate rage that any challenge to the colonialists' supremacy and security elicits.

The analogy between Gaza and Tijuana invites us to compare the settler-colonialisms of Israel/Palestine and the US/Mexico. We have several goals in mind in examining this apparently unlikely pairing. First, we flesh out the concept of settler colonialism, which can serve as a unifying framework for understanding US–Israeli relations. What are the similarities and differences between the two? How does this mode of conquest and subjugation work in diverse settings and across time? Second, by juxtaposing these colonial histories, we hope to highlight possible sites of solidarity. Solidarity based on comparative analysis is, of course, essential to any engagement in global human rights issues, but it is especially pertinent to any critique of Israeli policy towards Palestine. For not only is it imperative to challenge Israel: we also need to understand that imperative as continuous with the need to stop human rights abuses and imperialist projects on the part of the US. Our goal is to show how the common practices of settler colonialism in both regions operate to create extreme forms of human suffering and injustice. The first step in such an undertaking is to identify, describe, and compare how these particular forms of settler colonialism operate.

SETTLER COLONIALISM AND LAND APPROPRIATION

Settler colonialism is the practice of conquering land and then settling it with the victors. Such a population shift may be triggered by an expanding population, or by the need to assert economic and political control in the new territory; either way, it results in the dispossession and often the extermination of large parts of the "native" population, and the subsequent cultural, economic, and political subordination of the remainder. Their dispossession and subordination is counterpointed by the ever more vigorous assertion on the part of the settler of a *right* of possession, legitimized by appeals to manifest destiny, divine dispensation, or merely a civilizing mission. The displaced population's challenges to the settlers' claims are met with rage and a violence amplified by a siege mentality that never quite dissipates, even when the military force and numbers of the settler population vastly overwhelm the expropriated natives.

The expropriation of Palestinians has been relentless since the establishment of Israel, in 1948. In that year, by fiat of the United Nations and without consultation of the indigenous inhabitants of Palestine, the State of Israel received 56 percent of historic Palestine, although the Jewish population was at that time less than half of the Arab population. In the Arab-Israeli war that followed, some 60 percent of the Arab population was displaced, mostly expelled by force or by fear of the massacres inflicted by the Israeli forces. Over 500 villages were destroyed. In the subsequent sixty years, and in particular since 1967 and the occupation of Gaza and the West Bank, Israel has forcibly expanded to occupy over 93 percent of historic Palestine. In the occupied territories, Israel's colonial settlements—all illegal under international law—continue to expand, fragmenting what remains of Palestinian territory into islands of disjointed land, undermining any possibility of a viable Palestinian state. Increasingly, in a process of gradual ethnic cleansing or "silent transfer," the occupation makes life untenable for Palestinians, forcing them to abandon their homes and lands, which then fall under Israeli control.

The Mexican-American War was a classic instance of settler-colonial expansion, in which a dominant power deliberately provoked a war in order to acquire vast amounts of land, including access to the Pacific Ocean. Ultimately, through both the Mexican Cession and the Gadsden Purchase, Mexico lost over half of its national territory. While there was a clear economic motive for the war, it was fueled ideologically by "manifest destiny," which not only maintained that it was the US's birthright to expand across the continent, but that as a "white country" the US would provide enlightenment and civilization to barbarian Mexico. Given this ideology of white supremacy, expanding territory, and new communications, the war was extremely popular, and fought largely with volunteers.[1] The US consolidated control of its new possession by bringing millions of settlers to the region.

The Treaty of Guadalupe Hidalgo (1848) promised the conquered both citizenship and property rights. Instead, it inaugurated over 150 years of second-class citizenship and dispossession. Where Israel's occupation involves an ongoing process centered on the continual accrual of Palestinian territory, the US acquisition of Mexican territory was largely completed fairly quickly. With a few exceptions, once the US took over, individual landowners were dispossessed of their land within the next few decades. Individual and collective lands (land grants or *mercedes*) were lost through a variety of means, with legal fees being the most common.[2] Mexicans often found themselves in court defending their land claims against Anglo squatters, who were granted significant rights by the state in an effort to promote a wholesale transfer of land from Mexicans to Anglo-Americans.

Anglo-Americans have responded in multiple and complicated ways to the fact of conquest and the unceasing Mexican presence in the US. While there have been plenty of instances of settler-colonial rage unleashed upon the Mexican-origin population—lynchings, repatriation, Operation Wetback, English-only initiatives, Proposition 187, ICE raids—another strategy was simply the denial of this history. While many justify US appropriation of Mexican territory—indeed, numerous scholars have insisted that the terms of the 1848 Treaty were quite progressive and unprecedentedly liberal towards the conquered—the fact remains that the US deliberately and duplicitously initiated a war against Mexico with the intent of acquiring land and ocean access.

---

1 See John Michael Rivera, *The Emergence of Mexican America: Recovering Stories of Mexican Peoplehood in US Culture*, New York University Press, 2006: Chapter 2.

2 On the loss of Mexican land, see Malcolm Ebright, *Spanish and Mexican Land Grants and the Law*, Sunflower University Press, 1989, and Leonard Pitt, *The Decline of the Californios*, University of California Press, 1966. It should be noted that Spaniards and Mexicans were themselves interlopers on indigenous land in both Mexico and what is now the US Southwest.

Because of this deep history of the region, Chicana and Chicano activists have developed a familiar response to racist rhetoric: "We didn't come to the US, the US came to us." While this is literally true for a small minority (according to Richard Nostrand, there were approximately 80,000 Mexicans living in what is now the Southwestern US in 1850), subsequent migration to the US was driven by the wider cultural, political, and economic relations that emerged following the war and conquest, which themselves are rooted in settler colonialism. Its ideologies have intimately shaped the experiences of Mexican-Americans (and subsequent Latina and Latino groups) and life in the Southwest. Indeed, the fact that by 2005 there were 25,800,000 people of Mexican origin living in the US cannot be understood outside the context of the war.[3]

In Israel, by a rhetorical sleight of hand that seeks to preserve the image of Israeli democracy, Palestinians have Israeli citizenship (*ezrahut*, in Hebrew) but not "nationality" (*le'om*), on which crucial rights to property, movement, and settlement depend. Increasingly, what remains of Palestinian land in Israel and in occupied East Jerusalem is being expropriated, houses demolished, and Palestinians expelled or "transferred." Both the occupied territories and Israel itself now constitute a new form of apartheid regime, in many respects more draconian and destructive than South Africa's, and a new variant of settler colonialism, shored up by religious fanaticism and racial ideology. Meanwhile, whatever progressive elements there were in the Zionist colonial project have been eclipsed by the rise to political power of increasingly intransigent racist parties that argue openly for the ethnic cleansing of Palestinians from an Israel that would occupy virtually all of what remains of Palestine.[4]

---

3   Richard Nostrand, "Mexican Americans Circa 1850," *Annals of the Association of American Geographers* 65: 3 (1975): 378–90. On the contemporary demographics of the Mexican immigrant population, see Jeffrey Passel and D'Vera Cohn, "Mexican Immigrants: How Many Come? How Many Leave?" Pew Hispanic Center Reports, July 22, 2009, at pewhispanic.org.
4   On the apartheid nature of the Israeli occupation, see "SA Academic Study Finds that Israel is Practicing Apartheid and Colonialism in the Occupied Palestinian Territories," at a South African Human Sciences Research Council report, at hsrc.ac.za; and Karine MacAllister, "Applicability of the Crime of Apartheid to Israel," in *al-Majdal* 38 (Summer 2008), at badil.org.

FORMS OF DOMINATION

Still, there are economic and ideological reasons for the continued presence of the colonized in the conquered lands. Ideologically, the constant proclamation of the inferiority of the colonized serves to justify the colonizers' position of structural superiority. Economically, the presence of the colonized frees the colonizer from modes of labor that would be demeaning to his or her status. The Mexican has been the worker of choice in the Southwest (and increasingly the Southeast) for at least 100 years. Contemporary immigration is driven both by Mexico's inability to provide sufficient economic opportunity for its people and by the insatiable US demand for cheap, vulnerable labor. In many ways, immigrants, especially unauthorized ones, constitute the ultimate surplus labor force. But herein also lie the seeds of contradiction. Even as capital desperately wants to maintain surplus labor, the nation vehemently rejects Mexicans (and other poor Latinas and Latinos, especially Central Americans) as culturally and racially undesirable. In addition, the nation refuses to cover the costs of social reproduction associated with workers and their families.[5] As a result of such contradictions, anti-immigrant initiatives ebb and flow with economic and other national crises. Arizona's SB 1070, signed into law in 2010, is only the most notorious piece of legislation that further criminalizes unauthorized immigrants (and potentially all Latinas and Latinos) in order to make them disappear.

Globalization, with its new patterns of labor migration, may offer Israel a different and more total solution to the settler-colonial dilemma. Increasingly, since the second Intifada of 2000, the Palestinian workforce on which Israel had largely depended for construction and agriculture has been denied entry permits to Israel (and is, with bitter irony, increasingly employed in the construction of settlements and in the *maquiladora*-style enterprises through which Israeli corporations exploit the occupied West Bank). Palestinian labor has largely been replaced within Israel by migrant workers, mostly from Eastern Europe, South Asia, and the Philippines, who constitute an impermanent workforce of guest workers without claims on

---

5   Pierrette Hondagneu-Sotelo, "Women and Children First," *Socialist Review* 25 (1995): 169–90. Anna Gorman and Andrew Blankstein, "Massive Sweep Deports Hundreds," *Los Angeles Times*, October 3, 2007. Teresa Watanabe, "Humanizing Immigration Crackdowns," *Los Angeles Times*, November 24, 2007.

citizenship or permanent residency. A double regime of regulation of movement thus both controls Israel's colonial exploitation of labor and enables its ongoing displacement of Palestinians from their homeland, not least in the draconian network of checkpoints in the occupied territories and the separation or "apartheid" wall, which so strikingly resembles the US border fence with Mexico.[6]

Israel, as a bastion of "Western civilization" in the non-Western world, has become a laboratory for repression, and for military and carceral forms of population control and discipline, much as Northern Ireland and South Africa were in the 1970s and 1980s. The siege mentality of settler colonies positions them ideally to serve as experimental zones for counterinsurgency technologies and the control of subjugated and migrant populations. Consequently, Israel has become a vital resource in the "global war on terror"—a moniker that signifies the curtailment of human and civil rights and the refunctioning of colonial racial states. Israel has become the essential partner in the counterterrorism industry, an international academic-industrial complex whose positivistic lack of critical thinking would be breathtaking were it not so opportunistically self-serving.[7] The collaboration of US politicians with Israel's propaganda and security apparatuses signals not only the alliance of the US with Israel's colonial project, but the far more insidious normalization of the security state and its technologies and methods that Israel is pioneering, and that constitute an essential element of the repressive "knowledge economy" that involves the increasingly sinister collaboration of universities, the military, and private security corporations in a tight loop of economic self-interest. Meanwhile, there can be little doubt that Israeli expertise in the technologies of racial profiling, colonial policing, and border security will continue to be adapted with steady force to controlling black and brown populations throughout

---

6   See Uri Ram, "The Colonization Perspective in Israeli Sociology," in Ilan Pappe, ed., *The Israel/Palestine Question: A Reader*, 2nd ed., Routledge, 2007: 53–77; Saree Makdisi, *Palestine Inside Out: An Everyday Occupation*, Norton, 2008: 194–207; Eyal Weizman, *Hollow Land: Israel's Architecture of Occupation*, Verso, 2007: Chapter 6; and Neve Gordon, *Israel's Occupation*, University of California Press, 2008.

7   See, for example, the law-enforcement and military-training corporation ISI Inc., at isitrainingcenter.com.

the US Southwest. Kollsman Inc., a US-based subsidiary of Elbit Systems, is well known to supply surveillance equipment for the US–Mexican frontier, while numerous police departments, including that of the sheriff of Los Angeles County, Lee Baca, support Israel and draw on Israeli expertise to develop their own techniques of surveillance and control.[8]

THE EDUCATION AND ACADEMIC BOYCOTT

The intensified regulation and criminalization of the movement of people corresponds to ever-shrinking educational opportunities. Israel's targeting of Palestinian educational institutions has been systematic and unrelenting: the destruction in Operation Cast Lead of twenty-three educational sites in Gaza, ranging from the Islamic University to the American International School, a music school, and various UN facilities, is emblematic of ongoing interference with Palestinian education. Such interference ranges from the punitive closure of Palestinian universities for extended periods—a collective punishment for acts of resistance—to curtailing the movement of Palestinian students between their homes and their schools, all in violation of internationally accepted human rights norms. Palestinians comprise 20 percent of Israel's population (a proportion maintained by Zionist racial policies), compared with only 10 percent of university students and less than 1 percent of the faculty. Schooling is almost entirely segregated, to the material and cultural disadvantage of Palestinians—from discriminatory housing based on military service to the ideological pressures that face critics of Zionism, or even those who merely seek to recall the history of Palestinians in historic Palestine.[9]

US critics of Zionism as a colonial project have often been met with the charge of hypocrisy. The US, they are told, is not so different from Israel. Should the US, they are asked, relinquish possession of lands expropriated

---

8   On the Elbit Systems border contract, see "Israeli Firm Gets Mexico Border Wall Contract," *World War 4 Report*, November 8, 2006, at ww4report.com. On Lee Baca's support for Israel and visit there during Operation Cast Lead, see "En Route to Israel, Sheriff Lee Baca Slams Hamas Actions in Gaza Conflict," *Los Angeles Times*, January 8, 2009, at latimesblogs.latimes.com. On Israeli police training, see James Goldstein, "US Law Enforcement Officials Find Security in Israel," in Israel 21c, June 25, 2006, at israel21c.org.
9   See Makdisi, *Palestine Inside Out*: 150–1.

from indigenous people and send the others back to Europe? Similarly, given the discrimination in US education, the question is posed as to why Israeli educational institutions should be singled out for boycott. Neither question is to the point: to censure Israeli racism is not to condone US institutions, but rather to underscore links between them. What is demanded of Israel is not that its Jewish population "go home," but that its laws and practices protect, as almost every other constitution in the world demands, the equal rights of all its citizens, without respect to race or religion. What is demanded of the US is both the recognition that institutional racism exists, despite the popularity of colorblind ideologies, and a commitment to extending educational opportunities to those who live and work here—regardless of citizenship.

The boycott of Israeli institutions is called for on account of their systematic collusion with a racist occupation that deliberately denies to their Palestinian counterparts the rights Israeli scholars so abundantly enjoy, and that offers Israeli academics the resources and privileges they consider their right. The right to education is not partial or local, not conditioned by occupation or dispossession. Just as the condemnation of South Africa's apartheid system during the divestment movement of the 1980s opened out into the contestation of the continuing segregation of American campuses, so now—especially in a moment when the widespread process of educational defunding is leading to an extensive re-stratification of access to higher education, disadvantaging working-class students and students of color—the campaign against Zionist apartheid should highlight the relations between Israel's racist regime and the continuing effects of settler colonialism on the US racial state. The BDS slogan "right to education" has as much pertinence in the US as it does in Gaza or Jenin. The fight for human and civil rights against the mounting violence of the new security state is as urgent in the US or Europe, with their vicious anti-immigrant regimes and criminalization of minorities, as it is in Palestine. As with the divestment campaign against South Africa, the critique of Israel's racism against the Palestinian people should open the way to a renewed and global critique of the emerging racial state forms of the so-called civilized world. Recognition of the common histories and struggles that connect Palestine and the US Southwest is a critical dimension of that project.

13 THE HISTORY AND CONTEMPORARY STATE OF THE PALESTINIAN SEXUAL LIBERATION STRUGGLE

Haneen Maikey

When looking at the current sexuality discourse and organizing efforts in Palestine/Israel, the question of time and history becomes relevant. Understanding the larger historical context can explain the development of the queer Palestinian movement in the shadow of important political periods and events, and may offer a better perspective on the nature of queer organizing and the ways in which its political role was shaped. Most importantly, I hope this piece will shed light on the set of ideologies and strategies adopted by the Palestinian queer movement that emphasize the vision and understanding of intersections between struggles and oppressions in the larger Palestinian society and beyond. The Palestinian queer movement is perhaps one of few social and political movements that discuss (and practice), openly and clearly, the interlinked nature of sexual, social, and political realities and struggles.

Furthermore, when looking at the Palestinian queer movement, there are many interlinking relationships that should be taken into consideration: the relationship between Israel and Palestinian society; the relationship between queer Palestinians and Palestinian society; the relationship between queer Palestinians and the global community, the West, and the mainstream global media; and the relationship between queer Palestinians and Israel—in the form of both its military colonialism and queer, progressive Israelis and Israeli organizations. Hence, the active role Palestinian queer groups have taken in the Palestinian BDS movement in recent years cannot be understood as the result of a one-dimensional or simplistic process. It reflects our decade of organizing experience that adheres to the complexity of our real experience as queers living both in a traditional society and under occupation —an experience that contains our ambitions to be an integral and influential part of the larger Palestinian society. In addition, the clear and solid political framing and strategy that the BDS movement provides has become a main platform for Palestinian queer resistance.

WHEN SEXUALITY BECAME A POLITICAL ISSUE IN PALESTINE

Prior to the appearance of Palestinian LGBTQ groups, and especially after the Oslo Agreement in the mid 1990s, sexuality—and particularly homosexuality—began to emerge as a political issue in the region. In 1993, the Palestine Liberation Organization and the Israeli government signed the Declaration of Principles on Interim Self-Government Arrangements, also known as the Oslo Accords, which gave birth to the Palestinian Authority (PA) and, for the first time since 1948, gave Palestinians some authority over some of their land. This PA became accountable for various social, legal, and political matters.

At the same period, Israeli LGBT groups started to get organized, primarily in order to change Israel's anti-sodomy law criminalizing homosexual acts. The Israeli LGBT movement's organizing efforts were supported, and even led, by a number of Knesset members. Israeli LGBT groups were able to change the law in 1988. Absurdly, this new development added another aspect to the growing interest in LGBT legal status in the PA. In this dynamic, the colonizer's standards and achievements became the yardstick by which the colonized were measured, and to which they had to conform.

This new situation gave rise to a growing one-sided and stereotyping Western interest in the situation of sexual rights in Palestine. This interest included issues that were related to the LGBTQ community, although there were no formal LGBTQ groups or organizing attempts within Palestinian society at the time. International governments, human rights organizations, and Western LGBTQ organizations, along with the mainstream media, approached the emerging Palestinian state without showing any sensitivity to Palestinian culture, ideals, and morals around sexuality and same-sex behaviors. This one-sided and sometimes patronizing process was initiated at a time when neither Palestinian society in general nor the LGBTQ Palestinian community was ready to address the issues at stake.

If the Oslo period represented a peak in international interest in Palestine, and an important junction in pushing sexuality as a political issue into the public sphere, the processes that contributed the most to the development of the current Palestinian gay image, as perceived by the Palestinian LGBTQ community, Palestinian society, and the Western and other international media, actually began a few years beforehand, during the first Intifada.

During the first Intifada (1987–93)—the peak of underground political activism in Palestine–Israel began using blackmail as a tool in interrogations and to recruit collaborators. Any activities that were socially frowned upon in Palestinian society, including homosexuality and premarital or extra-marital sex, as well as drug or alcohol use, were utilized by Israel in order to threaten and coerce Palestinians into working with the Israeli authorities or facing the consequences. This Israeli tactic played a major role in the initial establishment of the image of the Palestinian queer as a collaborator and, later on, as someone who engages in "foreign" (and "Western") behavior.

This same tactic was used by the Palestinian leadership in the West Bank during the "anarchy" periods after the first Intifada, and both before and after the second Intifada (approximately 2000 to 2004). Political and armed groups informally adopted a "cleansing" strategy, and started using homosexuals and other outsiders to work with them, blackmailing them by threatening to disclose their sexuality. It is important to note that all such cases we know of have complicated backgrounds, and that the individuals involved were targeted not only because they were homosexual, but also because they were vulnerable in other ways. But most of this activity came to a close in the West Bank after Hamas won the election and the PA began to "control" the West Bank. There are hints that this same process is now taking place in Gaza, however; homosexuals who have been arrested there have been apprehended by "good" people, or by groups who want to aid in cleansing society (or simply to win some support from the authorities).

Palestinian queer groups began to organize during the second Intifada—one of the most pivotal political periods in recent Palestinian history, particularly for Palestinian citizens of Israel who, for the first time, took part in the new uprising and were victims of a brutal police attack that killed thirteen young demonstrators, known as the "October 2000 events." For many young Palestinians living within the 1948 borders, the second Intifada was a turning point in their conception of their identities as Palestinian, and redefined their deep connection and identification with the Palestinian liberation struggle. It was in this political climate that a Palestinian queer movement began to emerge. It started inside Israel, at the initiative of an Israeli Jewish organization, the Jerusalem Open House (JOH). Before the second Intifada, some LGBTQ Palestinians (mainly gay men) used to visit the JOH to participate in social events—the JOH center and Jerusalem were somewhat accessible to areas like Bethlehem, Ramallah, and East Jerusalem. After the second Intifada, however, Palestinian LGBTQ people stopped coming to Israeli queer spaces in general and to JOH in particular. JOH leaders began an outreach initiative to bring Palestinian queers back, while ignoring the reason behind this change in their attendance. This can be seen, in retrospect, as an attempt to depoliticize the Palestinian queer struggle, bringing it in line with an Israeli LGBT struggle that has been and continues to be largely apolitical.

Palestinian LGBTQ organizing was not able to distance itself from the political situation, and from questions about the relationship between queer politics and occupation. However, the internal and public debates about queer groups, and about local and regional politics in Palestine, began only with the 2006 war against Lebanon, in the same year that JOH was organizing WorldPride events in Jerusalem—a city at the heart of the political tension at that time. For the first time, Palestinian queer groups were required to respond publicly to political questions: How can we celebrate pride during the brutal 2006 war on Lebanon? How can we hold an apolitical WorldPride parade during such a period and in a place like Jerusalem, twenty minutes from the apartheid wall that separates us and hides the reality of sixty-four years of occupation and colonial domination? The main debate was between WorldPride organizers and radical queer groups, including some queer Palestinians. The 2006 war forced many queer groups to take a stance on the war, and on the position of queer groups with regard to it. The immediate result was a harsh clarification of the unbridged division between Palestinian queers and Israeli queer organizations. While Palestinian queer groups started to address questions of intersectionality (how different social categories such as race, class, gender, and disability contribute to social inequalities) and of gradually joining the anti-occupation struggle, Israeli queer groups instead "joined" the Israeli national project by promoting values such as militarism and heteronormativity as primary routes to acceptance by society—proving that Israeli LGBTQ groups were, after all, microcosms of an Israeli society based on decades of denial and complicity with state-based and systematic oppression.

In November 2005, in the shadow of the above developments, al-Qaws for Sexual and Gender Diversity in Palestinian Society (al-Qaws)—the largest LGBTQ Palestinian group—began a discussion of key questions of identity and the wider political and social context. WorldPride and the 2006 war gave new insight into the meaning and importance of investing major efforts in building a mature and aware Palestinian queer community that might, for the first time, be relevant to the real experience of most LGBTQ Palestinians. This reality was that their main struggle, in tandem with the sexual one, was living under occupation in the Palestinian territories, or as second-class citizens inside Israel. We believed that only in answering these questions could we define our ambitions to become an integral and important part of Palestinian society.

In late 2007, al-Qaws officially separated from the Jerusalem Open House. This can be seen as a natural and organic process. The decision to construct an independent Palestinian LGBTQ entity represented the first time a Palestinian group had sent a clear message emphasizing that a non-political space would no longer work, and that politics were part of our daily experience. It was a message of commitment to deal with intersectionality from within Palestinian sexual and gender activism. It was also a statement that highlighted the power and agency of Palestinian queer groups, rather than their victimization or instrumental usefulness. With the Gaza war in 2009, Palestinian queer groups started to promote a more radical political discourse, talking publicly about the war, organizing events for Gaza, and participating (though generally as individuals) in demonstrations. A few months later, in August 2009—just after Israel's massacre of hundreds of Gazans in Operation Cast Lead—there was a shooting in Bar-Noar, the gay youth space in Tel Aviv. Orthodox Jews had walked into the center and killed two gay Israeli youths. Palestinian queers who wanted to express solidarity and an anti–hate crime message, however, were banned from the main demonstration stage because they might "talk politics." The meaning of the exclusion of LGBTQ Palestinians from this event was made brutally clear when right-wing politicians proclaimed a "don't kill" message on the main stage, all the while ignoring their part in killing hundreds of Gazans only a few months earlier. This message was brought home when the organizers played the Israeli national anthem at the vigil—a song perceived by many Palestinians living in Israel as a reflection of its deep Zionist values. This celebration of nationalism vindicated the national identity of (progressive, gay-loving) Israelis, and further alienated the Palestinian crowd.

THE CURRENT CONFIGURATION OF LGBTQ POLITICS IN PALESTINE/ISRAEL: LIBERATION STRUGGLE VS HOMONATIONALISM

Over the course of this history, another factor has developed and risen to prominence in Israel: homonationalism, or the normalization and integration of certain "more acceptable" queers into the nationalist ideal. In Israel, homonationalism has taken many forms—such as the inclusion of gays in the military ("serving with pride"); the increasing appearance of Israeli flags at Pride demonstrations; and an increase in homonormativity, or queers assimilating to the mainstream social norms of a nuclear family unit based around marriage, children, and upward mobility. The rise of homonationalism in Israel has also served to further alienate Palestinian queers from Israeli queer groups and events, and has only clarified the divide between each group's ideas of queer politics and solidarity.

Homonationalist discourse and actions inside Israel have made it clear that it is increasingly impossible for queer Palestinians to take part in Israeli-organized queer events. For example, the distribution of 5,000 Israeli flags at the Tel Aviv pride parade in June 2010 sent the message that the event was as much about being a proud Israeli as it was about being a proud queer. The large nationalist demonstration that took place after the shooting in Tel Aviv is also a blatant example of this, of course. By aligning themselves with the same nation that has facilitated the institutionalized oppression of the Palestinian people for the last sixty-four years, the queer Israeli community has shrunk its ambitions from fighting for sexual freedom to being incorporated into the nation—and, by definition, has pushed the Palestinian queer movement to clearly redefine its political agenda, and therefore its relationship with the Israeli queer movement.

The division of politics and the distinctions made between different kinds of violence—accompanied by a denial of the link to broader politics, and specifically to occupation and apartheid—have made it obvious that the Palestinian and Israeli queer movements are heading in opposite directions: a struggle for liberation that links queer politics with broader struggles, on the one hand, and a struggle for nation-based acceptance that adopts nation-based values, on the other. In this context, solidarity also was subject to a process of redefinition—these ideological differences threw up questions of what solidarity meant to each side. While Palestinian queers perceived solidarity as an adherence to our concerns in a holistic way, in terms that we worked to develop during the last decade, Israeli queers defined and demanded a kind of solidarity promoting hierarchy among struggles, and forced us once again to compromise our struggles and identities, all the while leaving occupation, apartheid, racism, and daily human rights violations outside of the equation, as if these had nothing to do with the queer struggle.

PINKWASHING AND GAY TOURISM

While Israeli homonationalism has operated as another way of "othering" Palestinian queers, it has also led directly to yet another form of exploitation: pinkwashing. The rise of Israeli homonationalism and the subsequent alienation of Palestinian queers has opened the door for Israeli groups, queer or not, to use the tired trope of the victimized gay Palestinian and her/his implied helplessness, which they juxtapose with that of the integrated, normalized, liberated Israeli queer, in order to present Israel in the role of the savior while demonizing Palestinian society as backward and homophobic—all the while obscuring Israel's brutal treatment of *all* Palestinians. This tactic is employed not only by the Israeli government, but also by independent groups that hold strong Israeli nationalist ideologies. In short, pinkwashing is the cynical use of queer Palestinian voices and the gay rights struggle to vilify Palestinian society as barbaric and homophobic, while elevating Israel as a bastion of gay rights, and therefore human rights, in order to ignore and obscure Israeli oppression of Palestinians as a group, queer or otherwise. In vilifying Palestinian society as a whole, pinkwashing also serves to justify ongoing Israeli colonialism, apartheid, and oppression of Palestinians.

Pinkwashing also takes the form of the Israeli government's initiatives to promote gay tourism. This program stems directly from Israeli homonationalism, and conveniently glosses over Israel's numerous human rights violations, focusing instead on "our parties (something different and exciting happening every night), gay beach (the hottest and friendliest in the

Middle East), and lots of friendly locals always willing to extend hospitality to guests. Israel is a land of diversities with a never-ending and changing host of sites and activities to offer visitors—gay and straight alike." This initiative is not only a form of pinkwashing, but also a significant source of income for Israel; it not only abuses Palestinians to bolster Israel's image, but is also a means of generating revenue, and therefore of supporting and profiting directly from the Israeli apartheid system.

THE QUEER STRUGGLE: ANTI-OCCUPATION AND BDS ACTIVISM

The image of the Palestinian queer as a collaborator, which began during the first Intifada, was mobilized through abuse of the Palestinian queer cause and the instrumentalized, pinkwashed image of the Palestinian victim. The Gay International added salt to the wound by pressuring the PA and civil society organizations to respect gay rights, thus giving the cause the image of Western-imposed interference and of a Western attempt at changing our society. At the same time, a strong voice within Palestinian society remains—a voice that insists on prioritizing struggles and on a hierarchy of liberation, putting the Palestinian national struggle at the top of the list, while other struggles (women's rights, gender and sexuality rights, minority rights, and so on) come second. Hence, besides gay Palestinians' being seen as Israelized collaborators or Westernized intruders, the mere fact of their talking of the intersectionality of struggles, and of trying to break the hierarchy of struggles, is frowned upon within Palestinian society.

Working from within this complicated political and social context, and caught in the web of images produced of the Palestinian queer, it is difficult to address issues of homophobia within Palestinian society while simultaneously struggling against occupation and apartheid. These challenges have pushed us to develop new and creative methods of resistance, based on the deep understanding that the struggle against occupation and oppression is central to the queer Palestinian struggle. They have pushed us to define our visibility through political platforms, rather than through Western-imposed, apolitical pride parades. At the same time, having been proactive within our society for ten years, and having dealt with the victim image of us that pinkwashing efforts portray, we felt the need to speak out and dismantle the myths that are being used against our struggle: as Palestinians, and as Palestinian queers.

For these reasons, the Palestinian civil society call for BDS against Israel is the perfect platform for us to participate in the Palestinian struggle, and has become an essential mode of resistance for the Palestinian queer community. BDS has become a major rallying point not only because it is a proven method of ending such oppression (as it helped to do in apartheid South Africa), but also because it comes from Palestinians ourselves, and can be utilized by all Palestinians—whether we live in the occupied territories, the diaspora, or Israel. For these same reasons, BDS has been embraced by the Palestinian queer community.

One group that addresses this directly, and has taken an active and involved role in the BDS movement, is Palestinian Queers for BDS, or PQBDS. Founded in 2010 by a number of queer Palestinian activists, PQBDS works to support the BDS movement by addressing various international queer groups, as well as artists, activists, and musicians, calling upon them to boycott Israel, including any events held in Israel. A recent triumph for PQBDS was the decision of the International Gay and Lesbian Youth and Student Organization to relocate its General Assembly to Amsterdam from Tel Aviv, in response to a call to boycott the event issued by PQBDS. The leadership and success shown by PQBDS is a testament to the role that Palestinian queers have to play in the struggle against Israeli occupation and oppression. It shows not only that BDS is an effective and accessible means of resistance, but also that Palestinian queers can and do have a great deal of agency and relevance in the Palestinian struggle against Israeli occupation, apartheid, and colonization.

14 AFTER THE HOLOCAUST AND ISRAEL: CAN THE PROPHETIC HEAL TWO MARTYRED PEOPLES?

Marc H. Ellis

In the early 1970s, I was fortunate to study with Richard Rubenstein, one of the first Holocaust theologians in America. In 1966, Rubenstein published his groundbreaking *After Auschwitz: Radical Theology and Contemporary Judaism*. By the 1970s the field of Holocaust studies Rubenstein helped to pioneer was developing at a steady pace. During this time, Holocaust survivor Elie Wiesel and the late philosopher of the Holocaust Emil Fackenheim became known inside and outside of the academy. In the coming years both would become major players in Holocaust memorialization and public awareness, helping to define the American and global discourse on Jews and Judaism.

Looking back, the time was ripe for the blossoming of Holocaust consciousness. For Jews, the weeks preceding the 1967 Israeli-Arab war had evoked the anxiety of defeat, with the possible end of Israel and the annihilation of its Jewish population. Then the war came and ended quickly in Israel's favor, taking just six days to conclude. Considering the previous fear, some thought Israel's lightning victory a miracle.

Though American Jews were far from the battlefields in the Middle East, Israel's victory occasioned for many American Jews a newfound pride in being Jewish. Feeling empowered, Jews also named the tremendous suffering undergone at the hands of the Nazis decades before as the Holocaust. In the wake of the 1967 war, the Holocaust and Israel became linked in the Jewish imagination as the center of Judaism and Jewishness. They still are.

I lived through these days as a young college student, and from the special vantage point of studying with Rubenstein. In *After Auschwitz*, Rubenstein had already named the Holocaust as the central fact of contemporary Jewish existence. Israel was also central for Rubenstein, and, like the Holocaust, it was as yet unnamed by Jewish authorities. For Rubenstein, these two pivotal events had to be dealt with if the future of the Jewish people was to be analyzed. Jews suffered the Holocaust because they lacked power in Europe and had as yet been unable to come to terms with the changing face of modern violence. The lesson of the Holocaust was that never again could Jews be without power. Rubenstein saw Israel as the response to that powerlessness.

The inner core of Rubenstein's work had to do with his notion of *after*. For Rubenstein, *after* carried a variety of meanings relating to God, Judaism, Israel, and modernity. What can Jews say about God after Auschwitz? If God chose Jews as a people and promised to be with us, where was God at Auschwitz? Judaism as a religion was premised on God's presence, or at least the remembrance of God's presence in the liberation from Egypt and his promise of the land. Could Judaism be affirmed after Auschwitz without assigning an unacceptable punishing aspect to the Jewish God?

For Rubenstein, the state of Israel became the post-Holocaust embodiment of the will of Jews to protect Jewish lives from anyone who would do them harm. God did not protect the Jews of Europe, but, as Rubenstein pointed out, neither did humanity. The aloneness of European Jews in their time of dire need and their inability to protect themselves made Israel necessary.

As frightening for Rubenstein, however, was the *after* of modernity. For Rubenstein, the Nazis were barbarians and thoroughly modern at the same time. The combination of advanced technology, social organization, and bureaucracy that defined modernity made the extermination of Jews possible during the Nazi period, and made others, including Jews, vulnerable from that historical moment on. Since Rubenstein believed that anti-Semitism survived in modernity, Jews could be even more vulnerable in the future. Only Israel's ability to punish adversaries of the Jews could save them in a time of need. If Israel was defeated, at least the Jewish people would die as proud men and women. Unlike the Jews of the Holocaust, they would not go like sheep to the slaughter.

Listening to Rubenstein, I realized that the Holocaust and its lessons were fraught with disagreement and rivalry. I understood from Rubenstein that Wiesel and Fackenheim were his bitter enemies, but at first it was difficult for me to understand why. All three agreed on the weakness of Europe's Jews and the need for Jewish empowerment in Israel. They also agreed on the difficulty of speaking about God after Auschwitz. Fackenheim even introduced a new commandment that he felt epitomized the Jewish condition after the Holocaust in relation to Israel's centrality to the Jewish future. Noting that Orthodox Judaism had a core of 613 commandments given by God, Fackenheim posited a 614th commandment that came from the Jewish people in its struggle to survive the Holocaust and the Arab assault on Israel in the 1967 war: "The authentic Jew of today is forbidden to hand Hitler yet another posthumous victory."

For Fackenheim, the Commanding Voice of Sinai provided the 613 commandments of Judaism. However, that voice was silent during the Holocaust and Israel's endangerment. Refusing to be paralyzed by God's silence and to await God's reappearance, in the 1967 war the Jewish people rose up and took responsibility for its own fate. For Fackenheim, the 614th commandment came from the Jewish people. It was inspired by the Commanding Voice of Auschwitz.

Though the argument between Rubenstein, Wiesel, and Fackenheim lay beneath the bravado of claims and counterclaims made by each man, it was encapsulated in a one-on-one confrontation between Rubenstein and Wiesel in 1970, at one of the first Holocaust conferences held in the US. The issue between them was whether the six million Jews killed in the Holocaust were victims or martyrs. Rubenstein claimed the Holocaust dead were victims. Wiesel argued for martyrdom.

The battle over terminology may seem misplaced, even trite. After all, six million dead is six million dead. Does it matter what terms are used for their death? Rather, the terminology had to do with the importance of Jewish life and Jewish history, and whether or not it was worth the sacrifice involved to keep the Jewish people alive and intact. Is there a meaning to Jewish history that moves beyond the moment? Is there such a thing as Jewish destiny? If there is a meaning and destiny, what can be claimed of both after the Holocaust? Could Israel be the carrier of Jewish life and destiny, the only one possible, after the Holocaust?

For Rubenstein, Israel is the place where Jewish life is secured after the Holocaust. Though Jewish life is protected there, for Rubenstein there is no meaning for Jewish history after Auschwitz, and no inherent reason for

Jewish continuance. Wiesel felt otherwise. The designation of the victims of the Holocaust as martyrs gave their lives a retrospective function as providing the seeds for a Jewish future. For Wiesel, the concrete response to Jewish martyrdom and the hope of the Jewish future is found in Israel. Therefore, Israel demands the unqualified support of Jews everywhere.

In a time when God is distant, the Holocaust and Israel combine as the central affirmation of Jewish history and life. Otherwise, at least for Wiesel, the Holocaust dead and all of Jewish history will become null and void. Echoing Fackenheim's 614th commandment, Wiesel believes that seeing the Holocaust dead as victims, or even the thought of the world without a state of Israel, grants Hitler a posthumous victory.

CONSTANTINIAN JUDAISM, PROGRESSIVE JEWS, AND THE 615TH COMMANDMENT

As the debate about the place of the Holocaust and Israel was being played out in the 1970s, another unmentioned scenario was also taking place: the Israeli occupation and settlement of Jerusalem, the West Bank, and Gaza. Though unbeknownst to the Holocaust commentators at the time, and unfortunately even now, Israeli expansionism was undermining their very arguments. At least, it would make it more difficult for their arguments to be heard and considered. Would it also invalidate them completely?

Indeed, the taking of land and the ethnic cleansing of Palestinians had begun much earlier, with the founding of the state of Israel in 1948. For most American Jews, like me, this was unknown in the 1970s; or, if known, it was shrouded in the victims vs. martyrs debate that echoed throughout the Jewish world. Eventually Wiesel won his debate with Rubenstein, and his views, along with Fackenheim's 614th commandment, became normative in the American Jewish community and beyond.

Christians in America similarly adopted the conviction that, after the Holocaust, Israel was essential to Jewish survival and flourishing. Christians also came to believe that support for the State of Israel was part of Christian repentance for their historic sin of anti-Semitism. In some quarters, Holocaust theology became so pervasive that it became difficult to ascertain whether Holocaust theology was more important to Jews or to Christians. Like Jews, Christians in the main did not know—or at least did not care—that the displacement of Palestinians had begun much earlier than the aftermath of the 1967 war. In fact, along with many Jews, Christians hardly noticed the post-1967 taking of Palestinian land either. For Jews and Christians in America, Israel had been and remained innocent.

As the 1980s dawned and Israel settled permanently on ever more Palestinian land, Holocaust theology began to be challenged. The Israeli invasion of Lebanon, as well as Israel's crushing of the Palestinian uprising in the 1980s, also cautioned more than a few Jews and Christians that the question of Jewish martyrdom was being accompanied by the martyrdom of Palestinians. Could the two victimized and martyred peoples be reconciled, connected, and transformed together in two states, Israel and Palestine, existing side by side in peace?

This two-state possibility could be reconciled with the Holocaust/Israel consciousness that Rubenstein, Wiesel, and Fackenheim had pioneered as long as the innocence and redemptive quality of Jewish existence and the State of Israel were upheld. In fact, this became the position of progressive Jews in America and in Israel. For progressive Jews, Jewish and Israeli innocence was being compromised in the aftermath of the 1967 war by policies pursued by Israel and the American Jewish establishment. By ending the post-1967 occupation, they thought Jewish innocence could be reasserted. Yet the progressive Jewish movement, while pointing out the contradictions of the Jewish establishment, had its own contradictions as well. Progressive Jews refused to acknowledge the continuity in the displacement of Palestinians from 1948 onward, perhaps because it would be more difficult to support a two-state solution to the Israeli-Palestinian conflict. Besides, it would make Jews culpable from the beginning in the destruction of Palestine.

By the 1990s many Middle East experts recognized that Israel had embarked on a policy of expansionism that precluded any viable two-state solution. Yet progressive Jews clung to the position regardless. I began to think that the reason progressive Jews would not let go of the vanished two-state solution was because they actually mirrored the overall sensibilities of the Jewish establishment. I felt that progressive Jews had become the left wing of the Jewish establishment, thereby enabling their policies to continue while arguing for a moral solution to a conflict they knew meant Israel's victory over the Palestinians.

After the second Palestinian uprising, in 2000, it became clear that Israel and the Jewish establishment embodied a Constantinian formation—a formation resembling the movement in the fourth century as the nascent and marginal Christian community became the official religion of the Roman Empire. As the religion of the empire, Constantinian Christianity blessed the empire and received privileges from it. It occurred to me that something similar had happened to the Jewish community. Coming from the margins of European society and the suffering of the Holocaust, Jews had survived and flourished with our own state and power in America. To guarantee the continuance of that success, Jews blessed the state of Israel and America, and received privileges from both. Had we therefore adopted a Constantinian Judaism? Were progressive Jews, especially groups like Peace Now in Israel and the Tikkun community in the US, in actuality the left wing of Constantinian Judaism?

With the passage of time the terrain of Jewish life had shifted precipitously. Jews were now confronted with an expansionist Israel and the foreclosure of the two-state option. Still, the rhetoric and arguments within Israel and the American Jewish community remained in a Holocaust victims/martyrs mode that foreclosed any sense that Jewish culpability was in play. In fact, anyone who spoke about the plight of the Palestinians was deemed a Christian anti-Semite or a self-hating Jew. This Constantinian collusion of establishment and progressive forces made it even more difficult for Jews and others to think new thoughts about the meaning of Jewish survival and Jewish destiny.

As the first decade of the new millennium came to a close, even more information needed to be assimilated. In 2006, Israel invaded Lebanon a second time, with mixed results. The bombing of Lebanon left it burning, but the rockets fired into Israel by Hezbollah left Israel burning as well. In an era of sophisticated technology, were Israel and Jews really safe with an expansionist Israel? Then, in 2008, another Israeli invasion of Gaza occurred, which brought devastation to the people of Gaza and charges of war crimes against Israel. Even the UN's Goldstone Report on the war was initially condemned by many Jewish leaders in Israel and the US. Meanwhile, the people of Gaza continued to exist in a vast prison-like situation lacking the basic materials for a decent life.

During this time, a number of Jews began to think through the trajectory of the Holocaust and Israel, and where both had brought us as a people.

What did Jews need to do to break through the Constantinianism of the Jewish establishment and the progressive Jewish forces that collaborated with these policies? If Israel would not—perhaps could not—stop itself, could dissident Jews stop it? The Jewish ethical tradition had been advanced, and applied to Israel, for decades—but without success.

The discussion of the Holocaust had come full circle. Indeed, speaking and thinking about the Holocaust in light of Israel's expansionism and war was becoming ever more difficult. Some Jews began to see the Jewish ethical tradition as in danger of being destroyed. Was there a need for a 615th commandment to complement Fackenheim's 614th? That commandment might be stated thusly: "Thou shalt not dislocate, demean or destroy Palestinian life." Without this commandment, some Jews began to think that Hitler was being handed another posthumous victory.

JEWS OF CONSCIENCE

A third group of Israeli and American Jews has arisen over the last decade—Jews of conscience, like Gaza expert Sara Roy and Israeli reporter Amira Hass, both children of Holocaust survivors. These Jews feel that the Jewish future is imperiled by the power of Israel and the limitations that the Constantinian/progressive Jewish establishment places on what Jews and others are allowed to think regarding the Holocaust and Israel. Jews of conscience are aware of Jewish history—including the Holocaust—and are aware of the history Jews are creating—including the historic and contemporary policies of the State of Israel vis-à-vis the Palestinians.

For Jews of conscience, Jewish empowerment is not innocent, and Israel is not redemptive. But there is also a Jewish particularity that has been buffeted by history. While Jews cannot use power to oppress another people, Jews need some kind of power in the post-Holocaust world. Jews of conscience argue for an interconnected empowerment wherever Jews live, especially in Israel/Palestine, meaning that Jews need to be empowered alongside Palestinians. History exists: there was a Holocaust; there is a State of Israel. But the question is what is to be said and done after the Holocaust and Israel. How are Jews to mend the wrong done to Palestinians, and begin a new history with the Palestinian people?

Increasingly, as I travel among Jews of conscience, the Jewish prophets come to mind. Existing in ancient times, the prophets spoke to the leaders and the people about how they were turning their backs on Jewish destiny. The prophet's sense of Jewish destiny had to do with creating a different kind of society from the unjust Egyptian society they had been freed from, and also with their function as a light unto the nations.

True, in the Biblical account Israel was the Promised Land, but the prophets judged Israel's sojourn there by its actions. Once it had been judged as abridging justice, the sentence carried out was harsh. If the people of Israel did not heed the prophet's call, they became cut off from God, decimated and exiled from the land. With repentance, however, the people of Israel were welcomed back into God's good graces and allowed to return to the land.

Still, the shadow of the prophets loomed large. In fact, from that moment on, the prophets have accompanied Jewish life inside and outside of the land. Perhaps this is why Constantinian and progressive Jews argue the Jewish ethical tradition so vociferously even as the facts on the ground contradict their arguments. Perhaps this is also the reason that, despite the penalties attached to their views, Jews of conscience argue the case that the Jewish ethical tradition is being betrayed.

Jews have always been on both sides of the empire divide. While the people of Israel gave the prophets to the world, Jews have also been the great adversaries of the prophets. I see this age-old prophetic pattern when Constantinian and progressive Jews argue for Jewish empire, in harsh or soft tones, and when Jews of conscience take their prophetic stand against Jewish empire, even with the risks involved.

Increasing numbers of Jews of conscience argue that boycott, divestment, and sanctions from an expanding and occupying Israel are essential if the Jewish ethical tradition is to be upheld today. It is hard to argue against their standing in the tradition of the prophets. After all, the difficulties the prophets faced came precisely because they pointed the accusing finger inwards to Jews and the Jewish community.

This is where the prophets engage Jews at the deepest levels. By calling for justice within the empowered Jewish community, the prophets challenge Jews to reach their higher destiny. Like the prophets, Jews of conscience argue against the normalization of oppression, against empire that dislocates and destroys, and against the innocence that is always claimed by empire.

Like the prophets, Jews of conscience who argue for boycotts, divestment, and sanctions are charged with treason. And, again like the prophets, Jews of conscience are seen as imperiling the security of the State of Israel and of Jews everywhere. Those who call for concrete measures against the policies of the State of Israel, especially after the Holocaust, are seen as blasphemers by the powers that be. But then the prophets were seen in the exact same way.

When I hear some of the epithets of Jewish self-hatred leveled at Jews of conscience, I take comfort in reading the prophets. The words and actions of Isaiah, Jeremiah, Amos, and Ezekiel are even harsher than the ones Jews of conscience use today. Though the context is different, the similarities in viewpoints are striking. In the prophets, an empowered empire of Israel abusing its power, and thereby creating havoc in its relationship with God and society, is condemned by a justice-oriented ethical God and tradition. And though it is true that Jews of conscience rarely speak about God in the post-Holocaust world, the Biblical prophets themselves condemned the Jewish use of God-language in the context of empire. After all, biblically speaking, if Jews create injustice in the land, God is very far away from them. Without justice there is no God available to the people. Could Israel's oppression of Palestinians make it even more difficult to think God after the Holocaust?

If thinking God is too difficult, think healing. Jews of conscience realize that oppressing another people has led Jews to more insecurity and pain, more emphasis on the Holocaust and fear of anti-Semitism, and more anger within the Jewish community—not less. Has an expansionist Israel healed Jews of our Holocaust trauma, or deepened it?

It just may be that the movement of boycott, divestment, and sanctions is as much a struggle for healing as it is for justice. Could it be that justice is the only way to heal both martyred peoples, and that one's healing cannot take place without the healing of the other?

15 A MOMENT OF TRUTH: A DOCUMENT OF CHRISTIAN PALESTINIANS CALLING FOR BDS

Jamal Khader

At the beginning of 2008, a group of Christian Palestinians met for reflection and an exchange of opinion about the suffering in our country, under the Israeli occupation, and to reflect on our faith and God's divine providence for all the inhabitants of this land. The group was composed of laypeople and some clergy from different churches; they had in common their Christian faith and their preoccupation about the future of peace and justice in Palestine/Israel. Inspired by South Africa's "Kairos Document," written in 1985, in which South African theologians asked the churches of the world and the international community to join their struggle against apartheid, the group of Christian Palestinians came out with a document called: "A Moment of Truth: A Word of Faith, Hope and Love from the Heart of Palestinian Suffering."[1] We call ourselves Kairos Palestine.

Why now? The group noticed that today we have reached a dead end in the tragedy of the Palestinian people; the decision-makers content themselves with managing the crisis, rather than committing themselves to the serious task of finding a way to resolve it. The Palestinians keep asking: What is the international community doing? What are the political leaders in Palestine, in Israel, and in the Arab world doing? What is the church doing? The problem is not just a political one. It is a policy in which human beings are destroyed, and this must be of concern to the church.

---

1   See kairospalestine.ps.

THE REALITY ON THE GROUND

These days, everyone is speaking about peace in the Middle East, and about the peace process. So far, however, these are simply words; the reality is one of the Israeli occupation of Palestinian territories, of deprivation of our freedom, and of all that results from this situation.

The reality on the ground is a separation wall erected on Palestinian territory, and the confiscation of Palestinian land to build the wall or new settlements, or to enlarge existing settlements. Our towns and villages are turned into prisons, separating them from one another, rendering them dispersed and divided cantons. Gaza continues to live in inhuman conditions, under permanent blockade and cut off from the other Palestinian territories; Israeli settlements ravage our land, controlling our natural resources, including water and agricultural land, thus depriving hundreds of thousands of Palestinians, and constituting an obstacle to any political solution.

Our reality is one of daily humiliation, subjected to the military checkpoints as we make our way to jobs, schools, or hospitals. Even religious liberty is severely restricted; freedom of access to the holy places is denied under the pretext of security, and Jerusalem and its holy places are out of bounds for many Christians and Muslims from the West Bank and the Gaza Strip. The refugees are also part of our reality. Most of them are still living in camps under difficult circumstances; they have been waiting for fulfillment of their right of return, generation after generation. The thousands of prisoners languishing in Israeli prisons are also part of our reality.

Finally, Jerusalem continues to be emptied of its Palestinian citizens, Christians and Muslims. Their identity cards are confiscated, which means the loss of their right to reside in Jerusalem. Their homes are demolished or expropriated. Jerusalem, city of reconciliation, has become a city of discrimination and exclusion, a source of struggle rather than peace.

The State of Israel continues to disregard international law and international resolutions, and the Arab world and international community are paralyzed in the face of this contempt. Human rights are violated, and despite the various reports of local and international human rights organizations, the injustice continues.

In the face of this reality, Israel justifies its actions—including occupation, collective punishment, and all other forms of reprisals against the Palestinians—as self-defense. In our opinion, this vision is a reversal of reality. Yes, there is Palestinian resistance to the occupation. However, if there were no occupation, there would be no resistance, no fear, and no insecurity. This is our understanding of the situation. Therefore, we call on the Israelis to end the occupation. Then they will see a new world in which there is no fear, no threat, but rather security, justice, and peace.

The Palestinian response to this reality has been diverse. Some have responded through negotiations: that was the official position of the Palestinian Authority, but it did not advance the peace process. Some political parties have followed the way of armed resistance. Israel used this as a pretext to accuse the Palestinians of being terrorists, and was able to distort the real nature of the conflict, presenting it as an Israeli war against terror rather than an Israeli occupation faced by Palestinian legal resistance aiming at ending it.

In the midst of all this, what may be the Christian response? Kairos Palestine's response—this document—is a declaration of faith, hope, and love.

A WORD OF FAITH

After renewing our faith in a good and just God, creator of the universe and of humanity, who loves each one of his creatures, we affirmed our belief that every human being is created in God's image and likeness, and that everyone's dignity is derived from the dignity of the Almighty One. The Bible is often used to justify the policies of the State of Israel, including occupation and the dispossession of the Palestinians. Certain theologians in the West try to attach a biblical and theological legitimacy to the infringement of our rights. Thus, their interpretations have become a menace to our very existence. The "good news" in the Gospel itself has become a "harbinger of death" for us.

In light of the teachings of the Holy Bible, the promise of the land has never been a political program, but rather the prelude to complete universal salvation. Today we constitute three religions in this land—Judaism, Christianity, and Islam. So we believe it is our duty to liberate it from the evil of injustice and war. Our presence in this land, as Christian and Muslim Palestinians, is not accidental but rather deeply rooted in its history and geography, resonant with the connectedness of any other people to the land it lives in. Our connectedness to this land is a natural right.

In one of the strongest affirmations of "The Moment of Truth," we stated: "We declare that the Israeli occupation of Palestinian land is a sin against God and humanity because it deprives the Palestinians of their basic human rights, bestowed by God."

The document states the belief that occupation distorts the image of God in the Israeli who has become an occupier, just as it distorts this image in the Palestinian living under occupation.

ANY HOPE?

Without even a glimmer of positive expectation, the present situation does not promise any quick solution or the end of the occupation. Yes, the initiatives, the conferences, visits, and negotiations have multiplied, but they have not been followed up by any change in our situation or our suffering. The clear Israeli response, refusing any solution, leaves no room for positive expectations.

Despite all this, the document tries to base its hope on faith in God almighty, that His loving and goodness will one day be victorious over the evil. "What is the meaning of hope? Hope within us means first and foremost our faith in God and secondly our expectation, despite everything, for a better future. Thirdly, it means not chasing after illusions—we realize that release is not close at hand." From this vision derives the strength to be steadfast, remain firm, and work to change the reality. Hope means not giving in to evil, but rather standing up to it and continuing to resist it.

We may find some signs of hope in the church in our land which, despite her weakness and her divisions, can already be seen. Our parish communities are vibrant, and most of our young people are active apostles for justice and peace. We can add to this the numerous meetings for inter-religious dialogue, Christian–Muslim dialogue, which includes the religious leaders and a part of the people. There is dialogue among the three religions, Judaism, Christianity, and Islam. They all try to breach the walls imposed by the occupation and oppose the distorted perception of human beings in the hearts of their brothers or sisters.

Equally significant is the developing awareness among many churches throughout the world, and their desire to know the truth about what is going on here. In addition to that, we see a determination among many to overcome the resentments of the past and to be ready for reconciliation once justice has been restored. Public awareness of the need to restore political rights to the Palestinians is increasing, and Jewish and Israeli voices advocating peace and justice are raised in support of this, with the approval of the international community. True, these forces for justice and reconciliation have not yet been able to transform the situation of injustice, but they have their influence, and may shorten the time of suffering and hasten the time of reconciliation.

For the church, everything that happens in our land, everyone who lives there, all the pains and hopes, all the injustice and all the efforts to stop them, are part and parcel of the prayer of the church and the service of all her institutions. Thanks be to God that our church raises her voice against injustice despite the fact that some wish her to remain silent, closed in her religious devotions. If she does take sides, it is with the oppressed, to stand alongside them. Therefore, religion cannot favor or support any unjust political regime, but must rather promote justice, truth, and human dignity. It must exert every effort to purify regimes where human beings suffer injustice and human dignity is violated. Today, the church bears the strength of love rather than that of revenge, a culture of life rather than a culture of death.

THE COMMANDMENT OF LOVE: NONVIOLENT RESISTANCE TO EVIL

Jesus Christ said:

> You have heard that it was said, "You shall love your neighbor and hate your enemy." But I say to you, Love your enemies and pray for those who persecute you, so that you may be children of your Father in heaven; for he makes his sun rise on the evil and on the good, and sends rain on the righteous and on the unrighteous (Matthew 5:45–47).

Love is the commandment of Christ, and it includes both friends and enemies. This must be clear when we find ourselves in circumstances where we must resist evil. However, the commandment of love does not mean accepting evil or aggression on their part. Rather, this love seeks to correct the evil and stop the aggression.

The aggression against the Palestinian people which is the Israeli occupation is an evil that must be resisted. It is an evil and a sin that must be resisted and removed. Primary responsibility for this rests with the Palestinians themselves suffering occupation. Christian love invites us to resist it. However, love puts an end to evil by walking in the ways of justice. Responsibility lies also with the international community. Finally, responsibility lies with the perpetrators of the injustice; they must liberate themselves from the evil that is in them and the injustice they have imposed on others.

When we review the history of the nations, we see many wars and much resistance to war by war, to violence by violence. The Palestinian people have used violence as many peoples have, particularly in the first stages of its struggle with the Israeli occupation. However, it also engaged in peaceful struggle, especially during the first Intifada. The ways of force must give way to the ways of justice. This applies above all to the peoples that are militarily strong, mighty enough to impose their injustice on the weaker.

Our option as Christians in the face of the Israeli occupation is to resist; but it is resistance with love as its logic. It is thus a creative resistance, for it must find human ways that engage the humanity of the enemy to stop the injustice, and oblige the perpetrator to end his aggression and thus achieve the desired goal, which is getting back the land, freedom, dignity, and independence. The Christian commandment of love is a difficult one, yet it alone can stand firm in the face of the clear declarations of the occupation authorities that refuse our existence, and the many excuses these authorities use to continue imposing occupation upon us. Resistance to the evil of occupation is integrated, then, within this Christian love that refuses evil and corrects it. It resists evil in all its forms, with methods that enter into the logic of love and draw on all energies to make peace. We can resist through civil disobedience. We do not resist with death, but rather through respect for life.

Palestinian civil organizations, as well as international organizations, NGOs, and certain religious institutions call on individuals, companies, and states to engage in divestment and in an economic and commercial boycott of everything produced by the occupation. We understand this to incorporate the logic of peaceful resistance. These advocacy campaigns must be carried out with courage, openly and sincerely proclaiming that their object is not revenge, but rather an end to the existing evil, liberating both the perpetrators and the victims of injustice. The aim is to free both peoples from the extremist positions of the various Israeli governments, bringing both to justice and reconciliation. In this spirit and with this dedication we will eventually reach the longed-for resolution to our problems, as indeed happened in South Africa, and with many other liberation movements in the world.

Through our love, we will overcome injustices and establish foundations for a new society both for us and for our opponents. Our future and their future are one: either the cycle of violence that destroys both of us or peace that will benefit both. The document calls on the people of Israel to be partners in peace, and not in the cycle of interminable violence. Let us resist evil together—the evil of occupation and the infernal cycle of violence.

CALL TO JOIN OUR STRUGGLE FOR JUSTICE

The document ends with a call for all people to join in our vision for the future of peace and justice in Palestine/Israel. It begins with a word to the churches of the world, a word of gratitude for their solidarity and a call to revisit fundamentalist theological positions that support certain unjust political options with regard to the Palestinian people—not to offer a theological cover-up for the injustice.

The document condemns all forms of racism, whether religious or ethnic, including anti-Semitism and Islamophobia. At the same time, it demands the adoption of a position of truth with regard to Israel's occupation of Palestinian land. Again, the document reiterates its vision of boycott and disinvestment as tools of nonviolence for justice, peace, and security for all.

The document then addresses the international community, urging it to remove the principle of "double standards" and insist on the international resolutions regarding the Palestinian problem with regard to all parties. Selective application of international law threatens to leave us vulnerable to a law of the jungle. It legitimizes the claims by certain armed groups and states that the international community only understands the logic of force.

Therefore, the document calls for a response to what the civil and religious institutions have proposed, as mentioned earlier: the beginning of a system of economic sanctions and boycott to be applied against Israel. This is not revenge, but rather a serious action in order to reach a just and definitive peace that will put an end to Israeli occupation of Palestinian and other Arab territories, and will guarantee security and peace for all.

Finally, the religious and spiritual leaders, Jewish and Muslim, need to defend the oppressed and the dignity God has bestowed on them, to rise up above the political positions that have failed so far and continue to lead everyone on the path of failure and suffering. The document seeks to reach a common vision, built on equality and sharing—not on superiority, negation of the other, or aggression, using the pretext of fear and security. Peace is possible, and definitive reconciliation also. Thus, justice and security will be attained for all.

The idea of a religious state, Jewish or Islamic, suffocates the state, confines it within narrow limits, and transforms it into a state that practices discrimination and exclusion, preferring one citizen over another. Let the state be a state for all its citizens, with a vision constructed on respect for religion, but also on equality, justice, liberty, and respect for pluralism, and not on domination by a religion or a numerical majority.

The document was launched in December 11, 2009. Since then it has received a lot of positive reactions, both locally and internationally. Palestinian Christians have signed the document in support, as it speaks in their name, and others have endorsed it in a gesture of solidarity and support for its vision.

The document also received a lot of negative responses, accusing it of portraying a distorted vision of reality—which is, according to them, one of Islamic fundamentalism. The call for BDS was the reason why some international churches did not sign the document, and a reason for attacks against it. With the dead end we are facing, the call for BDS represents a nonviolent way of applying pressure, and of telling the world that this unjust situation must not continue.

16 ISRAEL/PALESTINE AND THE APARTHEID ANALOGY

Ran Greenstein

In the last decade, the Israeli system of political and military control has increasingly been compared to the apartheid system in South Africa. The comparison is invoked regularly by activists, and movements, including the BDS campaign, opposed to the 1967 occupation and other aspects of Israeli policies vis-à-vis Palestinians. It is denounced regularly by Israeli spokespersons. But the more empirical and theoretical discussion of the respective regimes and their historical trajectories has been marginalized in the process.[1] I wish to make three crucial distinctions to clarify the conceptual muddle afflicting the debate.

First, we need to consider which Israel is our topic of concern: Israel as it exists today, with boundaries extending from the Mediterranean to the River Jordan, or Israel as it existed before 1967, along the Green Line? Are the Palestinian territories occupied in 1967 part of the definition or an element external to it? Which boundaries (geographical, political, ideological) are we considering when we reference and analyze the analogy to apartheid?

The central question here is the relationship between three components: "Israel proper" (in its pre-1967 boundaries), "Greater Israel" (in its

---

1 Exceptions are Ran Greenstein, *Genealogies of Conflict: Class, Identity and State in Palestine/Israel and South Africa*, Wesleyan University Press, 1995; Mona Younis, *Liberation and Democratization: The South African and Palestinian National Movements*, University of Minnesota Press, 2000; Hilla Dayan, "Regimes of Separation: Israel/Palestine and the Shadow of Apartheid," in Adi Ophir, Michal Givoni, and Sari Hanafi, eds., *The Power of Inclusive Exclusion: Anatomy of Israeli Rule in the Occupied Palestinian Territories*, Zone Books, 2009.

post-1967 boundaries), and "Greater Palestine" (a demographic rather than geographic concept, including all Arabs with origins in pre-1948 Palestine).

Second, we need to distinguish between historical apartheid (the specific system that prevailed in South Africa between 1948 and 1994) and the more general definition of apartheid. Does Israel as an apartheid system need to be tackled in its own terms, independently of our understanding of South African history?

Third, what do the similarities and differences between the South African and Israeli systems mean for strategies of political change? To what extent can we apply political strategies from the former to the latter case? For that, we need to undertake a concrete analysis of Israeli and Palestinian societies, as well as their local and international allegiances, bases of support, and vulnerabilities.

WHAT IS APARTHEID?

The International Convention on the Suppression and Punishment of the Crime of Apartheid, adopted by the UN General Assembly in November 1973, regards apartheid as "a crime against humanity" and violation of international law. Apartheid means "similar policies and practices of racial segregation and discrimination as practised in southern Africa … committed for the purpose of establishing and maintaining domination by one racial group of persons over any other racial group of persons and systematically oppressing them." It lists many practices, including measures restricting particular groups from participating in political, social, economic, and cultural life, and that deliberately deny them their basic human rights and freedoms: the right to work, assemble, and organize; to education; to a nationality; to freedom of movement and residence; and to freedom of opinion and expression. It involves dividing the population along racial lines through reserves and ghettos; anti-miscegenation laws; and the expropriation of land on the basis of race.

Although this definition uses the notion of race, which is not applicable to Israeli–Palestinian relations, the International Convention on the Elimination of All Forms of Racial Discrimination, adopted by the UN in 1965, describes racial discrimination as "any distinction, exclusion, restriction or preference based on race, colour, descent, or national or ethnic origin which has the purpose or effect of nullifying or impairing the recognition, enjoyment or exercise, on an equal footing, of human rights and fundamental freedoms in the political, economic, social, cultural or any other field of public life."[2]

Putting together the two conventions, we can define apartheid as a set of policies and practices of legal discrimination, political exclusion, and social marginalization, based on racial, national, or ethnic origins. This definition draws on historical South African apartheid, but cannot be reduced to it.

IS ISRAEL AN APARTHEID STATE?

To answer this question, we must realize that it is impossible to look at Israel proper in isolation from Greater Israel and Greater Palestine. At the same time, we must recognize that the Israeli regime treats different groups of Palestinians differently. Those residing within Israel proper, or the pre-1967 boundaries, are citizens and have rights that were denied to the majority of black people in South Africa. That is, while they suffer discrimination in a variety of ways, ranging from lack of job opportunities and restricted access to land to far fewer social benefits than Jewish citizens, they do retain voting rights. Those in Greater Israel, or under Israeli occupation, are considered resident non-citizens and treated in much the same way as black South Africans (especially residents of the "homelands"): they are denied voting and social rights, face severe restrictions on their movements and access to land, and are subjects of foreign rule over which they have no control. Finally, refugees in Greater Palestine are non-resident non-citizens, and are excluded to an even greater degree than black South Africans: they cannot even set foot in the country, much less have a say in how it is governed. Considering apartheid in the general sense, Israeli policies and practices meet many of the criteria identified in the international convention on apartheid, though they are based on ethno-national rather than racial grounds. This does not mean that the Israeli state and system of control are identical to those of historical apartheid, although they do bear family resemblances. Anyhow, no case is ever quite like any other. While the technologies of rule (coercive, legal, and physical) used by Israel have largely converged with their apartheid counterparts, crucial differences remain.

---

2   Office of the United Nations High Commissioner for Human Rights, "International Convention on the Elimination of All Forms of Racial Discrimination," at www2.ohchr.org.

These involve ideological motivations, economic strategies, and political configurations. In all these respects, Israel/Palestine tends more towards exclusion than did South Africa.

To understand the reasons for this, we need to examine the historical trajectories of the two countries.[3]

For centuries, various colonial forces (the Dutch East India Company and the British Empire, Afrikaner and English settlers, missionaries, farming and mining lords) collaborated and competed to control the disparate indigenous groups in South Africa, resulting in disparate systems of domination, cooperation and resistance in different regions. Numerous political entities emerged as a result (British colonies, Boer republics, African kingdoms, missionary territories), characterized by a diverse array of forms of social organization (slavery, indentured labor, land and labor tenancy, sharecropping, and wage labor). It was not until the late nineteenth century that colonial policies were systematized to create a uniform mode of control, aimed at incorporating black people into the economy while keeping them politically excluded. Apartheid simply sought to entrench white domination as the foundation for white prosperity.

Unlike South Africa, settler Jews and indigenous Arabs had begun to consolidate their group identities—linked to broader ethno-national collectives—*before* the formation of the Israeli state in 1948, and the Israeli-Palestinian conflict that has unfolded ever since has simply deepened the divide between the communities. But the birth of Israel was also inextricably linked with the Nakba—the "ethnic cleansing" of the majority of the indigenous population living in the areas allocated to the new state.

As a result, the Zionist project has regarded indigenous people as an obstacle to be removed from the land in order to clear the way for Jewish immigration into the country. White settlers in South Africa, in contrast, focused on controlling resources and populations (land and labor) to enhance their prosperity. Political domination was a means to an economic goal in South Africa, whereas it has become a goal in its own right in Israel/Palestine.

The Nakba also produced two contradictory effects: on the one hand, the removal of most Palestinians from their land, coupled with the demotion

---

3   Extended discussion of these issues can be found in Greenstein, *Genealogies of Conflict*.

of Palestinians remaining in Israel to the status of minority, second-class citizens (who nonetheless retain voting rights), has allowed Israel to maintain the illusion that it is a democracy (albeit one premised upon Jewish demographic dominance). On the other hand, the Nakba also ensured that Israel would always henceforth view Palestinians dispossessed in 1948 as an external threat.

Neither scenario is reflected in the South African case. However, the 1967 occupation introduced another element to the picture, making it more like historical apartheid: a large number of Palestinians were incorporated into the Israeli labor market while remaining disenfranchised. The state was unwilling to extend to them the political and civil rights enjoyed by Palestinian citizens of Israel, yet also unable to impose on them another round of the 1948 ethnic cleansing. They remain in limbo, subject to a huge legal-military apparatus designed to ensure their subordination, without annexation and without ethnic "cleansing."

"APARTHEID OF A SPECIAL TYPE"

Is this apartheid in its generic sense? In crucial respects it is, but an apartheid of a special type. Back in the early 1960s, the South African Communist Party coined the term "colonialism of a special type" to refer to a system that combined the colonial legacies of racial discrimination, political exclusion and socio-economic inequalities, with political independence from the British Empire. It used this novel concept to devise a strategy for political change that regarded local white settlers as potential allies rather than as invaders to be removed from the territory.

The Israeli regime of separation is more complicated than that. The degree of legal-political differentiation (between citizens, occupied subjects, and refugees, and in the rules that apply to them) is greater, as it includes an array of formal and informal military regulations in the occupied territories, and policies delegating powers and resources to non-state institutions (the Jewish Agency, the Jewish National Fund), which act on behalf of the state to entrench domination, but in a more opaque manner. The relevant legal apparatuses also apply beyond Israeli boundaries (to Jews, all of whom are regarded as potential citizens, and to Palestinians, all of whom are regarded as prohibited persons). Hence we can view the regime in Israel/Palestine as "apartheid of a special type": a system that combines democratic norms, military rule, and exclusion/inclusion of extraterritorial populations. There are five reasons for this.

First, divisions are based on an ethno-national distinction between Jewish insiders and Palestinian Arab outsiders. This distinction has a religious dimension—the only way to join the Jewish group is through conversion—but is not affected by degree of religious adherence.

Second, Israel uses this distinction to expand citizenship beyond its territory (potentially to all Jews) and to limit citizenship within it (Palestinian residents of the occupied territories cannot become citizens). Thus, it is open to all nonresident members of one group, and closed to all nonresident members of the other group, regardless of their personal histories and actual links to the territory.

Third, Israel's physical boundaries are blurred, permanently temporary, and never fixed by law. They are also asymmetrical: porous in one direction (through the expansion of military forces and settlers into neighboring territories) and impermeable in the other direction (through severe restrictions or total prohibition on the entry of Palestinians).

Fourth, within the territories it controls, Israel combines different modes of rule: civilian authority and formal democracy within the Green Line, and military authority beyond it. In times of crisis, the military mode of rule tends to spill over the Green Line to apply to Palestinian citizens. At all times, civilian rule extends beyond the Green Line to apply to Jewish citizens. The distinction between the two sides of the Green Line is constantly eroding as a result, and norms and practices developed under the occupation filter back into Israel: as the phrase goes, the "Jewish democratic state" is "democratic" for Jews and "Jewish" for Arabs.

Finally, Israel is in fact a "Jewish demographic state." The fear that Jews may become a minority informs all state policy and structures, while all proposed solutions to the Israeli-Palestinian conflict are thus geared toward achieving a permanent Jewish majority, exercising political domination, in the State of Israel (whatever its boundaries may be).

Nonetheless, Israel's "apartheid of a special type" differs from South African apartheid in three major ways. First, South African apartheid was founded upon a racial distinction between whites and blacks (further divided into subgroups), rather than an ethno-national distinction. Racial groups were internally divided on the basis of language, religion, and ethnicity, and externally linked in various ways across the color line, which subsequently allowed for more diversity in practice and presented differing sites of division and cooperation, despite state organization around the single axis of race. More opportunities for social change were thus opened up.

This is not the case in Israel/Palestine. The rise of the Zionist movement and Arab nationalism in the twentieth century swallowed up other cross-cutting affiliations that existed early on, held by anti-Zionist orthodox Jews, Arabic-speaking Jews, and so on. State organization in Israel/Palestine thus mirrors social reality far more closely. But there is one exception: Palestinian citizens occupy a status somewhere between those of Jewish citizens and Palestinian noncitizens. They are the only segment of the entire population that is bilingual, familiar with political and cultural realities across the ethnic divide, and they have greater freedom to organize than other groups. As a minority group (15 to 20 percent of Israeli citizens *and* of Palestinian Arabs) they cannot drive change on their own, but may act as crucial catalysts for it.

Second, in South Africa, a key goal of the state was to ensure that black people continued to labor without making social and political demands. The strategy it used was to "externalize" blacks: to deny them their rights where their physical presence was economically necessary (in white homes, factories, farms, and service industries), and to have them exercise their rights elsewhere. Those with no economic function— children, women (especially mothers) and the elderly—were prevented from moving into the urban areas, or removed to the "reserves" (bantustans or homelands). Able-bodied blacks who worked in the cities were supposed to commute between the places where they had jobs (but no political rights) and the places where they had political rights (but no jobs).

This system of migrant labor opened up a contradiction between political and economic imperatives. Apartheid broke down families and the social order, hampered efforts to create a skilled labor force, reduced productivity, and gave rise to crime and social protest. To control people's movements, the state created a bloated and expensive repressive apparatus, which put a constant burden on state resources and capacities. Domestic and industrial employers faced increasing difficulties in meeting their labor needs. What was initially viewed as an economic asset eventually became an economic liability, and had to go.

In contrast, the economic imperative of the Israeli system has been to create employment for Jewish immigrants. Palestinian labor was used by certain groups at certain times, but has never been central to Jewish prosperity in Israel. With the first Intifada, in the late 1980s, and under conditions of globalization, it could be replaced by foreign workers. A massive wave of Russian Jewish immigration in the 1990s helped this process. The externalization of Palestinians—through denial of rights, ethnic cleansing, and "disengagement"—has presented few economic problems for Israeli Jews.

Finally, apartheid was just one in a series of regimes in which settlers dominated indigenous people in South Africa through military power, technological superiority, and "divide and rule" strategies. Numerical dominance was never a serious concern, so long as security of person, property, and investment could be guaranteed. When repression proved increasingly counterproductive, a deal exchanging political power for ongoing prosperity became acceptable to most whites. Can such a deal be offered to Israeli Jews, for whom demography is key to political survival on their own terms? Unlikely.

PROSPECTS AND SOLUTIONS

What does all of this imply? With the two ethno-national groups in the country divided by language, political identity, religion, and ethnic origin (though all Palestinian citizens are bilingual, they make up only about 10 percent of the total population), South Africa's rainbow nation is unlikely to be replicated in Israel/Palestine. The multiplicity of identities and lack of a single axis of division to align them all in South Africa made it possible to adopt English as the lingua franca of politics, business, and education, and Christianity as a religious umbrella, but the starker divisions in Greater Israel/Palestine seem to make a two-state solution more natural. But things are slightly more complex.

Israel proper, considered in isolation, is similar to South Africa. Here, veteran Ashkenazi and Mizrahi Jews, Russian and Ethiopian immigrants, and Palestinian citizens use Hebrew in their daily interactions and share similar social habits and cultural tastes. In Haifa, Jaffa, and Acre some neighborhoods are mixed, with Jews and Arabs living together and sharing similar lifestyles. They have more in common than white suburbanites have with rural black South Africans, during apartheid or now. As the tent protests of summer 2011 proved, meaningful political links between Jewish and Palestinian citizens can be forged, though not easily. Perhaps this can be the foundation for binationalism within a single state. In Greater Israel, the two groups live in a combination of mixed and homogeneous areas. Israel's demographic engineering has created a patchwork quilt of mono-ethnic and bi-ethnic regions, separated by political intent rather than geographical logic. But for such a state to become a foundation for an overall solution, common citizenship for all residents should be established, the 1967 occupation must be terminated, and the rights of the 1948 refugees recognized.

Still, we cannot consider Israel proper in isolation, and links of common identity and citizenship between Jews and Palestinians, both refugees and those under occupation, will be much more difficult to establish. A fundamental change to the boundaries of citizenship would require a radical realignment of the political scene, which currently has no serious political advocates; nor is it a substitute for the struggle against the occupation.

The occupation remains the largest obstacle in Israeli–Palestinian relations. Futile negotiations over the last two decades have only intensified its daily presence in the lives of Palestinians, both in Gaza and the West Bank. This has given rise to localized resistance against restrictions on movement, access to land, economic activity, water use, study, and construction—which are bound to continue and intensify, irrespective of the state of negotiations between Israel and the Palestinian Authority, or the recognition of Palestinian statehood by the United Nations. The South African transition teaches us that subordinating local struggles to the requirements of diplomacy helped to bring the ANC to power, but failed to address the many concerns that gave rise to the struggle in the first place.

The rights of refugees in Greater Palestine will present the greatest challenge to the boundaries of Israeli citizenship and control. Two steps could be taken immediately to begin the process of solution. First, the "present absentees" (Palestinians who were removed from their original homes in 1948 but have become citizens) could be given access to their property and confiscated land. This would not affect Israel's current demographics, nor involve changes in citizenship status. Second, the original 1948 refugees could be invited back. Fewer than 100,000 are still alive, meaning no more than a 1 to 2 percent increase in Israel's population. Both these steps will be resisted by Israeli Jews, who fear any recognition—even symbolic and limited—of the right of return. Change will thus only be possible through ongoing educational, political, and legal campaigns.

We must focus on the crucial difference between apartheid in Israel and in South Africa: Palestinians are not strategically located within the Israeli economy, and therefore lack the crucial weapon of struggle used by black South Africans. Most Palestinians operate outside the boundaries of the Israeli system, and lack a strategy of change from within. While Palestinian citizens can organize resistance to the system from within, and play a key role in transforming it, in order to realize their goals they will need the mobilization of dissident Jews in Israel, the ongoing struggle against the occupation, and the solidarity of regional and international forces.

On the positive side, the status quo is becoming increasingly more unstable. The Zionist project's drive towards geographical expansion is undermining Israel's demographic imperative to ensure a Jewish majority. Changing international tides are eroding support for the regime. For two decades Israel benefited from the collapse of the Soviet bloc, with its alliance with "progressive" Third World governments, and more recently from positioning itself as the frontline in the "global war on terror." These have served to entrench its hold on the occupied territories. But the Arab Spring of 2011, along with the shifting strategies of Turkey and Egypt, have begun to isolate Israel and weaken the hold over the region of its sponsor, the US. The growing international solidarity movement, and rising internal dissatisfaction with the ever-rising costs of maintaining the occupation, are eating away at support for Israel's apartheid policies. Only by combining internal and external pressure will the struggle against Israel's "apartheid of a special type" be successful.

17 JUSTICE FOR PALESTINE: A CALL TO ACTION FROM INDIGENOUS AND WOMEN-OF-COLOR FEMINISTS

Between June 14 and 23, 2011, a delegation of eleven scholars, activists, and artists visited occupied Palestine. As indigenous and women-of-color feminists involved in multiple social justice struggles, we sought to affirm our association with the growing international movement for a free Palestine. We wanted to see for ourselves the conditions under which Palestinian people live and struggle against what we can now confidently name as the Israeli project of apartheid and ethnic cleansing. Each and every one of us—including those members of our delegation who grew up in the Jim Crow South, in apartheid South Africa, and on Indian reservations in the US—was shocked by what we saw. In this statement we describe some of our experiences and issue an urgent call to others who share our commitment to racial justice, equality, and freedom.

During our short stay in Palestine, we met with academics, students, youth, leaders of civic organizations, elected officials, trade unionists, political leaders, artists, and civil society activists, as well as residents of refugee camps and villages that have recently been attacked by Israeli soldiers and settlers. Everyone we encountered—in Nablus, Awarta, Balata, Jerusalem, Hebron, Dheisheh, Bethlehem, Birzeit, Ramallah, Umm el-Fahem, and Haifa—asked us to tell the truth about life under occupation and about their unwavering commitment to a free Palestine. We were deeply impressed by people's insistence on the linkages between the movement for a free Palestine and struggles for justice throughout the world; as Martin Luther King Jr. insisted throughout his life, "Justice is indivisible. Injustice anywhere is a threat to justice everywhere."

Traveling by bus throughout the country, we saw vast numbers of Israeli settlements ominously perched in the hills, bearing witness to the systematic confiscation of Palestinian land in flagrant violation of international law and UN resolutions. We met with refugees across the country whose families had been evicted from their homes by Zionist forces, their land confiscated, their villages and olive groves razed. As a consequence of this ongoing displacement, Palestinians comprise the largest refugee population in the world (over five million), the majority living within a hundred kilometers of their natal homes, villages, and farmlands. In defiance of UN Resolution 194, Israel has an active policy of opposing the right of Palestinian refugees to return to their ancestral homes and lands, on the grounds that they are not entitled to exercise the Israeli Law of Return, which is reserved for Jews.

In Sheikh Jarrah, a neighborhood in eastern occupied Jerusalem, we met an 88-year-old woman who was forcibly evicted in the middle of the night; she watched as the Israeli military moved settlers into her house a mere two hours later. Now living in the small back rooms of what was once her large family residence, she defiantly asserted that neither Israel's courts nor its military could ever force her from her home. In the city of Hebron, we were stunned by the conspicuous presence of Israeli soldiers, who maintain veritable conditions of apartheid for the city's Palestinian population of almost 200,000, as against its 700 Jewish settlers. We passed several Israeli checkpoints designed to control Palestinian movement on West Bank roads and along the Green Line. Throughout our stay, we met Palestinians who, because of Israel's annexation of Jerusalem and plans to remove its native population, have been denied entry to the holy city. We spoke to a man who lives ten minutes away from Jerusalem, but who has not been able to enter the city for twenty-seven years. The Israeli government thus continues to wage a demographic war for Jewish dominance over the Palestinian population.

We were never able to escape the jarring sight of the ubiquitous apartheid wall, which stands in contempt of international law and human rights principles. Constructed of 25-foot-high concrete slabs, electrified cyclone fencing, and winding razor wire, it almost completely encloses the West Bank, and extends well east of the Green Line marking Israel's pre-1967 borders. It snakes its way through ancient olive groves, destroying the beauty of the landscape, dividing communities and families, severing farmers from their fields, and depriving them of their livelihood. In Abu Dis, the wall cuts across the campus of al-Quds University, through the soccer field. In Qalqilya, we saw massive gates built to control the entry and access of Palestinians to their lands and homes, including a gated corridor through which Palestinians with increasingly rare Israeli-issued permits are processed as they enter Israel for work, sustaining the very state that has displaced them. Palestinian children are forced through similar corridors, lining up for hours twice each day to attend school. As one Palestinian colleague put it, "Occupied Palestine is the largest prison in the world."

An extensive prison system bolsters the occupation and suppresses resistance. Everywhere we went, we met people who had either been imprisoned themselves or had relatives who had been incarcerated. Of the 20,000 Palestinians locked inside Israeli prisons, at least 8,000 are political prisoners, and more than 300 are children. In Jerusalem, we met with members of the Palestinian Legislative Council who are being protected from arrest by the International Committee of the Red Cross. In Umm el-Fahem, we met with an Islamist leader just after his release from prison, and heard a riveting account of his experience on the Mavi Marmara and the 2010 Gaza Flotilla. The criminalization of their political activity, and that of the many Palestinians we met, was a constant and harrowing theme.

We also came to understand how overt repression is buttressed by deceptive representations of the State of Israel as the most developed social democracy in the region. As feminists, we deplore the Israeli practice of "pinkwashing"—the state's use of ostensible support for gender and sexual equality to dress up its occupation. In Palestine, we consistently found evidence and analyses of a more substantive approach to an indivisible justice. In Nablus, we met the president and the leadership of the Arab Feminist Union and several other women's groups, who spoke about the role and struggles of Palestinian women on several fronts. We visited one of the oldest women's empowerment centers in Palestine, In'ash al-Usra, and learned about various income-generating cultural projects. We also spoke with Palestinian Queers for BDS, young organizers who frame the struggle for gender and sexual justice as part and parcel of a comprehensive framework for self-determination and liberation. Feminist colleagues at Birzeit University, An-Najah University, and Mada al-Carmel spoke to us about the organic linkage of anticolonial resistance with gender and sexual equality, as well as about the transformative role Palestinian institutions of higher education play in these struggles.

We were continually inspired by the deep and abiding spirit of resistance in the stories people told us; in the murals inside buildings such as Ibdaa Center in Dheisheh Refugee Camp; in slogans painted on the apartheid wall in Qalqilya, Bethlehem, and Abu Dis; in the education of young children; and in the commitment to emancipatory knowledge-production. At our meeting with the Boycott National Committee—an umbrella alliance of over 200 Palestinian civil society organizations, including the General Union of Palestinian Women, the General Union of Palestinian Workers, the Palestinian Academic and Cultural Boycott of Israel, and the Palestinian Network of NGOs—we were humbled by their appeal: "We are not asking you for heroic action or to form freedom brigades. We are simply asking you not to be complicit in perpetuating the crimes of the Israeli state."

Therefore, we unequivocally endorse the BDS campaign. The purpose of this campaign is to pressure Israeli state-sponsored institutions to adhere to international law, basic human rights, and democratic principles as a condition for just and equitable social relations. We reject the argument that to criticize the State of Israel is anti-Semitic. We stand with Palestinians, an increasing number of Jews, and other human rights activists all over the world in condemning the flagrant injustices of the Israeli occupation.

We call upon all of our academic and activist colleagues in the US and elsewhere to join us by endorsing the BDS campaign and by working to end US financial support, at $8.2 million daily, for the Israeli state and its occupation. We call upon all people of conscience to engage in serious dialogue about Palestine, and to acknowledge connections between the Palestinian cause and other struggles for justice. Injustice anywhere is a threat to justice everywhere.

Angela Y. Davis
Rabab Abdulhadi
Ayoka Chenzira
Gina Dent
Melissa Garcia
Anna Romina Guevarra

Beverly Guy-Sheftall
Premilla Nadasen
Barbara Ransby
Chandra Talpade Mohanty
Waziyatawin

Part IV CASE FOR SANCTIONS AGAINST ISRAEL

18 WHY BOYCOTT ISRAEL?

Lisa Taraki and Mark LeVine

Mark LeVine: What is the "Boycott, Divestment, and Sanctions" movement, and how is it related to the academic and cultural boycott movement? How have both evolved in the past few years in terms of their goals and methods?

Lisa Taraki: The BDS movement can be summed up as the struggle against Israeli colonization, occupation, and apartheid. BDS is a rights-based strategy to be pursued until Israel meets its obligation to recognize the Palestinian people's inalienable right to self-determination and complies with the requirements of international law.

Within this framework, the academic and cultural boycott of Israel has gained considerable ground in the seven years since the launching of the Palestinian Campaign for the Academic and Cultural Boycott of Israel (PACBI) in 2004. The goals of the academic and cultural boycott call, like the aims of the Palestinian Civil Society Call for Boycott, Divestment and Sanctions issued in 2005, have remained consistent: to end the colonization of Palestinian lands occupied in 1967; to ensure full equality of Palestinian citizens of Israel and end the system of racial discrimination; and to realize the rights of Palestinian refugees to return to their homes and properties, as stipulated in UN Resolution 194.

The logic of the BDS movement has also remained consistent. The basic logic of BDS is the logic of pressure—not diplomacy, persuasion, or dialogue. Diplomacy as a strategy for achieving Palestinian rights has proved futile, due to the protection and immunity Israel enjoys from hegemonic world powers and those in their orbit.

Second, the logic of persuasion has also shown its bankruptcy, since no amount of "education" of Israelis about the horrors of occupation and other forms of oppression seems to have turned the tide. Dialogue between Palestinians and Israelis, which remains very popular among Israeli liberals and Western foundations and governments that fund the activities, has also failed miserably. Dialogue is often framed in terms of "two sides to the story," in the sense that each side must understand the pain, anguish, and suffering of the other, and accept the narrative of the other.

This presents the "two sides" as if they were equally culpable, and deliberately avoids acknowledgment of the basic colonizer–colonized relationship. Dialogue does not promote change, but rather reinforces the status quo, and in fact is mainly in the interest of the Israeli side of the dialogue, since it makes Israelis feel that they are doing something, while in fact they are not. The logic of BDS is the logic of pressure. And that pressure has been amplifying.

The Palestinian-led academic and cultural boycott is an institutional boycott; that is, it does not target individual scholars or artists. This point has also remained the same since the inception of the BDS movement. Yet it is important to state here that all Israeli universities and virtually the entire spectrum of Israeli cultural institutions are complicit in the state's policies, and are thereby legitimate targets of the boycott. Guidelines and criteria for boycott, however, have been elaborated since the founding of the movement, as more experience is gained on the ground, and in response to requests for guidance from conscientious academics and cultural workers wishing to respect the Palestinian boycott call. PACBI in particular expends a great deal of effort guiding and advising international solidarity activists. Consistency is achieved through adhering to the guidelines developed by PACBI, in cooperation with other elements in the Palestinian BDS movement.

World-renowned public intellectuals, academics, writers, artists, musicians, and other cultural workers have now endorsed the academic and cultural boycott call; their names are too many to note here, but the interested reader can consult the PACBI website. In addition, several campaigns for academic and cultural boycott have been established around the world: in the UK, the US, France, Pakistan, Lebanon, Germany, Norway, India, Spain, South Africa, and Australia, and many other countries. The newly established European Platform for the Academic and

Cultural Boycott of Israel (EPACBI) is an important coordinating body in Europe.

The lethal Israeli assault on the Gaza Strip in the winter of 2008–09 and the murder of Turkish solidarity activists aboard the Mavi Marmara in May 2010 served as further catalysts in the tremendous spread of BDS actions around the world, which include cancellations of artistic performances in Israel, protests against complicit Israeli institutions' performances abroad (such as the past and current protests around performances by the Israel Philharmonic Orchestra), and many more creative forms of protest and boycott of Israeli and Brand Israel projects and institutions.

ML: The Israelis have recently passed a so-called "anti-Boycott law," which opens Israelis who support any form of boycott, even if it's limited to settlement products, to significant civil penalties and lawsuits to force them to stop their actions. Can you comment on this whole discourse, especially the commentary in the Israeli press critical of it, claiming it represents a move against democracy, towards fascism, and similar responses which seem to suggest these are unprecedented measures?

LT: The Palestinian BDS movement is encouraged by the adoption of the logic of BDS, and boycott in particular, by sections of the Israeli left, and feels it has been vindicated in its argument that pressure—and not persuasion—is the best way to make Israelis realize that the system of occupation, apartheid, and colonialism must end. Having said this, I must note that there are at least two disturbing aspects to the new surge of activity surrounding the new anti-boycott law passed by the Israeli Knesset recently.

First, the boycott being defended by leftist and liberal Israelis targets institutions (such as the University Center of Samaria and the cultural center in Ariel) and products of the Israeli colonies in the West Bank only. This boycott, then, is silent on the complicity of all mainstream Israeli institutions—and indeed many industries, such as the weapons industry—in maintaining and legitimizing the structures of oppression.

Second, this boycott is often cast in terms of "saving Israeli democracy." It is thus an Israel-centered discourse and project, and its point of reference is neither Palestinian rights as stipulated by international law nor an acknowledgment that they are heeding the call of the Palestinians. One outstanding exception is the Israeli group Boycott from Within, which explicitly endorses the Palestinian BDS call and considers it the basic point of reference for its agenda of activism—such as urging artists and musicians not to perform in Israel, supporting a military embargo of Israel, advocating for different divestment campaigns, and many other activities that target all complicit Israeli institutions. Other Israeli groups, such as the Coalition of Women for Peace, ICAHD, and others have also endorsed the Palestinian BDS call publicly.

ML: What is your impression of what happened with the latest Gaza flotilla [in July 2011]? Some commentators have argued that the "successful" use of supposedly "nonviolent" strategies by the government of Israel to put pressure on other governments to stop the flotilla before it got anywhere near Gaza represents a defeat for the rising tide of nonviolent resistance, showing that the Israelis have learned the lessons and are now able to beat the activists at their own game.

LT: I don't agree with that assessment at all. I think the main aim of the flotillas, which has been to highlight, resist, and protest Israel's illegal siege of the Gaza Strip, has been realized, despite Israeli efforts to [bring] extreme pressure [to bear] against governments to prevent the vessels from sailing. The ridiculous Israeli response to the [July 2011] "Welcome to Palestine" campaign did more to publicize the campaign than would otherwise have happened.

You are right to frame the flotilla movement as a part of the international movement to isolate, expose, and place pressure upon Israel to respect international law and end its system of colonization, occupation, and apartheid. That this movement—still in its early stages—has achieved world recognition is attested to by the state of disarray in official Israeli and Zionist circles. Already, several conferences and strategy papers have been launched in Israel and abroad to counter what is being marketed as the "delegitimization threat." If BDS, the annual and growing Israeli Apartheid Week events, and other resistance actions such as the waves of flotillas are mere nuisances, I doubt that so much effort would be invested merely out of an "academic" interest in them. Strong-arm tactics with some governments may have prevented the flotillas from reaching Gaza, but the strength of the BDS movement—and other solidarity actions—is that they are built on people's initiatives. [These] cannot be easily suppressed, despite intimidation, legal threats and lawsuits, and other silencing tactics.

ML: In the BDS literature, there is a critique of those, like myself, who argue that anyone who wants to join BDS for Palestine should also adopt similar actions vis-à-vis other countries involved in massive systematic oppression and/or occupation (China, India, the US, to cite the most obvious examples), and that the need to think systemically is not merely an ethical imperative but a strategic one as well. Your response, when we last met in Ramallah, was that this strategy is utopian, that Palestinians have enough trouble getting people to engage in BDS merely against Israel, and that enlarging it would be untenable.

Can you explain how BDS can become more effective without thinking of joining with other movements against oppression and occupation that might call for a similar campaign?

LT: The BDS movement does operate with a conceptual framework, of course. This includes an analysis of global and regional power relations. BDS is predicated on the fact that the collusion of the hegemonic or major world powers of the so-called "international community" with Israeli impunity is the single most important factor that enables Israel to continue flouting international law. The hegemonic powers not only shield Israel from censure; they have also often turned a blind eye to grievous offences committed by their allies—but only when it serves their own interests. The inconsistency of US and European foreign policy is not something I need to stress, I believe. Plenty of rogue regimes continue to oppress and suppress their citizenry without international censure, as we all know.

What is important to note, however, is that when an oppressed people decide to appeal to the world to help them achieve self-determination and freedom through boycotts and other pressure mechanisms, as the vast majority of Palestinian civil society has done, then the response of all conscientious people would usually be to respect that appeal directly and immediately. It certainly was the case in South Africa. I don't think anyone had the temerity to suggest, during the anti-apartheid struggle in that country, that the existence of a full-throttle anti-imperialist movement would be the precondition for supporting the boycotts called for by the oppressed in South Africa, or that a boycott of the US, the UK, and indeed Israel, was the only principled course of action to take. That would have been a recipe for paralysis.

Israel, unlike many other oppressive states, enjoys the full support of the hegemonic powers, as I have noted. Precisely because of this, since there is no other impetus for change, it is incumbent upon forces that support justice to heed the Palestinian call. If there were a robust BDS movement in China or in Morocco today urging a boycott of the existing regimes, then certainly it would be an obligation to respect the call of the oppressed.

ML: It seems increasing numbers of diaspora and Israeli Jews are support-ing BDS, at least in principle—although, as you [suggested], what they imagine BDS is and what it actually means can differ significantly. How is the growing support impacting the success of BDS? Do you think it is pen-etrating more into Israeli society? And have you seen any changes in the way the Israeli government deals with nonviolent protest in the last year or so, given the increasing success of the movement?

LT: My comments concerning the Israeli boycott of the colonies in the West Bank are relevant in this context as well. I think most Israelis are very far from becoming convinced that BDS is an effective strategy for radical change of the status quo, and that is because Israeli society has no incen-tive to change the status quo. Only pressure, in the form of various BDS measures, can move the Israeli body politic. That is the logic of BDS, after all. As for the treatment of protests by the Israeli government and military, it's obvious that they are continuing to reassess their on-the-ground tactics in the face of the continuing escalation of protests, both by Palestinians and international and Israeli supporters. The use of force has been a constant for several decades now, and is nothing new. During the first Intifada, which was a form of civil resistance and disobedience, the response of the Israeli military was deadly and violent, just as it is today. The language of force will not be abandoned. That is the logic of a colonial power, after all.

ML: Can you elaborate a bit more on what the initiators of the BDS move-ment mean when they describe institutions, or artists and academics, who "serve Brand Israel." What is Brand Israel, and whose interests does it serve?

LT: Brand Israel is a worldwide campaign launched in 2005 by some agencies of the Israeli government and major pro-Israel groups internationally, primarily in the US. It's a diffuse and diverse effort, but the main idea behind it is to portray and promote Israel as a normal country for tourism, youth culture, enjoyment of the fine arts, sports, and all other "normal" and "civilized" pursuits. Public relations firms have played an important role in crafting the Israeli brand. In addition, Israeli consulates and embassies, as well as Jewish and Zionist organizations (such as Hillel in the US), are actively involved in promoting Israeli art, scientific accomplishments, and other "achievements" abroad. The modernity, diversity, and vitality of Israel are stressed in Brand Israel promotional activities.

I may add that the Israeli writer Yitzhak Laor has uncovered evidence of official Israeli sponsorship of Brand Israel–type activities, and with a price tag attached; in an article published in 2008, he revealed that any Israeli artist or cultural worker accepting financial support from the Israeli Foreign Ministry for exhibiting or showcasing his or her work abroad was obligated to sign a contract stipulating that he or she "undertakes to act faithfully, responsibly and tirelessly to provide the Ministry with the highest professional services. The service provider is aware that the purpose of ordering services from him is to promote the policy interests of the State of Israel via culture and art, including contributing to creating a positive image for Israel."

What this reveals, then, is that, in light of the bad press Israel has been receiving in past years, it has been deemed necessary to make sure that artists and other cultural workers—perhaps because of their reputation as idiosyncratic or even eccentric—know what is expected of them when they accept state funding of their tours abroad. They are supposed to act as "cultural ambassadors" for Israel, which, in large part, is to become apologists for Israeli policies and practices that oppress the Palestinians.

ML: In terms of the academic boycott, if I have a student who needs to come to Israel to develop her or his Hebrew in order to better understand the dynamics of the occupation and can only afford to do this through various programs such as Erasmus or Education Abroad Programs that involved affiliation with Israeli universities, or wants to do research at Israeli archives on the country's history that require students to be affiliated to Israeli universities to obtain research clearance, what is the official position of PACBI towards this?

LT: The PACBI guidelines for the implementation of the academic boycott, which apply to international academics and students, are clear: any interaction with Israeli universities, regardless of the content or form (studying there, accessing archives, giving a course, attending a conference, conducting research) violates the academic boycott if such an interaction entails official contact with the institution.

This can include accepting an invitation to attend a conference, registering for a course, accepting employment or agreeing to conduct seminars, or conducting research in affiliation with such institutions. While using a university facility such as a library does not strictly violate the boycott, doing so in the framework of affiliation with the university would.

Institutional study abroad schemes, research activity conducted in the framework of institutional cooperation agreements—such as the various EU-funded programs, including Erasmus Mundus—violate the boycott. Regarding the study of Hebrew, I think that the international options for pursuing that are very wide indeed; most universities in the West offer Hebrew instruction.

In general, conscientious scholars and students are encouraged to familiarize themselves with the logic and aims of the boycott and to abide by its spirit if situations other than the ones noted above are encountered. Since Palestinians—including academics and their representative body, the Palestinian Federation of Unions of University Employees—have called for an academic boycott, it becomes a responsibility of conscientious academics and students considering visiting the area for research or study purposes to become familiar with the context, which includes thinking seriously about the meaning of their affiliation with Israeli universities in light of the boycott call.

ML: Critics might say that this response is explicitly putting politics—however worthy—ahead of the advance of scholarship. For historians, for example, it is impossible to produce new knowledge without accessing archives. For student historians, their degree depends on their access to archives. If the archives are controlled by the state, then does the mere fact of using them mean complicity with the state?

LT: This is not putting politics above scholarship; it is about applying ethical principles to the practice of scholarship. No scholarly activity takes place in a vacuum, and every scholar must consider the consequences of his or her research strategies when pursuing scholarly activity. State control of some archives does not necessarily preclude using them, as I noted earlier; usually, it is enough to prove one's academic credentials to gain access to them. It is the same as using Israeli medical facilities or any other public service. The main issue is institutional affiliation.

ML: Are there any lessons from the so-called Arab Spring, or from other mass mobilizations globally against oppression in the past year or two, that can inform and even help the BDS movement and Palestinian resistance more broadly? Do the events of the last eight months give you hope, or is the situation in Palestine different enough—being at once a colonial situation and an internal struggle for democracy within both Israeli and Palestinian societies—that these other mass mobilizations can't really help beyond inspiring Palestinians to stay the course?

LT: The revolutionary spirit that has ignited the Arab world will no doubt make the question of Palestine more urgent than before, both in those countries that have begun the process of revolutionary transformation and those in which struggles for freedom and democracy are still unfolding. Once there are free and unrigged elections for new parliaments in Egypt and Tunisia, as well as other Arab countries, the new parliaments will have to be sensitive to the views of the people—unlike the situation that has hitherto prevailed.

It is well known that Palestine is an Arab question, and that includes widespread rejection of Israel's destructive role in the region. The forces of counterrevolution may try to combat popular sentiment, and there will be continuous contestation and ongoing struggles, but the policies of Arab countries will not be the same now that the revolutionary spirit has taken hold of the imagination of the Arab people.

ML: How do you think the sudden rise of the protest movement in Israel for "social justice" will impact the BDS movement and Palestinian resistance to the occupation more broadly? Especially with the likely coincidence of renewed protests in Israel next month [in September 2011] and a major Palestinian push for statehood at the UN, is there a space for Palestinians to make a significant intervention in the protest discourse inside Israel that helps reshape it towards broader ends? And if so, what role would BDS play in this?

LT: From all indications, the protest movement in Israel has nothing to say about justice for Palestinians, either as citizens or as occupied people. The Palestinian BDS movement does not address the Israeli public directly in order to persuade it or to appeal to its sense of justice. That is not the logic of BDS. It is up to Israeli political forces to make that connection and to influence their public. We expect that pro-BDS Israelis, however small their numbers might be, will be taking this up within their society.

19 ISRAEL: BOYCOTT, DIVEST, SANCTION

Naomi Klein

It's time. Long past time. The best strategy to end the increasingly bloody occupation is for Israel to become the target of the kind of global movement that put an end to apartheid in South Africa.

In July 2005 a huge coalition of Palestinian groups laid out plans to do just that. They called on "people of conscience all over the world to impose broad boycotts and implement divestment initiatives against Israel similar to those applied to South Africa in the apartheid era." The campaign Boycott, Divestment, and Sanctions—BDS for short—was born.

Every day that Israel pounds Gaza brings more converts to the BDS cause, and talk of ceasefires is doing little to slow the momentum.[1] Support is even emerging among Israeli Jews. In the midst of the assault, roughly 500 Israelis, dozens of them well-known artists and scholars, sent a letter to foreign ambassadors stationed in Israel. It calls for "the adoption of immediate restrictive measures and sanctions," and draws a clear parallel with the anti-apartheid struggle. "The boycott on South Africa was effective, but Israel is handled with kid gloves … This international backing must stop."

Yet many still can't go there. The reasons are complex, emotional, and understandable. And they simply aren't good enough. Economic sanctions are the most effective tools in the nonviolent arsenal. Surrendering them verges on active complicity. Here are the top four objections to the BDS strategy, followed by counterarguments.

---

1 Editor's note: This piece was written in January 2009, when Operation Cast Lead was underway.

1. PUNITIVE MEASURES WILL ALIENATE RATHER THAN PERSUADE ISRAELIS

The world has tried what used to be called "constructive engagement." It has failed utterly. Since 2006 Israel has been steadily escalating its criminality: expanding settlements, launching an outrageous war against Lebanon, and imposing collective punishment on Gaza through the brutal blockade. Despite this escalation, Israel has not faced punitive measures—quite the opposite. The weapons and $3 billion in annual aid that the US sends to Israel is only the beginning. Throughout this key period, Israel has enjoyed a dramatic improvement in its diplomatic, cultural, and trade relations with a variety of other allies. For instance, in 2007 Israel became the first non–Latin American country to sign a free-trade deal with Mercosur. In the first nine months of 2008, Israeli exports to Canada went up 45 percent. A new trade deal with the European Union is set to double Israel's exports of processed food. And on December 8, 2008, European ministers "upgraded" the EU–Israel Association Agreement, a reward long sought by Jerusalem.[2]

It is in this context that Israeli leaders started their latest war: confident they would face no meaningful costs. It is remarkable that over seven days of wartime trading, the Tel Aviv Stock Exchange's flagship index actually went up by 10.7 percent. When carrots do not work, sticks are needed.

2. ISRAEL IS NOT SOUTH AFRICA

Of course it isn't. The relevance of the South African model is that it proves that BDS tactics can be effective when weaker measures (protests, petitions, backroom lobbying) have failed. And there are indeed deeply distressing echoes: the color-coded IDs and travel permits, the bulldozed homes and forced displacement, the settler-only roads. Ronnie Kasrils, a prominent South African politician, has said that the architecture of segregation that he saw in the West Bank and Gaza in 2007 was "infinitely worse than apartheid."

---

2   On January 14, in response to Israel's aggression in Gaza, the EU called off its plans to upgrade the EU–Israel Association Agreement, a sign of growing understanding that political sanctions can be brought to bear to bring an end to the war.

3. WHY SINGLE OUT ISRAEL WHEN THE UNITED STATES, BRITAIN, AND OTHER WESTERN COUNTRIES DO THE SAME THINGS IN IRAQ AND AFGHANISTAN?

Boycott is not a dogma; it is a tactic. The reason the BDS strategy should be tried against Israel is practical: in a country so small and trade-dependent, it could actually work.

4. BOYCOTTS SEVER COMMUNICATION; WE NEED MORE DIALOGUE, NOT LESS

This one I will answer with a personal story. For eight years, my books have been published in Israel by a commercial house called Babel. But when I published *The Shock Doctrine*, I wanted to respect the boycott. On the advice of BDS activists, I contacted a small publisher called Andalus. Andalus is an activist press, deeply involved in the anti-occupation movement, and the only Israeli publisher devoted exclusively to translating Arabic writing into Hebrew. We drafted a contract that guarantees that all proceeds go to Andalus's work, and none to me. In other words, I am boycotting the Israeli economy but not Israelis.

Coming up with this plan required dozens of phone calls, emails, and instant messages, stretching from Tel Aviv to Ramallah to Paris to Toronto to Gaza City. My point is this: as soon as you start implementing a boycott strategy, dialogue increases dramatically. And why wouldn't it? Building a movement requires endless communicating, as many in the anti-apartheid struggle well recall. The argument that supporting boycotts will cut us off from one another is particularly specious given the array of cheap information technologies at our fingertips. We are drowning in ways to rant at one another across national boundaries. No boycott can stop us.

Just about now, many a proud Zionist is gearing up for major point-scoring: Don't I know that many of those very high-tech toys come from Israeli research parks, world leaders in infotech? True enough, but not all of them. Several days into Israel's Gaza assault, Richard Ramsey, the managing director of a British telecom company, sent an email to the Israeli tech firm MobileMax. "As a result of the Israeli government action in the last few days we will no longer be in a position to consider doing business with yourself or any other Israeli company."

When contacted by the *Nation*, Ramsey said his decision wasn't political.

"We can't afford to lose any of our clients, so it was purely commercially defensive."

It was this kind of cold business calculation that led many companies to pull out of South Africa two decades ago. And it is precisely the kind of calculation that is our most realistic hope of bringing justice, so long denied, to Palestine.

20 THE BOYCOTT WILL WORK: AN ISRAELI PERSPECTIVE

Ilan Pappe

I have been a political activist for most of my adult life. In all these years, I have believed deeply that the unbearable and unacceptable reality of Israel and Palestine could only be changed from within. This is why I have been ceaselessly devoted to persuading Jewish society—to which I belong and into which I was born—that its basic policy in the land was wrong and disastrous. As for so many others, the options for me were clear: I could either join politics from above, or counter it from below.

I began by joining the Labor Party in the 1980s, and then the Democratic Front for Peace and Equality (Hadash), when I declined an offer to join the Knesset. At the same time, I focused my energies on working alongside others within educational and peace NGOs, even chairing two such institutions: the left-Zionist Institute for Peace Studies in Givat Haviva, and the non-Zionist Emil Touma Institute for Palestinian Studies. In both circles, veteran and younger colleagues alike sought to create constructive dialogue with our compatriots, in the hope of influencing present policy for future reconciliation. It was mainly a campaign of information about crimes and atrocities committed by Israel since 1948, and a plea for a future based on equal human and civil rights.

For an activist, the realization that change from within is unattainable not only grows from an intellectual or political process, but is more than anything else an admission of defeat. And it was this fear of defeatism that prevented me from adopting a more resolute position for a very long time.

After almost thirty years of activism and historical research, I became convinced that the balance of power in Palestine and Israel pre-empted any possibility for a transformation within Jewish Israeli society in the foreseeable future. Though rather late in the game, I came to realize that the problem was not a particular policy or a specific government, but one more deeply rooted in the ideological infrastructure informing Israeli decisions on Palestine and the Palestinians ever since 1948. I have described this ideology elsewhere as a hybrid between colonialism and romantic nationalism.[1]

Today, Israel is a formidable settler-colonialist state, unwilling to transform or compromise, and eager to crush by whatever means necessary any resistance to its control and rule in historical Palestine. Beginning with the ethnic cleansing of 80 percent of Palestine in 1948, and Israel's occupation of the remaining 20 percent of the land in 1967, Palestinians in Israel are now enclaved in mega-prisons, bantustans, and besieged cantons, and singled out through discriminatory policies. Meanwhile, millions of Palestinian refugees around the world have no way to return home, and time has only weakened, if not annihilated, all internal challenges to this ideological infrastructure. The Israeli settler state continues to further colonize and uproot the indigenous people of Palestine, even as this book goes to press.

Admittedly, Israel is not a straightforward case study in colonialism,[2] nor can the solutions to either the 1967 occupation or the question of Palestine as a whole be easily described as decolonization. Unlike most colonialist projects, the Zionist movement had no clear metropolis, and because it far predates the age of colonialism, describing it in that way would be anachronistic. But these paradigms are still highly relevant to the situation, for two reasons. The first is that diplomatic efforts in Palestine since 1936 and the peace process that began in 1967 have only increased the number of Israeli settlements in Palestine, from less than 10 percent of Palestine in 1936 to over 90 per cent of the country today. Thus it seems that the message from the peace brokers, mainly Americans ever since 1970, is that peace can be achieved without any significant limit being placed on the settlements, or colonies, in Palestine. True, settlers have periodically been evicted from Gaza settlements and some other isolated outposts, but this did not alter the overall matrix of colonial control, with all its systematic daily abuses

---

1   Ilan Pappe, "Zionism as Colonialism: A Comparative View of Diluted Colonialism in Asia and Africa," *South Atlantic Quarterly* 107: 4 (2008): 611–33.
2   See Gabriel Piterberg, *The Returns of Zionism: Myths, Politics and Scholarship in Israel*, Verso, 2009.

of civil and human rights. The occupation of the West Bank and the Gaza Strip, the oppression of the Palestinians inside Israel, and the denial of the refugees' right of return will continue as long as these policies (occupation, oppression, and denial) were packaged as a comprehensive peace settlement to be endorsed by obedient Palestinian and Arab partners.

The second reason for viewing the situation through the lens of colonialism and anti-colonialism is that it allows us a fresh look at the raison d'être of the peace process. The basic objective, apart from the creation of two separate states, is for Israel to withdraw from areas it occupied in 1967. But this is contingent upon Israeli security concerns being satisfied, which Prime Minister Netanyahu has articulated as the recognition of Israel as a Jewish state, and the rest of Israel's political center has articulated as the existence of a demilitarized future Palestinian state only in parts of the occupied territories. The consensus is that, after withdrawal, the army will still keep an eye on Palestine from the Jewish settlement blocs, East Jerusalem, the Jordanian border, and the other side of the walls and fences surrounding the West Bank and the Gaza Strip.

Whether or not the Quartet, or even the present US administration, seeks a more comprehensive withdrawal and a more sovereign Palestinian state, no one in the international community has seriously challenged the Israeli demand that its concerns first be satisfied. The peace process only requires a change in the Palestinian agenda, leaving the Israeli agenda untouched. In other words, the message from abroad to Israel is that peace does not require any transformation from within. In fact, it even leaves Israel room for interpretation: the Israeli government, apprehensive of the reaction of hardline settlers, was unwilling to evict them from isolated posts in the occupied territories.

That even the weak Palestinian leadership has refused to accept this rationale has allowed the Israelis to claim that the Palestinians are stubborn and inflexible, and therefore that Israel is entitled to pursue unilateral policies to safeguard its national security (the infamous "ingathering policy," as coined by Ehud Olmert).[3]

Therefore, it seems safe to conclude that the peace process has actually deterred the colonizer and occupier from transforming its mentality and ideology. As long as the international community waits for the oppressed

3   Ilan Pappe, "Ingathering," *London Review of Books*, April 20, 2006: 15.

to transform their positions, while validating those upheld by the oppressor since 1967, this will remain the most brutal occupation the world has seen since World War II.

The annals of colonialism and decolonization teach us that an end to the military presence and occupation was a *conditio sine qua non* for meaningful negotiations between colonizer and colonized even to begin. An unconditional end to Israel's military presence in the lives of more than three million Palestinians should be the precondition for any negotiations, which can only develop when the relationship between the two sides is not oppressive but equal.

In most cases, occupiers have not decided to leave. They were forced out, usually through a prolonged and bloody armed struggle. This has been attempted with very little success in the Israel-Palestine conflict. In fewer cases, success was achieved by applying external pressure on the rogue power or state in the very last stage of decolonization. The latter strategy is more attractive. In any case, the Israeli paradigm of "peace" is not going to shift unless it is pressured from the outside, or forced to do so on the ground.

Even before one begins to define more specifically what such outside pressure entails, it is essential not to confuse the means (pressure) with the objective (finding a formula for joint living). In other words, it is important to emphasize that pressure is meant to trigger meaningful negotiations, not take their place.

So while I still believe that change from within is key to bringing about a lasting solution to the question of the refugees, the predicament of the Palestinian minority in Israel, and the future of Jerusalem, other steps must first be taken for this to be achieved.

What kind a pressure is necessary? South Africa has provided the most illuminating and inspiring historical example for those leading this debate, while, on the ground, activists and NGOs under occupation have sought nonviolent means both to resist the occupation and to expand the forms of resistance beyond suicide bombing and the firing of Qassam missiles from Gaza.

These two impulses produced the BDS campaign against Israel. It is not a coordinated campaign operated by some secret cabal. It began as a call from within the civil society under occupation, endorsed by other Palestinian groups, and translated into individual and collective actions worldwide.

These actions vary in focus and form, from boycotting Israeli products to severing ties with academic institutes in Israel. Some are individual displays of protest; others are organized campaigns. What they have in common is their message of outrage against the atrocities on the ground in Palestine—but the campaign's elasticity has made it into a broad process powerful enough to produce a new public mood and atmosphere, without any clear focal point.

For the few Israelis who sponsored the campaign early on, it was a definitive moment that clearly stated our position vis-à-vis the origins, nature, and policies of our state. But in hindsight, it also seems to have provided moral sponsorship, which has been helpful for the success of the campaign.

Supporting BDS remains a drastic act for an Israeli peace activist. It excludes one immediately from the consensus and from the accepted discourse in Israel. Palestinians pay a higher price for the struggle, and those of us who choose this path should not expect to be rewarded or even praised. But it does involve putting yourself in direct confrontation with the state, your own society, and quite often friends and family. For all intents and purposes, this is to cross the final red line—to say farewell to the tribe. This is why any one of us deciding to join the call should make such a decision wholeheartedly, and with a clear sense of its implications.

But there is really no other alternative. Any other option—from indifference, through soft criticism, and up to full endorsement of Israeli policy—is a willful decision to be an accomplice to crimes against humanity. The closing of the public mind in Israel, the persistent hold of the settlers over Israeli society, the inbuilt racism within the Jewish population, the dehumanization of the Palestinians, and the vested interests of the army and industry in keeping the occupied territories—all of these mean that we are in for a very long period of callous and oppressive occupation. Thus, the responsibility of Israeli Jews is far greater than that of anyone else involved in advancing peace in Israel and Palestine. Israeli Jews are coming to realize this fact, and this is why the number who support pressuring Israel from the outside is growing by the day. It is still a very small group, but it does form the nucleus of the future Israeli peace camp.

Much can be learned from the Oslo process. There, the Israelis employed the discourse of peace as a convenient way of maintaining the occupation (aided for a while by Palestinian leaders who fell prey to US–Israeli deception tactics). This meant that an end to the occupation was vetoed not only by the "hawks," but also the "doves," who were not really interested in stopping it. That is why concentrated and effective pressure on Israel needs to be applied by the world at large. Such pressure proved successful in the past, particularly in the case of South Africa; and pressure is also necessary to prevent the worst scenarios from becoming realities. After the massacre in Gaza in January 2009, it was hard to see how things could get worse, but they can—with no halt to the expansion of settlements, and continuing assaults on Gaza, the Israeli repertoire of evil has not yet been exhausted.

The problem is that the governments of Europe, and especially the US, are not likely to endorse the BDS campaign. But one is reminded of the trials and tribulations of the boycott campaign against South Africa, which emanated from civil societies and not from the corridors of power. In many ways, the most encouraging news comes from the most unlikely quarter: US campuses. The enthusiasm and commitment of hundreds of local students have helped in the last decade to bring the idea of divestment to US society—a society that was regarded as a lost cause by the global campaign for Palestine. They have faced formidable foes: both the effective and cynical AIPAC, and the fanatical Christian Zionists. But they offer a new way of engaging with Israel, not only for the sake of Palestinians, but also for Jews worldwide.

In Europe, an admirable coalition of Muslims, Jews, and Christians is advancing this agenda against fierce accusations of anti-Semitism. The presence of a few Israelis among them have helped to fend off these vicious and totally false allegations.

I do not regard the moral and active support of Israelis like myself as the most important ingredient in this campaign. But connections with progressive and radical Jewish dissidents in Israel are vital to the campaign. They are a bridge to a wider public in Israel, which will eventually have to be incorporated. Pariah status will hopefully persuade Israel to abandon its policies of war crimes and abuses of human rights. We hope to empower those on the outside who are now engaged in the campaign, and we are empowered ourselves by their actions. All of us, it seems, need clear targets, and to remain vigilant against simplistic generalizations about the boycott being against Israel for being Jewish, or against the Jews for being in Israel. That is simply not true. The millions of Jews in Israel must be reckoned with. It is a living organism that will remain part of any future solution. However, it is first our sacred duty to end the oppressive occupation and to prevent another Nakba—and the best means for achieving this is a sustained boycott and divestment campaign.

21 WHY A BOYCOTT?

John Berger

The boycott is an active protest against two forms of exclusion which have persisted, despite many other forms of protestations, for over sixty years—for almost three generations.

During this period the State of Israel has consistently excluded itself from any international obligation to heed UN resolutions or the judgment of any international court. It has already defied countless Security Council resolutions.[1]

As a direct consequence, seven million Palestinians have been excluded from the right to live as they wish on land internationally acknowledged to be theirs; and now increasingly, with every week that passes, they are being excluded from their right to any future at all as a nation.

As Nelson Mandela has pointed out, boycott is not a principle, it is a tactic depending upon circumstances. A tactic which allows people, as distinct from their elected but often craven governments, to apply a certain pressure on those wielding power in what they, the boycotters, consider to be an unjust or immoral way. (In white South Africa yesterday and in Israel today, the immorality was, or is being, coded, into a form of racist apartheid.)

---

1   Editor's note: In the original version of this piece, Berger wrote that Israel "has defied 246 Security Council resolutions." The actual number is unclear—in most cases, the language of the resolution is open to interpretation—but 246 is likely an overexaggeration, one inherited from John Pilger's *Freedom Next Time*. Stephen Zunes made very conservative estimate in 2002, excluding resolutions too open to interpretation, and came up with thirty-two ("United Nations Security Council Resolutions Currently Being Violated by Countries Other than Iraq," *Foreign Policy in Focus*, October 1, 2002).

Boycott is not a principle. When it becomes one, it itself risks becoming exclusive and racist. No boycott, in our sense of the term, should be directed against an individual, a people, or a nation as such. A boycott is directed against a policy and the institutions which support that policy, either actively or tacitly. Its aim is not to reject, but to bring about change.

How to apply a cultural boycott? A boycott of goods is a simpler proposition, but in this case it would probably be less effective, and speed is of the essence, because the situation is deteriorating every month (which is precisely why some of the most powerful world political leaders, hoping for the worst, keep silent).

How to apply a boycott? For academics it's perhaps a little clearer—a question of declining invitations from state institutions and explaining why. For invited actors, musicians, jugglers, or poets it can be more complicated. I'm convinced, in any case, that its application should not be systematized; it has to come from a personal choice based on a personal assessment.

For instance: an important mainstream Israeli publisher today is asking to publish three of my books. I intend to apply the boycott with an explanation. There exist, however, a few small, marginal Israeli publishers who expressly work to encourage exchanges and bridges between Arabs and Israelis, and if one of them should ask to publish something of mine, I would unhesitatingly agree and furthermore waive any question of author's royalties. I don't ask other writers supporting the boycott to come necessarily to exactly the same conclusion. I simply offer an example.

What is important is that we make our chosen protests together, and that we speak out, thus breaking the silence of connivance maintained by those who claim to represent us, and thus ourselves representing, briefly by our common action, the incalculable number of people who have been appalled by recent events but lack the opportunity of making their sense of outrage effective.

22 BOYCOTT ISRAEL

Neve Gordon

Israeli newspapers this summer are filled with angry articles about the push for an international boycott of Israel. Films have been withdrawn from Israeli film festivals, Leonard Cohen is under fire around the world for his decision to perform in Tel Aviv, and Oxfam has severed ties with a celebrity spokesperson—a British actress who also endorses cosmetics produced in the occupied territories. Clearly, the campaign to use the kind of tactics that helped put an end to the practice of apartheid in South Africa is gaining many followers around the world. Not surprisingly, many Israelis—even peaceniks—are not signing on. A global boycott inevitably elicits charges, however specious, of anti-Semitism. It also brings up questions of a double standard (why not boycott China for its egregious violations of human rights?) and the seemingly contradictory position of approving a boycott of one's own nation.

It is indeed not a simple matter for me as an Israeli citizen to call on foreign governments, regional authorities, international social movements, faith-based organizations, unions, and citizens to suspend cooperation with Israel. But today, as I watch my two boys playing in the yard, I am convinced that it is the only way that Israel can be saved from itself.

I say this because Israel has reached a historic crossroads, and times of crisis call for dramatic measures. I say this as a Jew who has chosen to raise his children in Israel, who has been a member of the Israeli peace camp for almost thirty years, and who is deeply anxious about the country's future.

The most accurate way to describe Israel today is as an apartheid state. For more than forty-two years, Israel has controlled the land between the Jordan Valley and the Mediterranean Sea. Within this region, about six million Jews and close to five million Palestinians reside. Out of this population, 3.5 million Palestinians and almost half a million Jews live in the areas Israel occupied in 1967—and yet, while these two groups live in the same area, they are subject to totally different legal systems. The Palestinians are stateless and lack many of the most basic human rights. By sharp contrast, all Jews—whether they live in the occupied territories or in Israel—are citizens of the state of Israel.

The question that keeps me up at night, both as a parent and as a citizen, is how to ensure that my two children, as well as the children of my Palestinian neighbors, do not grow up in an apartheid regime.

There are only two moral ways of achieving this goal.

The first is the one-state solution: offering citizenship to all Palestinians, and thus establishing a binational democracy within the entire area controlled by Israel. Given the demographics, this would amount to the demise of Israel as a Jewish state; for most Israeli Jews, it is anathema.

The second means of ending our apartheid is through the two-state solution, which entails Israel's withdrawal to its pre-1967 borders (with possible one-for-one land swaps), the division of Jerusalem, and a recognition of the Palestinian right of return, with the stipulation that only a limited number of the 4.5 million Palestinian refugees would be allowed to return to Israel, while the rest could return to the new Palestinian state.

Geographically, the one-state solution appears much more feasible, because Jews and Palestinians are already totally enmeshed; indeed, "on the ground," the one-state solution (in an apartheid manifestation) is a reality.

Ideologically, the two-state solution is more realistic, because fewer than 1 percent of Jews and only a minority of Palestinians support binationalism.

For now, despite the concrete difficulties, it makes more sense to alter the geographic realities than the ideological ones. If at some future date the two peoples decide to share a state, they can do so, but currently this is not something they want.

So, if the two-state solution is the way to stop the apartheid state, then how does one achieve this goal?

I am convinced that outside pressure is the only answer. Over the last three decades, Jewish settlers in the occupied territories have dramatically increased their numbers. The myth of the united Jerusalem has led to the creation of an apartheid city where Palestinians are not citizens and lack basic services. The Israeli peace camp has gradually dwindled, so that today it is almost nonexistent, and Israeli politics are moving increasingly to the extreme right.

It is therefore clear to me that the only way to counter the apartheid trend in Israel is through massive international pressure. The words and condemnations from the Obama administration and the European Union have yielded few results—only a limited and temporary settlement freeze, and no decision to withdraw from the occupied territories.

Consequently, I have decided to support the BDS movement that was launched by Palestinian activists in July 2005, and has since garnered widespread support around the globe. The objective is to ensure that Israel respects its obligations under international law, and that Palestinians are granted the right to self-determination.

In Bilbao, Spain, in 2008, a coalition of organizations from all over the world formulated the ten-point BDS campaign, meant to pressure Israel in a "gradual, sustainable manner that is sensitive to context and capacity." For example, the effort begins with sanctions on and divestment from Israeli firms operating in the occupied territories, followed by actions against those that help sustain and reinforce the occupation in a visible manner. Along similar lines, artists who come to Israel in order to draw attention to the occupation are welcome, while those who just want to perform are not.

Nothing else has worked. Putting massive international pressure on Israel is the only way to guarantee that the next generation of Israelis and Palestinians—my two boys included—does not grow up in an apartheid regime.

23 YES TO BDS! AN ANSWER TO URI AVNERY

Michael Warschawski

The call for BDS has finally reached Israeli public opinion. The decision of Norway to divest capital from Israeli corporations involved in settlement-building made the difference, and provided the first big success for that important campaign. Moreover, the group of Israelis supporting BDS under the label "Boycott from Within" is gaining some momentum, thanks, among other things, to a public appeal by Naomi Klein to Israeli activists when she came to Tel Aviv to launch the Hebrew version of her *Shock Doctrine*.

The fact that there is an Israeli voice—albeit small—in support of the international BDS campaign makes a difference, if only because it helps to disarm the infamous accusation of anti-Semitism raised by the Israeli propaganda machine against everyone who dares to criticize the colonial policies of the Jewish State. Moreover, as I will argue below, the Israeli supporters of BDS are in fact expressing the true and long-term interests of the Israeli people.

Reading two texts written recently by Uri Avnery,[1] who criticizes BDS, convinced me that it was important to clarify the importance of this campaign, and why it should be supported by as many Israelis as possible. I sometimes disagree with Avnery's opinions, but I have great respect for the man, the journalist, the activist, and the analyst. Since the bankruptcy of Peace Now during the Oslo process, we have been closely active together; I might even say that we became friends. This is why I feel compelled to react to his rejection of the BDS campaign.

---

1   Uri Avnery is a veteran political activist and journalist, former Member of the Knesset, and former chief editor of *HaOlam HaZeh* weekly.

Avnery writes: "I have no argument with people who hate Israel. That's entirely their right. I just don't think that we have any common ground for discussion. I would only like to point out that hatred is a very bad advisor. Hatred leads nowhere, but to more hatred." He then adds that the comparison with South Africa is misplaced.

We have no debate on these two issues. Hatred is indeed a very bad advisor, and I will be the last to disagree with him. I know also that he will agree with me if I add that, in our political context, hatred is understandable. And of course Israel is not South Africa, and each concrete reality is different from every other. Nevertheless, these two countries have some similarities: both are racist states with different kinds of apartheid systems (the literal meaning of apartheid being "structural separation"). Both countries were established as "European states" in a national/ethnic environment composed of non-Europeans who were considered to constitute a hostile environment—and rightly so.

We also agree—and this is even more important—that in order to achieve substantial results in our struggle, we need to build a coalition between the Palestinian national resistance, the Israeli anti-occupation forces, and the international solidarity movement. Ten years ago, I called it "the winning triangle."

I willingly follow Avnery until this point, but then our paths begin to part. First, he misrepresents his political opponents. "[They] have despaired of the Israelis," he says, referring to the supporters of the BDS. If it were indeed so, then why do Israeli BDS campaigners spend so much of their time building, together with Uri Avnery, an Israeli movement against war, occupation, and colonization? The true debate is not between those who aim to "change the Israeli society" and those who do not, but about how to go about it, and for what purpose.

Avnery's political goal is "an Israeli-Palestinian peace," by which he means a compromise that would satisfy the majority of the two communities, on a symmetrical basis (in another important article, he called it "truth against truth"). Such symmetry is the result of another key political assumption held by Avnery: namely, that the conflict in Palestine is a conflict between two national movements with equal legitimacy.

Many supporters of the BDS campaign disagree with both assumptions: our goal is not peace as such, because "peace" in itself has no meaning (almost every war in modern history was initiated under the pretext of achieving peace). Peace is always the reflection of relations of forces when one side cannot impose on the other what it considers its legitimate rights. Unlike Avnery, our goal is the fulfillment of certain values, including basic individual and collective rights, an end of domination and oppression, decolonization, equality, and as much justice as possible. Within that framework, we obviously may support "peace initiatives" that can reduce the level of violence and/or achieve a certain measure of rights. In our strategy, however, this support of peace initiatives is not a goal in itself, but merely a means to achieve a series of values and rights.

That difference between "peace" and "justice" is connected to our disagreement with Avnery's second assumption—namely, of the symmetry between two equally legitimate national movements.

For us, Zionism is not a national liberation movement but a colonial movement, and the State of Israel is and has always been a settler-colonial state. Peace—or, better yet, justice—cannot be achieved without a total decolonization (one can say de-Zionization) of the Israeli state; it is a precondition for the fulfillment of the legitimate rights of the Palestinians—refugees, those living under military occupation, and the second-class citizens of Israel. Whether the final result of that decolonization will be a "one-state" solution, two democratic states (i.e. not a "Jewish state"), a federation, or any other institutional structure is secondary, and will ultimately be decided by the struggle itself, and by the level of participation of Israelis, if any.

Avnery is accordingly wrong when he states that our divergence is about "one state" or "two states." As explained above, the divergence is on the questions of rights and decolonization, and the principle of full equality. The form of the solution is, in my opinion, irrelevant as long as we are speaking about a solution in which the two peoples are living in freedom (without colonial relationships) and equality.

Another important divergence with Avnery concerns the Israeli psyche and the dialectics between the Palestinian national liberation agenda and the so-call Israeli peace camp. While it is obvious that the Palestinian national movement needs as many Israeli allies as possible to achieve liberation as quickly as possible, and with as little suffering as possible for both people, one cannot expect the Palestinian movement to wait until Avnery and the other Israeli anticolonialists can convince the majority of the Israeli public that colonialism is wrong. First, because popular national movements do not wait to fight oppression and colonialism, and, second, because history has taught us that changes within the colonialist society have always been the result of the liberation struggle, and not the other way round. When the price for occupation becomes too high, growing numbers of people will understand that it is not worth continuing.

Generally speaking, one can say that the Jewish Israeli psyche is shaped by two realities—or, more accurately, one reality and one perception of reality. The first is the colonial reality of Israeli existence, the feeling of being surrounded by a hostile environment which, to say the least, feels threatened by the dynamics of Zionist colonization. The other factor shaping Israeli collective mentality is anti-Semitism (real and constructed), strengthened by the experience of the Nazi judeocide.

Like any other people, the Israelis want to be accepted, even loved. They have, however, a twofold difficulty: to pay the price for this acceptance—i.e. to behave in a civilized manner—and to trust the other to normalize relations with them.

Yes, a hand extended in the name of coexistence is needed, but together with an iron fist fighting for rights and freedom. The failure of the Oslo process confirms a very old lesson of history: that any attempt for reconciliation before the fulfillment of rights strengthens the continuation of the relationship of colonial domination. Without a price to be paid, why should Israelis stop colonization? Why should they risk a deep internal crisis?

This is precisely why the BDS campaign is so relevant: it offers an international framework to act in order to help the Palestinian people achieve their legitimate rights, both on the institutional level (states and international institutions) and on the level of civil society. On the one hand, the campaign addresses the international community, calling upon it to impose sanctions on a state that is systematically violating international law, UN resolutions, the Geneva Conventions, and signed agreements. On the other hand, it calls upon international civil society to act, as individuals as well as social movements (trade unions, parties, local councils, popular associations, and so on) to boycott goods, official representatives, and institutions that represent the colonial State of Israel.

All three strategies—boycott, divestment, and sanctions—will eventually pressure the Israeli people, pushing them to understand that occupation and colonization have a price, and that violating the international rules may, sooner or later, make the State of Israel a pariah, unwelcome among the civilized community of nations—not unlike South Africa in the last decades of apartheid. Precisely in this sense, and disproving Avnery's claim, BDS is addressed to the Israeli public. At this historical juncture it is the only way to provoke a change in Israel's attitude toward occupation and colonization. If one compares it to the anti-apartheid BDS campaign that took twenty years to start bearing real fruit, one cannot but be surprised how efficient the anti-Israeli occupation campaign has already been—even in Israel, we can already witness its first effects.

The BDS campaign was initiated by a broad coalition of Palestinian political and social movements. No Israeli who claims to support the national rights of the Palestinian people can, decently, turn his or her back on this campaign. After having claimed for years that "armed struggle is not the way," it will be outrageous if this strategy too is disqualified by those Israeli activists. On the contrary, Israelis interested in a just peace should join the Boycott from Within campaign in order to provide an Israeli backup to that Palestinian initiative. It is the minimum we can do; it is the minimum we should do.

24 *LOOKING FOR ERIC*, MELBOURNE FESTIVAL, AND THE CULTURAL BOYCOTT

Ken Loach, Rebecca O'Brien, and Paul Laverty

When we decided to pull our film *Looking for Eric* from the Melbourne Film Festival following our discovery that the festival was in part sponsored by the Israeli state, we wrote to the festival's director, Richard Moore, with our detailed reasons. Continually he has dishonestly misrepresented us and does so again[1] by stating that "to allow the personal politics of *one* filmmaker to proscribe a festival position … goes against the grain of what festivals stand for." Later, "Loach's demands were beyond the pale." Once again, Mr. Moore, this decision was taken by three filmmakers (director, producer, writer), not in some private abstract bubble, but after long discussion between us and in response to a call for a cultural boycott, including film festivals, from a wide spectrum of Palestinian civil society, including writers, filmmakers, cultural workers, human rights groups, journalists, trade unions, women's groups, student organizations, and many more besides. As Moore should know by now, the Palestine Campaign for the Academic and Cultural Boycott of Israel was launched in Ramallah in April 2004, and its aims, reasons, and constituent parts are widely available on the internet. This in turn is part of a much wider international movement for BDS against the Israeli state.

Why this growing international movement? Over the last sixty years Israel, backed by the US, has shown contempt for hundreds of UN resolutions and for the Geneva Convention, and has continually broken international law. It has demonstrated itself to be a violent and ruthless state, as was clearly shown by the recent massacres in Gaza, and was even prepared to challenge

---

1   Richard Moore, "Censorship Has No Place in Film," *Guardian*—Comment Is Free, August 27, 2009, at guardian.co.uk.

international law further by use of phosphorous weapons. It flouts public opinion around the world, and no clearer example can be found than its determination to continue to build the wall through Palestinian territories despite the recent decision of the International Court of Justice. What does the international community do? Nothing but complain. What does the US do? It continues to voice its "grave concern" while subsidizing the Israeli state to the tune of some three billion dollars a year. Meanwhile, "on the ground" (a good title for a film), Israeli settlers continue, day by day, to take over more Palestinian homes and lands, making a viable Palestinian homeland impossible. Normal life, with basic human rights, is now a virtual dream for most Palestinians.

Given the failure of international law and the impunity of the Israeli state, there is no alternative but for ordinary citizens to try their best to fill the breach. Desmond Tutu has said, "The end of apartheid stands as one of the crowning accomplishments of the past century, but we would not have succeeded without the help of the international community—in particular the divestment movement of the 1980s. Over the past six months, a similar movement has taken shape, this time aiming at the end of the Israeli occupation."

Naomi Klein makes a very good point when she says that there is no exact equivalency between Israel and South Africa. She says,

> the question is not "Is Israel the same as South Africa?"; it is "Do Israel's actions meet the international definition of what apartheid is?" And if you look at those conditions which includes the transfer of people, multiple tiers of law, official state segregation, then you see that, yes, it does meet that definition—which is different than saying it is South Africa. No two states are the same. It's not the question, it's a distraction.[2]

Not long after the Gaza invasion, we spoke to the head of the human rights organization there, who told us that the Israelis were refusing enough chemicals to adequately treat the civilian water supply—a clear example of vindictive collective punishment delivered to one half of the population.

Neve Gordon, a Jewish political professor teaching in an Israeli university,

---

2   "Transcript of Naomi Klein Lecture in Ramallah," July 10, 2009, at bdsmovement.net.

recently commented, "The most accurate way to describe Israel today is as an apartheid state."[3] As a result, he too is supporting the international campaign of divestment and boycott. Maybe in the future there will be grave contradictions and grey areas as to whether a particular project is hit by the cultural boycott or not, but we feel duty bound to take advice from those living at the sharp end inside the country. We would also encourage other filmmakers and actors invited to festivals to check for Israeli-state backing before attending, and if it pertains, to respect the boycott. Israeli filmmakers are not the target. State involvement is. In the grand scale of things it is a tiny contribution to a growing movement, but the example of South Africa should give us heart.

Ken Loach (director)
Rebecca O'Brien (producer)
Paul Laverty (writer)
August 27, 2009

---

3   See Chapter 22.

25 AN EFFECTIVE WAY OF SUPPORTING THE STRUGGLE

Ra'anan Alexandrowicz and Rebecca Vilkomerson

Ra'anan Alexandrowicz is a highly respected Israeli filmmaker. His previous films include *The Inner Tour*, a documentary from 2001 that follows a group of Palestinians in the West Bank who take an Israeli tour in order to visit their home villages; and *James' Journey to Jerusalem*, a dark comedy about the spiritual and physical journey of an African migrant worker in Israel. His most recent movie, *The Law in These Parts*, won the Best New Documentary award at the Jerusalem Film Festival in July 2011, where he spoke out against Israel's anti-boycott law, which had just passed in the Knesset, making it illegal for Israeli citizens to advocate a boycott of Israel or its settlements. *The Law in These Parts* is a stunning indictment of the system of Israeli military law, used primarily in the West Bank. Developed over decades of occupation, in the film it is deconstructed by interviews with former Israeli military judges.

Ra'anan also takes part in anti-occupation activities, primarily with Ta'ayush in the South Hebron Hills and in Silwan, East Jerusalem. For several years now, we have been discussing BDS as an effective strategy, especially in the context of Israeli artists. It was not until the Israeli anti-boycott law was first proposed that Ra'anan decided that he would endorse the Palestinian boycott call (should the law be passed), despite his discomfort with some aspects of BDS. In August, we talked via Skype about Ra'anan's next steps, and how to act with integrity in the current circumstances as an Israeli.

Rebecca Vilkomerson: Why, until now, have you held back from endorsing BDS efforts?

Ra'anan Alexandrowicz: As an Israeli, the idea of "holding the stick" from both ends is difficult for me. I live on the easy side of this conflict. Anyone who lives in any society exists somewhere in the "pyramid of privileges" of that society. When I talk about society in this country I don't mean just the Jewish society. I mean everyone who exists here: Jewish, Muslim, occupier, occupied, "legal" or "illegal." The reality is that I am from the part of society that enjoys the most freedom and prosperity in the current political situation. The reality is that I benefit from the current political order even if I don't agree with it at all.

I am Israeli; I get the privileges of an Israeli; that's what I am. One can argue that in terms of basics, like paying taxes, getting water or education for your children, it is unavoidable. But when you talk about a filmmaker, or an academic like my partner—people who have extra privileges which only a very small part of the society enjoys—there is an active choice to participate in it or not; and I do. I get a lot of privileges from living in this society, and I use them. The best example is using public funds to make films, or the fact that for three years I have financially benefited from a scholarship that my partner gets from the state while she pursues her PhD. Therefore I feel there is a double standard, or a contradiction in on the one hand taking what society offers me, but on the other hand trying to be on the right side of history.

Another privilege I had, as a Jewish Israeli, was to not pay a price for cultivating ideas that contest the ideology of the state. For people like me, the Israeli system allows a wide range of freedom of speech, but this is definitely a privilege not everyone in society has.

RV: What do you consider to be the best way to act in solidarity with the Palestinian struggle?

RA: To participate in Palestinian actions that you agree with, that are coherent for you—which feel right for you to participate in. I think it is important to share the struggle and the risk. There are two main reasons why we don't always live up to our expectations of ourselves when we "struggle" in solidarity. One is that sometimes we won't so willfully give up our privileges—or our children's privileges, for that matter—nor willfully expose ourselves to the highest risk. The truth is that most Israelis who are engaged in the struggle are struggling from a different position than the Palestinians, not with our backs to the wall, but from a choice, and it creates many differences in what we will or will not do.

And then there is the second reason—which is perhaps an outcome of the first. Sometimes we as Israelis are not welcome to be part of the struggle. I feel that the majority of Palestinian society does not welcome Israeli solidarity anymore. There is a Palestinian saying: "One hand slaps you, and the other puts your hat back on…"

But, to get back to your question, the best way to participate in the Palestinian struggle is to do as much as possible what Palestinians you agree with ask of you.

RV: Through the BDS call, Palestinians have been asking Israelis of good faith to publicly support their efforts since 2005. What has changed for you?

RA: If we are talking about the BDS campaign, when I look at it from the Palestinian perspective, it is totally legitimate and logical and timely to work in this direction now. I legitimize it totally, as an Israeli.

But I also have reservations about the coherence of the stand of supporters of BDS. I talked about my perspective as an Israeli, but now I am referring to the international supporter, the average one—not the person who devotes his life to the Palestinian struggle, or the person that actually could have worked with Israeli funding, or [done] business with the Israeli government, and decided not to do that and pay a real price. I am referring to the aware, conscious, liberal person who is what I think most international supporters are. Endorsing the boycott at the click of a button is somehow an easy action to take, isn't it? Maybe I don't know enough; maybe it's a hard action to take and I don't realize it from here. But I am sure there is some inconsistency involved. Theoretically, an action is legitimate if you would apply the same standards on other similar cases, and I wonder if BDS supporters in the US and UK struggle with this?

You can take on BDS because it is timely and it can have an effect on Israel, but you should probably, in theory, be boycotting your own country too. And this of course would be useless (and perhaps less comfortable). So it is set aside as "impractical." So, looking at it from this perspective, boycotting is not some moral stand. It is a weapon used in a war of resistance. You use the most effective tool, because the situation demands it.

So even if I understand that this is not a moral position but a tactic—a tactic I legitimize and I understand and see as timely, as an Israeli—until our new law passed, I preferred to stay purely on the boycotted side. That was my responsibility, given my role in society. It is my job to be boycotted, because I willingly take the privileges this society offers me.

The new law changes this situation. Now the people who endorsed the BDS call are in legal danger. Endorsing the call, which is a legitimate political stance, became illegal. So now the balance between what I felt was hypocrisy—to take advantage of what this society offers and yet denounce its policies—and the need for solidarity has shifted, so that solidarity has become more important.

So when I spoke publicly about this law, I said that this is a law we must break. Just like other laws that must be broken—the law of entry into Israel, the Nakba law, the law of the acceptance committees.

The Nakba law and some of the aspects of the entrance law—these are the kind of laws that prove that, while the state wishes to define itself as "Jewish and democratic," the correct definition is actually that it is a democracy for Jews. And the boycott law goes even further—it is a democracy for anyone who is willing to accept racist rules and support expansionism.[1]

RV: In the US, there are more and more attempts to distinguish between boycotts of the settlements or the occupation, and boycott of Israel generally.

RA: In terms of my personal position, I do see a difference. When it comes to the settlements, it is in terms of what I can do. As an Israeli I already actively choose as much as possible not to enjoy the fruits of the occupation. I won't go hiking in the West Bank, I try not to consume things manufactured there, I won't take my child to a friend's house if it is in the West Bank; I've been offered to screen films for payment in the West Bank for settlers, but I wouldn't. Boycotting the settlements is coherent with how I live. I refused to do military reserve duty in the West Bank before I refused totally.

---

1   The Nakba law, passed by the Knesset on March 22, 2011, prohibits state funding for any organizations that mourn the displacement and expulsion of Palestinians associated with the creation of the state of Israel in 1948.

When I try to see it from an American perspective, I guess there is a difference between the two types of boycott. I can imagine that the settlement boycott is endorsed by people who are critical of our politics but feel a part of Israel somehow. Perhaps I am wrong about this. But the interesting thing is that the law (some aspects of which could apply to foreign nationals) actually erases the line between the two groups as far as the Israeli perspective goes, and makes boycotting the settlements equal to boycotting Israel.

RV: What are the best ways, in your view, for internationals to support the Palestinian struggle?

RA: The way I analyze the situation now, I think endorsing BDS is a very effective way of supporting the Palestinian struggle. Academic and cultural boycott is the one thing that really seems to work now because it is a) very easy to do, and b) it actually hurts us Israelis, and it hurts Israel. That's why it's effective. Of course, to be involved in direct action and changing people's minds is important.

RV: Do you have any specific concerns about how the BDS movement will affect Israel or Israelis?

RA: Israelis who refute the boycott or are offended by it can't say that other measures weren't tried. It seems that we don't move unless we're pushed very strongly.

I think the passing of the anti-boycott law is proof that the people who initiated the BDS movement knew what they were doing. It unmasks the Israeli government, and will eventually make the Israeli society look in the mirror. And that means it is effective.

I imagine there are people who must feel some satisfaction with every escalation of the boycott, and I can see the positive political aspect, but it doesn't give me such a great feeling; in fact it makes me sad. But the important thing, the highest priority, is to bring some change to this very sick political situation.

I see the new law as a bad sign in the sense that I'm afraid of what is coming. It's another one of the signs that the near future will bring some frightful things with it. As the pressure mounts it will be directed inward, toward the Palestinians and toward the Israeli "traitors." We see more and more signs that this is what will happen, and this is both sad and frightening. I am not sure that, once tension mounts and the next round of heightened violence erupts, it can be controlled. I am not sure that these processes will be undone so easily, and I am not even sure what they will actually lead to. But on the other hand, because I don't see any chance for things advancing without a crisis, then I guess that in this sense it's an indication that at least something is moving.

26 LIGHTING A TORCH WITHIN: ANTI-COLONIAL ISRAELI SUPPORT FOR BDS[1]

Omar Barghouti

The historic call by Palestinian civil society for boycott, divestment and sanctions against Israel until it fully complies with its obligations under international law contains a rarely noticed dimension inspired by struggle against South African apartheid. It invites "conscientious Israelis to support this Call, for the sake of justice and genuine peace,"[2] thereby confirming that principled anti-colonial Jewish Israelis who support the Palestinian people's inalienable right to self-determination, and who uphold freedom, justice, and equality for all as the bases for a just, comprehensive, and sustainable peace, are regarded as partners in the struggle.

Principled Israeli anti-colonialists committed to Palestinian rights as stipulated in international law have played a significant and growing role in the struggle for Palestinian rights, despite their still small numbers. Many of them, aside from their unequivocal commitment to comprehensive Palestinian rights, realize that Israelis cannot possibly have normal lives without first shedding their colonial character and recognizing Palestinian rights. The words of the Brazilian educator, Paulo Freire, on how the oppressed can also re-humanize their oppressors, are relevant here:

> Because it is a distortion of being more fully human, sooner or later being less human leads the oppressed to struggle against those who made them so. In

---

1   Parts of this chapter are based on text published in Omar Barghouti, *Boycott, Divestment, Sanctions: The Global Struggle for Palestinian Rights*, Haymarket, 2011.
2   See Chapter 4.

order for this struggle to have meaning, the oppressed must not, in seeking to regain their humanity (which is a way to create it), become in turn oppressors of the oppressors, but rather restorers of the humanity of both.[3]

In 2009, Boycott! Supporting the Palestinian BDS Call from Within (or "Boycott from Within," for short),[4] a growing movement in Israel, fully adopted the Palestinian call for BDS, and committed to its principles, showing the way for genuine Israeli opposition to occupation and apartheid. Israeli groups that have endorsed the BDS call include, among others, the Alternative Information Center (AIC),[5] the Israeli Committee Against House Demolition (ICAHD),[6] and Who Profits from the Occupation? (a project of the Coalition of Women for Peace),[7] all of which have played vital roles in providing political, moral, and often logistical and information support to the global BDS movement. Who Profits?, for instance, has kept an updated database of Israeli and international corporations involved in the occupation, a list that is often used by stockholders of pension funds, banks, and international institutions to select their BDS targets and build their cases against them.

In contrast to this principled Israeli support for BDS, some writers and academics on the Zionist "left" in Israel and the West have a tendency to frame the struggle as Israel-centric. They focus on ending the occupation alone, thus ignoring the basic rights of the majority of the Palestinian people, and they base their support for withdrawing from most of the occupied Palestinian territory on the argument that it would be in Israel's best interest, above everything else, as if that should be the overriding concern for anyone seeking justice and human rights. A common factor in their work is the omission or sidelining of the Palestinian origins of the movement, the

---

3 Paulo Freire, *Pedagogy of the Oppressed*, available at laconstituciondel peru.org.

4 Boycott! Supporting the Palestinian BDS Call from Within, at boycottisrael. info.

5 Alternative Information Center, at alternativenews.org.

6 Israeli Committee Against House Demolitions, "About ICAHD," at icahd. org.

7 Who Profits? Exposing the Israeli Occupation Industry, at whoprofits.org.

BDS National Committee (BNC)[8] and the BDS call, along with an attempt to design their own guidelines for applying the boycott—guidelines whose entrenched colonial attitude is hard to miss.

The BNC always welcomes initiatives calling for a partial or selective boycott of Israel and its complicit institutions, so long as they do not undermine or negate the basic rights of the Palestinians. Some Zionists now calling for a selective boycott of Israeli academic and cultural institutions based in colonial settlements, after decades of silence in the face of a brutal system of occupation and apartheid, are doing so explicitly in order to undermine or circumvent the wider, more principled, and far more morally consistent BDS campaign. Rather than weakening BDS, though, such campaigns are in fact contributing to making the ground more fertile for its future growth, by vindicating the logic of BDS—namely, that *pressure*, not appeasement, is the only effective way to end Israel's violations of international law.

Soft Zionists have always tried to maintain a gate-keeping role in channeling solidarity with Palestinians and reducing it to focus specifically on a small subset of Palestinian rights, while actively opposing any attempt to develop an independent, Palestinian-led resistance strategy based on the quest for self-determination and justice.

With the advance of BDS, this Zionist gate-keeper hegemony is largely in tatters. Soft Zionists are taking this quite harshly, some going as far as to accuse Palestinian civil society of "betraying" them, and harming its own interests in the process. In their self-centered worldview, typical of apologists for colonialism anywhere, they think that if they withdraw their support, Palestinians will lose their only hope for emancipation. But this patronizing, colonial discourse has been largely discredited, and increasingly revealed as a fraud, feeding the egos of its proponents while safeguarding Israeli apartheid.

The BDS movement totally rejects the "save Israeli apartheid" view, for it strives to end the occupation alone without addressing the internationally recognized right of the great majority of the Palestinian people, the refugees, to return to their homes and receive reparations, and omits any mention of the need to end Israel's legalized and institutionalized system of racial discrimination, or apartheid, against the indigenous Palestinians—i.e.

---

8   Palestinian BDS National Committee, at bdsmovement.net.

"non-Jews"—who hold Israeli citizenship. This school of thought seeks, often quite overtly, to strengthen apartheid demographically by getting rid of some four million Palestinians (in the occupied territories), thus maintaining Israel's character as an ethnocentric, racist, and exclusivist state for decades longer. The litmus test for any Israeli group claiming to support human rights and a sustainable peace based on justice and international law is, therefore, whether it is ready to support the most basic right to full equality for the indigenous Palestinians. "Equality or nothing," as the late Edward Said insisted.

COEXISTENCE VS CO-RESISTANCE[9]

The struggle over Palestine, as Edward Said argued,[10] is not a symmetric struggle where "both sides" are in "conflict"; it is a case of settler colonialism that is now increasingly recognized as entailing both occupation and apartheid.[11] Advocacy of dialogue and coexistence to overcome "entrenched hatred" and reach a compromise on "competing claims," as is often rehearsed in the mainstream Western media, is therefore entirely misplaced, and based on false premises. Above all, the struggle is one for freedom, justice, and self-determination for *the oppressed*, which in turn might liberate the oppressor. Only through an end to oppression can there be any real potential for what I call ethical coexistence—coexistence based on justice and full equality for everyone, not a master–slave type of "coexistence" that many in the "peace industry"[12] advocate.

The boycott criteria adopted by Palestinian civil society and advocated by the BNC set two conditions without which relations between a Palestinian side and an Israeli side would be regarded as constituting normalization. Normalization, in the Arab—including Palestinian—context, is defined

---

9   This section is based on Chapter 16 of Barghouti, *Boycott, Divestment, Sanctions.*

10   Edward W. Said, *The Question of Palestine*, Vintage, 1992.

11   For more on this, see "United Against Apartheid, Colonialism, and Occupation: Dignity & Justice for the Palestinian People," Palestinian Civil Society's Strategic Position Paper for the Durban Review Conference, Geneva, April 20–24, 2009, at bdsmovement.net.

12   For more on this, see Faris Giacaman, "Can We Talk? The Middle East Peace Industry," *Electronic Intifada*, August 20, 2000, at electronicintifada.net.

as the development of joint relations and projects with an Israeli side that gives the false impression of normalcy despite the continuation of colonial oppression.[13] Such projects and relations, by definition and in effect, attempt to ignore or sidestep, and therefore normalize, the abnormal: Israel's colonial oppression. The two conditions guaranteeing a normalization-free relationship, as set by the Palestinian Campaign for the Academic and Cultural Boycott of Israel (PACBI) and adopted by the great majority of Palestinian civil society since November 2007, are 1) the Israeli side must recognize the internationally sanctioned and inalienable rights of the Palestinian people, including the right to self-determination; and 2) the project itself, regardless of its exact nature (cultural, academic, environmental, medical, feminist, or whatever), must have as one of its main objectives resistance against the occupation and apartheid. As one Palestinian youth activist puts it, under conditions of colonial oppression genuine coexistence between the communities of oppressors and oppressed should entail *co-resistance* (that is Israeli alongside Palestinian resistance) to oppression.[14]

CIRCLING THE WAGONS

Some skeptics have argued that, far from winning over Israelis or weakening support in Israel for the state's violations of Palestinian rights, boycotts tend to trigger acute paranoia among Israelis, as well as inducing an aggressive siege mentality. This may be true at first—as in every colonial society, where the oppressor community sets aside internal discord and bands together, or "circles the wagons," against perceived external threats of isolation that can lead to a pariah status. At that stage, prospects for the internal struggle to challenge the structures of colonialism and apartheid seem remote at best, if

---

13 The full definition of normalization, in Arabic, can be found in "A Call from Palestine: Palestinian Students' Campaign for the Academic Boycott of Israel," at pacbi.org. The definition of normalization, in short, is "participating in any project, initiative or activity whether locally or internationally, that is designed to bring together—whether directly or indirectly—Palestinian and/or Arab youth with Israelis (whether individuals or institutions) and is *not* explicitly designed to resist or expose the occupation and all forms of discrimination and oppression inflicted upon the Palestinian people."

14 Maath Musleh, "Opinion: Co-resistance vs. Co-existence," *Maan News Agency*, July 17, 2011, at maannews.net

not altogether delusional. But when the internal struggle, led by Palestinians and supported by conscientious Israelis, combines with the struggle from outside to generate sustainable and effective pressure that sharply raises the price of oppression, this seemingly invincible garrison-based unity starts to crack. The fact that BDS is categorically opposed to all forms of racism and racist ideology, including anti-Semitism, can only enhance the prospects of this transformative process. The courageous Israeli BDS group, Boycott from Within, is keenly aware of this equation, which is known to be true from struggles across the world—in South Africa, France during the Algerian liberation struggle, the US in Vietnam, and so on.

A tipping point will be reached in which Israel's oppression is met with substantial resistance—primarily from the Palestinian people, but also from the wider Arab World and the world at large, and particularly in the form of sustainable BDS campaigns leading to comprehensive UN sanctions (as was the case in the struggle against South African apartheid). When such a point is reached, Israel's economy will suffer tremendously, at which point the BDS movement inside Israel will gain substantial momentum. At that stage, ordinary, apolitical Israelis will start rethinking whether they want to continue "living by the sword," as Sharon put it, as a world pariah in a state that lacks economic prospects and that is shunned and widely boycotted by international civil society, and even by other states. Then, under overwhelming pressure from both within and without, the natural human quest for normalcy, for a peaceful and economically viable life, will lead many of those Israelis to withdraw their support for Israeli apartheid and occupation. Many may even actively join movements that aim to end both. The collapse of the multi-tiered Israeli system of oppression will then become only a matter of time. The experience of the South African anti-apartheid struggle, despite obvious differences, demonstrates this pattern of events.

ISRAEL'S ANTI-BOYCOTT LAW[15]

Viewing BDS as a "strategic threat"[16] to the Israeli establishment, as a leading Israeli think tank and several ranking officials have done, and frustrated at

---

15   This section is based on Omar Barghouti, "Dropping the Last Mask of Democracy," Al Jazeera, August 3, 2011, at english.aljazeera.net.
16   "Eroding Israel's Legitimacy in the International Arena," January 28, 2010, at reut-institute.org.

its utter failure to hinder the fast spread of the movement on a global scale, Israel has decided to use legal measures to suppress support for BDS, at least under its jurisdiction.

Much controversy has arisen since July 2011, when the Israeli parliament passed legislation effectively criminalizing support for any boycott against Israel or its institutions, under threat of heavy penalties (at minimum), without the need to prove "guilt," or even correlation between the expression of support for the boycott and any claimed damages.[17] Dozens of Israeli civil society organizations and leading legal scholars, including many opposing the boycott, have resolutely opposed this exceptionally authoritarian law on diverse grounds, ranging from the most principled to the straightforwardly pragmatic.

Mostly missing from the debate has been the Palestinian perspective. Given that this law was entirely motivated by the spectacular growth in recent years of the global BDS movement against Israel, and the corresponding growth of support within Israel for BDS or for various selective boycotts that refer to international law, this absence is highly significant.

While expressing alarm at this latest repressive attempt by Israel to crush peaceful Palestinian resistance, as well as support for it among conscientious Israelis, a BNC statement[18] expressed confidence that this law would bolster the spread of BDS even faster among liberal communities the world over. According to Hind Awwad, a coordinator of the BNC, "This new legislation, which violates international law, is testament to the success of the rapidly growing global BDS movement and a realization within political elites inside Israel that the state is becoming a world pariah in the way that South Africa once was."[19]

Eilat Maoz, coordinator of the Coalition of Women for Peace, was quoted in the Hebrew-language *Maariv*[20] as follows: "An illegitimate government passes an illegitimate law to protect an illegitimate occupation,

---

17   "Knesset Passes Boycott Law; ACRI Plans to Appeal," July 12, 2011, at acri.org.il.
18   "Leadership of Palestinian Boycott Campaign Responds to New Law," July 12, 2011, at bdsmovement.net.
19   Ibid.
20   Arik Bender, "'Boycott Law Passes Second and Third Reading in the Knesset," *Maariv*, July 11, 2011 (Hebrew).

while complaining about delegitimization. We will continue boycotting, protesting, demonstrating, and resisting the occupation—and we call on everyone else to do so." The BNC stood by its Israeli partners, saying, "We stand in solidarity with all principled Israeli citizens and organizations who are the primary target of this law, and who may be fined and even imprisoned for exercising their fundamental right to speak out and act nonviolently in order to bring their state into compliance with international law."

Amnesty International[21] condemned the new Israeli bill, saying it would have "a chilling effect on freedom of expression." Members of the European Parliament raised similar concerns, while the EU itself, typically submissive to Israeli–US interests, expressed alarm at the law's implications for basic rights. Even a *New York Times* editorial slammed it[22] as undemocratic. All this will do further damage to Israel's already low standing in international public opinion.[23]

It is as if Israel, by passing this law, has pushed the fast-forward button in the process of digging the grave of its own occupation and apartheid policies. The passage of this exceptionally draconian law, which blatantly stifles free speech, shows that Israel is ready to sacrifice one of its very last masks of "democracy" for the sake of crushing the BDS movement with an iron fist. This provides further irrefutable evidence of the level of panic in the Israeli establishment at the dramatic expansion and rising impact of the movement. It also proves, once again, the futility of all the other unsavory weapons in Israel's massive arsenal of intimidation, smears, threats, and bullying in combating BDS—which, as a nonviolent, morally consistent

---

21   "Israel Anti-Boycott Law an Attack on Freedom of Expression," July 12, 2011, at amnesty.org.
22   "Not Befitting a Democracy," *New York Times*, July 17, 2011, at nytimes.com.
23   A BBC poll of international public opinion conducted in March 2011 revealed that Israel's influence was among the most negatively rated, competing with that of North Korea, Iran, and Pakistan. Significantly, the study shows that, while positive ratings for Israel in the US, its closest ally and patron, have remained quite stable compared with results in 2010, at 43 percent, negative ratings have climbed by ten points, to 41 percent, making the US public "divided rather than favourable," as the BBC states. BBC World Service, "Positive Views of Brazil on the Rise in 2011 BBC Country Rating Poll," March 7, 2011, at worldpublicopinion.org.

movement, has dragged Israel into a "battlefield" where even its daunting nuclear weapons are rendered ineffective.

The Israeli establishment's attempt to justify its repressive new law in the cause of countering a movement bent on "delegitimizing" it and calling into question its very existence has failed to convince any significant portion of world public opinion. Most observers cannot but ask, why was the anti-apartheid boycott of South Africa not considered a threat to the *existence* of the state? Similarly, did ending segregation in the southern states of the US delegitimize whites, or end their existence? In fact, the only things that justice and equality delegitimize are injustice and inequality. BDS aims to "delegitimize" Israel's occupation and colonial policies and structures. And it seems many in international civil society are gradually moving in the direction of supporting the movement and bringing closer Israel's South Africa moment.

To those who may say that this law will corrupt Israel's democracy, one can only ask whether a state that has dozens of laws discriminating against its "non-Jewish" citizens based solely on their religious-ethnic identity can be called a democracy. Can a state involved in occupation, forced displacement, siege, and denial of the basic rights of refugees be regarded as a democracy? The prominent Israeli historian, Ilan Pappe, calls Israel a "herrenvolk democracy"—a democracy only for the masters.[24]

Finally, Israel's claim that BDS is somehow against Jews is best refuted by Avraham Burg, former chairman of the Jewish Agency and for many years speaker of the Israeli Knesset, where this latest legislation only underlines the pivotal role the Knesset has consistently played in maintaining Israeli colonial oppression:

> Israel sweeps all the criticism against it, both justified and unjustified, under the same anti-Semitic rug. It is actually we who are repeatedly mixing up proper criticism of Israel with anti-Semitism. The reason is to avoid at any price having to confront the situation and make tough existential decisions: the occupation, the injustices, the discrimination, the persecution of the non-Jewish minority in our midst ... There is no other country in the Western world from which the international community has been willing to put up

---

24   Frank Barat, "Reframing the Israel-Palestine Conflict," *New Internationalist*, at newint.org.

with acts of state violence for five decades, other than Israel … And there is no other colonialist left in the world, other than "the only democracy in the Middle East." The world is still putting up with all this, but not for much longer—it will soon be over.[25]

If Palestinian activists learned anything from the South African struggle, it is that the darkest moment is the one that precedes dawn. In an ironic way, this new Israeli law may be a harbinger for that darkest moment, with no masks or pretense, and beyond which the light of freedom and justice will become visible.

While the BDS movement is not an ideological or centralized political party, it does have a Palestinian leadership, the BNC, and a well developed and clearly articulated set of objectives that comprehensively and consistently affirm Palestinian rights in terms of universal principles of international law and human rights. The heart of the call for BDS is not the diverse and contextualized boycotting acts it urges, but this rights-based approach addressing the three basic, UN-sanctioned rights corresponding to the main segments of the Palestinian people. Ending Israel's occupation, ending its apartheid, and ending its denial of the right of refugees to return—together, these constitute the minimal requirements for justice and the realization of the inalienable right of Palestinians to self-determination. Support for the BDS movement entails the upholding of freedom, justice, and equality as an irreducible basis for a just and sustainable peace. Lighting the torch of dissent by building support for this movement in Israel represents an indispensable part of the struggle.

---

25   Avraham Burg, "When the Walls Come Tumbling Down," *Haaretz*, April 1, 2011, at haaretz.com.

CHRONOLOGY

1987–1993

During the first intifada, Palestinians initiate a series of organized protests against Israel, consisting of general strikes, tax revolts, boycotts of Israeli products, and refusal to recognize Israeli rule. Israeli forces responded with arrests, beatings, curfews, and sieges.

September 25 and October 4, 1997

Israeli group Gush Shalom places advertisements in *Haaretz* calling for a boycott of settlement products.

April 2001

Under the name Matzpun ("conscience"), an Israeli letter is circulated calling for "the world community to organize and boycott Israeli industrial and agricultural exports and goods, as well as leisure tourism, in the hope that it will have the same positive result that the boycott of South Africa had on Apartheid."

September 14, 2001

The Executive Committee of the World Council of Churches calls for an international boycott of Israeli settlement products.

April 6, 2002

British professors Hilary and Steven Rose publish an open letter signed by 125 academics calling for an academic boycott of Israel.

May 6, 2002
Professors at Harvard University and MIT issue a petition calling for their institutions to "divest from Israel, and from US companies that sell arms to Israel."

March 2004
An open letter signed by nearly 300 academics calls for Israeli academics to oppose "Israeli government action against Palestinian education and academic freedom" or face a boycott.

April 2004
The Palestinian Campaign for the Academic and Cultural Boycott of Israel (PACBI) is founded, endorsed by dozens of Palestinian civil society organizations.

June 2004
The General Assembly of the Presbyterian Church USA adopts a resolution to "initiate a process of phased, selective divestment in multinational corporations operating in Israel." Following international pressure, the policy is altered in June 2006 to call for investing "in only peaceful pursuits."

November 21, 2004
Human Rights Watch calls on Caterpillar Inc. to suspend sales of its D9 bulldozers to the Israeli military, as "Caterpillar's continued sales will make the company complicit in human rights abuses."

January 27, 2005
The Israeli Committee Against House Demolitions (ICAHD) calls for "a multitiered campaign of strategic, selective sanctions against Israel until the Occupation ends."

February 21, 2005
The World Council of Churches encourages its 340 member churches to consider divestment strategies to apply "economic pressure" on Israel.

April 22, 2005
The council of the UK Association of University Teachers (AUT) votes to boycott University of Haifa and Bar-Ilan University. The boycott is rescinded a month later following international pressure.

June 11, 2005
The New England Conference of the United Methodist Church passes a resolution to support divestment from companies that support the Israeli occupation.

July 9, 2005
On the one-year anniversary of the International Court of Justice's advisory opinion against the West Bank wall, over 170 Palestinian civil society organizations issue a call for boycott, divestment, and sanctions, marking the official beginning of the international BDS movement.

February 6, 2006
The Church of Enlgand votes to divest from Caterpillar. Despite ensuing criticism, the Church quietly withdraws its £2.2 million from Caterpillar in December 2008.

May 27, 2006
The Ontario division of the Canadian Union of Public Employees (CUPE) passes a resolution supporting BDS "until Israel meets its obligation to recognize the Palestinian people's inalienable right to self-determination."

December 15, 2006
A letter written by John Berger and signed by an additional 93 authors, filmmakers, musicians and performers calls for a cultural boycott of Israel. The signatories include Arundhati Roy, Eduardo Galeano, and Brian Eno.

November 2007
Activists from Adalah New York begin targeting the businesses of Israeli billionaire Lev Leviev for his involvement in Israeli settlement construction. This will lead to numerous divestments from Leviev's Africa Israel Investments company and UNICEF severing its ties to Leviev. Africa

Israel will later announce that it is no longer involved in settlement construction.

April 2008
The Canadian Union of Postal Workers (CUPW) passes a resolution supporting BDS on Israel.

February 5, 2009
Under the banner of the Congress of South African Trade Unions (COSATU), South African dock workers refuse to offload a ship carrying Israeli goods. COSATU calls on the international community to "isolate apartheid Israel."

February 7, 2009
Hampshire College approves a proposal by Students for Justice in Palestine (SJP) to divest from six companies profiting from the Israeli occupation, thus becoming the first US college to implement BDS on Israel. Although the college administration denies that the divestments relate to Israel, the companies targeted were the ones proposed by SJP.

April 23, 2009
The Scottish Trade Union Congress votes overwhelmingly to endorse BDS on Israel.

June 2009
CODEPINK begins campaign to boycott Ahava products, which are sourced from a West Bank settlement.

June 30, 2009
The Norwegian Government Pension Fund divests from the Israeli military company Elbit Systems.

July 1, 2009
Activists the Yes Men announce the withdrawal of their film *The Yes Men Fix the World* from the Jerusalem Film Festival "in solidarity with the Boycott, Divestment and Sanctions campaign."

September 2, 2009
Dozens of prominent artists and writers issue a letter to the Toronto International Film Festival (TIFF), declaring their opposition to the TIFF's involvement in the Brand Israel campaign. Among the signers to the "Toronto Declaration" are John Berger, Harry Belafonte, Naomi Klein, David Byrne, Eve Ensler, Alice Walker, and Viggo Mortensen.

September 17, 2009
The British Trades Union Congress, representing 6.5 million workers across the UK, votes overwhelmingly to endorse BDS on Israel.

September 22, 2009
Palestinian activist Mohammed Othman is arrested by Israeli authorities while returning home from a trip to Norway, where he discussed BDS with Norwegian officials. He is released four months later, following an international campaign in which Amnesty International threatened to declare Othman a prisoner of conscience. No charges were leveled against him.

December 2009
Palestinian Christian institutions issue the Kairos Palestine Document, modeled after the South African Kairos Document, calling for BDS.

December 16, 2009
Jamal Juma', coordinator for the Stop the Wall campaign and secretariat member of the Palestinian BDS National Committee, is arrested by Israeli forces and held without charges. Following an international campaign, Juma' is released on January 13, 2010, along with BDS activist Mohammed Othman.

January 28, 2010
Musician Carlos Santana cancels an upcoming performance in Israel. The show's Israeli promoter, Shuki Weiss, attributes the cancellation to the boycott campaign.

March 18, 2010

The Student Senate of the University of California–Berkeley votes to divest from General Electric and United Technologies for profiting from the Israeli occupation. The move is later vetoed by the senate president, thus forcing a supermajority vote. In the ensuing debate over the nonbinding resolution, several prominent writers, activists, and Nobel laureates from around the world express their support for the resolution, while the Israeli government and a coalition of pro-Israel organizations oppose the resolution. Eventually the veto survives by one vote.

April 24, 2010

Artist Gil Scott-Heron announces that he will cancel an upcoming tour date in Israel, acknowledging the boycott campaign.

May 2010

Two major Italian supermarket chains, COOP and Nordiconad, suspend sales of goods by the Agrexco Export Company, stating that it cannot be ascertained whether Agrexco products marked as originating from Israel actually orginate from the occupied territories.

May 15, 2010

Elvis Costello announces his cancellation of two upcoming performances in Israel, stating that "there are occasions when merely having your name added to a concert schedule may be interpreted as a political act that reso-nates more than anything that might be sung and it may be assumed that one has no mind for the suffering of the innocent … One must at least con-sider any rational argument that comes before the appeal of more desperate means. Sometimes a silence in music is better than adding to the static and so an end to it."

May 31, 2010

In the aftermath of the Israeli raid on the Gaza Freedom Flotilla, numer-ous artists and entertainers cancel their scheduled appearances in Israel. Cancellations come from Hollywood actors Dustin Hoffman and Meg Ryan and musicians Klaxons, Gorillaz Sound System, Devendra Banhart, Leftfield and the Pixies.

June 1, 2010
Britain's largest union, Unite, unanimously passes a motion to boycott and divest from Israeli companies.

June 2, 2010
The Swedish Port Workers Union announces a blockade of ships carrying Israeli cargo from June 15 until June 24.

June 3, 2010
The South African Transport and Allied Workers Union (SATAWU) calls for an "an escalation of the boycott of Israeli goods and call upon our fellow trade unionists not to handle them." Meanwhile, students at the Evergreen State College in Olympia, Washington, vote by an overwhelming majority to divest from companies profiting from the Israeli occupation and to ban Caterpillar equipment from the college campus due to Caterpillar's complicity in the occupation.

June 4, 2010
The Central Executive Committee of the South African Municipal Workers Union (SAMWU) unanimously passes a motion to "immediately work towards every municipality in South Africa [becoming] an Apartheid Israel free zone."

June 16, 2010
Jewish Voice for Peace launches campaign to compel pension fund TIAA-CREF to divest from five companies crucial to the Israeli occupation.

June 20, 2010
In Oakland, CA, hundreds of labor and community activists enact a twenty-four-hour blockade of the port to prevent the unloading of an Israeli Zim Line ship.

July 15, 2010
The Olympia Food Co-op in Olympia, Washington, becomes the first US grocery store to publicly honor the boycott of Israeli goods.

July 18, 2010

The Israeli security service Shin Bet summons prominent Israeli activist Yonatan Shapira for questioning about the global BDS movement. During questioning, Shapira asks if his phone is being tapped. A Shin Bet officer responds, "You won't talk about BDS. Why should I tell you?"

late August 2010

Dozens of Israeli actors, directors, and playwrights sign a letter declaring their refusal to perform in a newly constructed cultural center located in the West Bank settlement of Ariel. Soon after, over 150 Israeli academics issue their own letter of support. Jewish Voice for Peace also issues a letter of support signed by 150 artists in theater, film, and television, including Julianne Moore, Wallace Shawn, Theodore Bikel, and Eve Ensler.

October 2010

In the US, the Jewish Federations of North America and the Jewish Council for Public Affairs pledge $6 million for the establishment of an Israel Action Network designed to combat BDS. Jewish Federation CEO Jerry Silverman calls BDS the second most dangerous threat to Israel after Iran.

October 25, 2010

Israeli media report that Caterpillar Inc. is suspending delivery of D9 bulldozers to Israel for the duration of the trial of the Rachel Corrie lawsuit in Israel.

December 4, 2010

The Greens Party of New South Wales announces its support of BDS. A year later, following relentless attacks on the party, the Greens withdraw official support for BDS but continue to recognize BDS as a legitimate political tactic.

March 23, 2011

The Senate of the University of Johannesburg, South Africa, votes to end its formal ties with Ben Gurion University, following a campaign endorsed by Desmond Tutu, Breyten Breytenbach, and John Dugard.

July 11, 2011

The Israeli Knesset passes legislation making endorsement of BDS a civil offense. Those endorsing a boycott of Israel or Israeli settlements may be held liable for financial damages, real or hypothetical, by boycott targets.

RESOURCES

Boycott Israeli Goods Campaign
bigcampaign.org
The BDS website of the UK Palestine Solidarity Campaign (palestine campaign.org).

Boycott! Supporting the Palestinian Call from Within (Boycott from Within)
boycottisrael.info
Website for Israeli supporters of the Palestinian BDS call.

Electronic Intifada
electronicintifada.net
News, analysis, and reports on Palestine/Israel.

International Solidarity Movement (ISM)
palsolidarity.org
Palestinian-led movement that invites people from around the world to participate in nonviolent direct action against the occupation.

Jewish Voice for Peace
jvp.org
Jewish Voice for Peace is spearheading a US campaign to compel the financial services organization TIAA-CREF to divest from five companies profiting from the occupation. See also wedivest.org.

Mondoweiss
mondoweiss.net
Popular blog for news and analysis on Palestine/Israel, edited by Phil Weiss and Adam Horowitz.

Palestinian BDS National Committee (BNC)
bdsmovement.net
The Palestinian coordinating body for the global BDS movement.

Palestinian Campaign for the Academic and Cultural Boycott of Israel (PACBI)
pacbi.org
Contains guidelines and parameters for implementing academic and cultural boycott.

Palestinian Queers for BDS (PQBDS)
pqbds.com
Palestinian queers, at the intersection between the struggle for sexual and gender diversity and the Palestinian struggle for freedom, promoting BDS and combating Israeli pinkwashing.

Popular Struggle Coordination Committee
popularstruggle.org
Coalition of the popular committees waging active resistance to the Israeli occupation in villages and towns across the West Bank.

Stolen Beauty: Boycott Ahava Campaign
stolenbeauty.org
Code Pink's campaign to boycott settlement-produced Ahava products.

US Campaign for the Academic and Cultural Boycott of Israel (USACBI)
usacbi.org
US campaign focused on the promotion of academic and cultural boycotts.

US Campaign to End the Israeli Occupation

endtheoccupation.org

Coalition of Palestine solidarity organizations throughout the US. The website contains many BDS resources.

Who Profits from the Occupation?

whoprofits.org

A project of the Israeli Coalition of Women for Peace, Who Profits? maintains an extensive and growing database of companies directly involved in the Israeli occupation.

ACKNOWLEDGMENTS

Neve Gordon and Roane Carey shaped this book in its early stages, and Phan Nguyen provided essential wisdom and advice throughout. Many thanks to each of them, though any errors and oversight are my own.

Several chapters also appeared in earlier forms:

Chapter 1, Mustafa Barghouthi, "Freedom in Our Lifetime," appeared in earlier versions as "What We Palestinians Need," *Al-Ahram Weekly*, August 13–19, 2009; and "When Will It Be Our Time?," *New York Times*, December 16, 2009.

Chapter 3, Slavoj Žižek, "What Goes On When Nothing Goes On?," appeared in an earlier version in *Living in the End Times*, Verso, 2010.

Chapter 5, Omar Barghouti, "The Cultural Boycott: Israel vs. South Africa," is excerpted from *Boycott, Divestment, Sanctions: The Global Struggle for Palestinian Rights*, Haymarket, 2011.

Chapter 10, Noura Erakat, "BDS in the USA, 2001–2010," appeared in an earlier version in *Middle East Report* 255, Summer 2010.

Chapter 12, David Lloyd and Laura Pulido, "In the Long Shadow of the Settler: On Israeli and US Colonialisms," appeared in an earlier version in *American Quarterly* 62:4, December 2010.

Chapter 16, Ran Greenstein, "Israel/Palestine and the Apartheid Analogy: Critics, Apologists and Strategic Lessons," appeared in an earlier version on the website of *Monthly Review*, August 22 and 27, 2010, at mrzine.monthly review.org.

Chapter 18, Lisa Taraki and Mark Levine, "Why Boycott Israel?," originally appeared on the Al Jazeera website, August 13, 2011, at Aljazeera.com.

Chapter 19, Naomi Klein, "Israel: Boycott, Divest, Sanction," originally appeared in the *Nation*, January 26, 2009.

Chapter 21, John Berger, "Why a Boycott," originally appeared as "We Must Speak Out," in the *Guardian*—Comment Is Free, December 15, 2006.

Chapter 22, Neve Gordon, "Boycott Israel," originally appeared in the *Los Angeles Times*, August 20, 2009.

Chapter 23, Michael Warschawski, "Yes to BDS! An Answer to Uri Avnery," originally appeared on the Alternative Information Center website, August 25, 2010, at alternativenews.org.

Chapter 24, Ken Loach, Rebecca O'Brien, and Paul Laverty, "*Looking for Eric*, Melbourne Festival, and the Cultural Boycott," originally appeared as "Boycotts Don't Equal Censorship," the *Guardian*—Comment Is Free, September 1, 2009.

CONTRIBUTORS

Ra'anan Alexandrowicz is an Israeli filmmaker and activist.

Hind Awwad is a coordinator with the Palestinian BDS National Committee.

Mustafa Barghouthi is the Secretary General of the Palestinian National Initiative, the president of the Palestinian Medical Relief Society, a member of the Palestinian Legislative Council, and a nonviolence democracy leader based in Ramallah.

Omar Barghouti is a human rights activist, founding member of the Palestinian Campaign for the Academic and Cultural Boycott of Israel and the BDS movement, and author of *Boycott, Divestment, Sanctions: The Global Struggle for Palestinian Rights*.

Dalit Baum and Merav Amir are project coordinators of Who Profits from the Occupation? in the Coalition of Women for Peace.

Joel Beinin is Donald J. McLachlan Professor of History at Stanford University.

John Berger is a novelist, essayist, screenwriter, dramatist and critic. His many books include *Ways of Seeing*, the Booker Prize–winning novel *G*, the Man Booker–longlisted *From A to X*, and *A Seventh Man*.

Nada Elia teaches Global and Gender Studies at Antioch University in Seattle. She is a member of the Organizing Collective of USACBI, the US Campaign for Academic and Cultural Boycott of Israel.

Marc H. Ellis is University Professor of Jewish Studies, Professor of History and Founding Director of the Center for Jewish Studies at Baylor University. He is the author and editor of more than twenty books, including *Encountering the Jewish Future.*

Noura Erakat is a human rights attorney and Adjunct Professor of International Human Rights Law at Georgetown University.

Neve Gordon is an Israeli academic and the author of *Israel's Occupation.*

Ran Greenstein works at the University of the Witwatersrand, Johannesburg, South Africa.

Ronnie Kasrils is a former South African government minister and was an activist during the anti-apartheid struggle. Among other positions, he was chief of military intelligence of the ANC's military wing. Today he writes and lectures, is active in the Palestinian solidarity movement, and is a noted author whose recent book *The Unlikely Secret Agent* won the country's prestigious Alan Paton Award.

Father Jamal Khader is Chairperson of the Department of Religious Studies, Bethlehem University, Palestine.

Naomi Klein is an award-winning journalist, syndicated columnist, fellow at the Nation Institute and author of *The Shock Doctrine.*

Mark LeVine is a Professor of Middle East History at the University of California, Irvine, and author of *Heavy Metal Islam: Rock, Resistance, and the Struggle for the Soul of Islam* and *Impossible Peace: Israel/Palestine Since 1989.*

David Lloyd is a Professor of English and Comparative Literature at the University of Southern California, and **Laura Pulido** is a Professor of American Studies and Ethnicity at the University of Southern California.

Ken Loach is the director of *The Wind That Shakes the Barley* and *Looking for Eric*. **Rebecca O'Brien** and **Paul Laverty** were the producer and writer, respectively, for the latter film.

Haneen Maikey is cofounder and Director of al-Qaws for Sexual and Gender Diversity in Palestinian Society, and cofounder of Palestinian Queers for Boycott, Divestment and Sanctions.

Ilan Pappe is a Professor of History at the University of Exeter. His many books include *The Ethnic Cleansing of Palestine*, *Gaza in Crisis* (with Noam Chomsky) and, most recently, *The Idea of Israel*.

Jonathan Pollak is an Israeli activist who has been involved in the Palestinian popular struggle since 2002

Lisa Taraki is a Sociologist at Birzeit University in the occupied Palestinian territories, and a founding member of the Palestinian Campaign for the Academic and Cultural Boycott of Israel.

Rebecca Vilkomerson is the Executive Director of Jewish Voice for Peace.

Michael Warschawski is a journalist, political analyst, and veteran Israeli anticolonial activist. He is also the cofounder of the Alternative Information Center.

Slavoj Žižek is the author of *Living in the End Times, First as Tragedy, Then as Farce, In Defense of Lost Causes*, and many more